Holiness and the World

*Studies in the
Teachings of Blessed Josemaría Escrivá*

Holiness
and
the World

*Studies in the
Teachings of Blessed Josemaría Escrivá*

Edited by
M. Belda, J. Escudero, J. L. Illanes
and P. O'Callaghan

SCEPTER PUBLISHERS • PRINCETON
FOUR COURTS PRESS • DUBLIN
MIDWEST THEOLOGICAL FORUM • CHICAGO

This is a translation of *Santità e mondo*.
Atii del Convegno teologico di studio sugli insegnamenti del Beato Josemaría Escrivá (Roma, 12–14 ottobre 1993)

© 1994 Libreria Editrice Vaticana, 00120 Vatican City
© 1994 Pontifico Ateneo della Santa Croce
© 1997 English version, Midwest Theological Forum

Published by:

Scepter Publishers, Inc.
20 Nasau St.
Princeton, NJ 08542

Four Courts Press
Fumbally Lane,
Dublin 8, Ireland

Midwest Theological Forum
712 S. Loomis St.
Chicago, Illinois 60607
Tel. (312) 421-8135
Fax (312) 421-8129
e-mail: jsocias@msn.com

All rights reserved.

Without limiting the rights under copyright reserved above, no part of this publication may be reproduced, stored in or introduced into a retrieval system, or transmitted in any form or by any means (electronic, mechanical, photocopying, recording or otherwise), wihout the prior written permission of both the copyright owner and the publishers of this book.

First American Edition: 1997
Translation: Michael Adams 1997
Printed in the United States of America

ISBN 1-890177-04-0

VOLVMEN HOC ACTORVM
THEOLOGICI CONGRESSVS
QVEM ROM. PONT. IOANNES PAVLVS II
SVA DIGNATVS EST ALLOCVTIONE CONCLVDERE
DE IIS QVÆ BEATVS IOSEPHMARIA ESCRIVA
VITA VERBIS SCRIPTIS
DOCVIT AC TRADIDIT
ATHENÆI ROMANI SANCTÆ CRVCIS
PROFESSORES ALVMNI ADMINISTRI
EXC.MO AC REV.MO D.NO ALVARO DEL PORTILLO
EPISCOPO OPERIS DEI PRÆLATO
EIVSDEMQVE ATHENÆI MAGNO CANCELLARIO
QVINQVAGESIMVM AGENTI ANNVM
EX QVO
PRESBYTERORVM ORDINI EST AGGREGATVS
IN SIGNVM GRATI ANIMI OFFERVNT
ID SIMVL OMINANTES
VT
SANCTISSIMA DEI GENETRICE INTERCEDENTE
BEATI QVOQVE IOSEPHMARIÆ DEPRECATIONE
CAELESTIVM DONORVM COPIAM
BENIGNVS EI DOMINVS LARGIATVR
XI MARTII AN. A REP. SAL. MCMXCIV

Contents

List of Contributors	12
Preface by *José-Luis Illanes*	13
Papal audience	15
Address by his holiness *John Paul II*	15
Greeting by *Bishop Alvaro del Portillo*	19
Opening ceremony	21
Address by *Bishop Alvaro del Portillo*	21
Message from *Joseph Cardinal Ratzinger*	25

Part I : Holiness

The vocation to holiness in Christ and in the Church
Fernando Ocáriz — 33

I. Calls to holiness in Christ	33
II. The vocation to holiness is addressed to all	39
III. A vocation in the Church	45
IV. The vocation to holiness and the mission to reconcile creation to God	49

Holiness and ordinary life in the teaching of Blessed Josemaría Escrivá
William May   53

   I. The ultimate basis for the universal call to holiness: Baptism and our divine filiation   54

   II. In what does sanctification consist? The primacy of grace   60

   III. Ordinary life as the place and means of sanctification   64

      1. The centrality of this truth, its context, and the dynamic unity of Blessed Josemaría's thought   64

      2. Why is ordinary life the place and means of sanctification?   70

      3. Work, the value of 'little things', marriage and family life   73

         a. The meaning of work   73

         b. The value of 'little things'   80

         c. Marriage and family life   81

   IV. Conclusion   85

Part II : Spiritual Life

Prayer and the basic structure of faith
Georges Cottier   89

Awareness of divine filiation
Jutta Burggraf   107

   I. Experience of divine love   107

   II. The dogmatic basis   111

      1. The indwelling of the Blessed Trinity   111

      2. The elevation of human nature   114

   III. Implications for Christian life   116

      1. The 'Trinity on earth'   117

      2. The audacity of divine filiation   119

    3. 'Tension' between spiritual childhood
       and spiritual maturity   122

The Christian, *alter Christus, ipse Christus*, in the thought of Blessed Josemaría Escrivá
Antonio Aranda   127

  I. Introduction   127
  II. Bases for a theological reflection   132
    1. Roots in New Testament revelation   132
    2. Roots in theological-dogmatic tradition   137
      a. Christ, the Anointed; the Christian, a new Christ   137
      b. From the theology of anointing to the theology of character   144
      c. The anti-Lutheran controversy of priesthood   146
      d. '*Sacerdos alter Christus*' in 20th-century Magisterium   149
    3. Roots in spiritual tradition   151
  III. '*Alter Christus, ipse Christus*' in the thought of Josemaría Escrivá   157
    1. '*Alter Christus, ipse Christus*': the texts   159
      a. Verbal forms used   159
      b. The subject of the description   162
    2. '*Alter Christus, ipse Christus*': the context   169
      a. Broader context: following, imitating and identifying with Christ   170
        - Following Christ   171
        - Imitation of Christ   174
        - Identification with Christ   177
      b. The immediate context: phrases accompanying the description   181
  IV. Conclusion: his underlying image of Christ   185

Part III : Sanctification of Work

Christians, the life of the world
Giuseppe Dalla Torre — 191
- I. Introduction — 191
- II. Christianity and the world — 194
- III. Christians, the life of the world — 199
- IV. The Church and Christians, the life of the world — 204
- V. Between tradition and renewal — 208

Work, justice, charity
José-Luis Illanes — 211
- I. Work, the core element in Blessed Josemaría Escrivá's spiritual teaching — 212
- II. Professional work and Christian living — 219
- III. At the summit of all human activities — 225
- IV. On developments in the theology of work — 234
- V. Social responsibility, charity, justice — 242

Responsibility to the world, and freedom
Jean-Luc Chabot — 251
- I. Introduction — 251
- II. Christianity brings mankind to fulfillment — 253
  1. Christ-centred human and social advancement — 253
     - a. Christ, the perfection of human nature — 253
     - b. 'No one can surpass the Christian in human nature.' — 254
  2. The Christian revolution and rejection of ideologies — 256
     - a. 'The greatest revolution of all time' — 256
     - b. The reductive anti-humanism of ideology — 257

III. The social impact of a genuine Christian life	260
1. The 'unity of life' principle and its social effect	260
a. 'These world crises are crises of saints'	261
b. 'We cannot lead a double life'	262
2. Putting Christ at the summit of all human activities	264
a. An eager sense of being responsible for the world and all creation	264
b. Sanctification of the world by the citizen and by the Christian worker	265
c. Human advancement through Christian apostolate	267
IV. Personal freedom is essential in the Christian life	268
1. The freedom of persons, and the truth that sets one free	269
a. The two stages of freedom: 'Veritas liberabit vos'	269
b. 'Freedom of consciences' and respect for persons	272
2. Unity of faith, and freedom of opinion	274
a. There are no dogmas in the area of matters of opinion	274
b. Respect for legitimate pluralism	275
V. Conclusion	277

By way of conclusion
Bishop Alvaro del Portillo

	279
I. Holiness in the world	281
II. Being sons and daughters of God. Being Christ.	287
III. Putting Christ at the summit	291

List of Contributors

Bishop Alvaro del Portillo (1914–1994) was Prelate of Opus Dei and Chancellor of the Roman Atheneum of the Holy Cross.

Joseph Cardinal Ratzinger is Prefect of the Sacred Congregation for the Doctrine of the Faith.

Fernando Ocáriz is a professor of the Pontifical Roman Atheneum of the Holy Cross.

William May is a professor of the Washington, D.C. section of the John Paul II Institute for the Study of Marriage and the Family.

Georges Cottier is Theologian of the Papal Household.

Jutta Burggraf is a professor of the International Academic Institute for the Study of Marriage and the Family at Medo, Rolduc, The Netherlands.

Antonio Aranda is Dean of the Faculty of Theology at the Pontifical Roman Atheneum of the Holy Cross.

Guiseppe dalla Torre is the Rector of the Libera Università Maria SS. Assunta, Rome.

José-Luis Illanes is a professor of the University of Navarre.

Jean-Luc Chabot teaches at the University of Grenoble.

Preface

The Roman Atheneum of the Holy Cross,[1] which owed so much, in terms of its origin and inspiration, to Monsignor Josemaría Escrivá, feeling obliged to contribute something to the celebrations which followed his beatification on May 17, 1992, decided that it should do so in the form of some sort of academic event. And so it was, that in the days immediately after May 17 it was decided to organize a symposium to study, from a theological point of view, some aspects of the spiritual message of Opus Dei. Over the months that followed the plans for a symposium were laid.It was obvious from the start that the symposium could not attempt to cover all aspects of Blessed Josemaría's teaching: a single scholarly meeting simply would not be enough. So it was decided to focus the sessions on a few important themes.

Because the symposium was being held to mark the beatification, one of these themes clearly had to be that of holiness—particularly if one takes into account the fact (as the Pope said in the beatification mass) that one of Blessed Josemaría's main contributions to the history and life of the Church was the part he played in proclaiming the universal call to holiness, that is, in the recognition that all Christians (in fact every man and woman), whatever their position in life, are called to union with God.

To speak of union with God is to speak of a personal experience of the divine, of a vital, real encounter with God One and Triune who, in Christ and in the Holy Spirit, draws near to man: it means, therefore, talking about prayer. It is in prayer that the Christian becomes aware of the nearness and strength of grace. And, therefore, it is in prayer that he comes to see his own position and mission in the world, which, in the case of the ordinary Christian, means that he realizes that he is called to give earthly things their fullest meaning.

---

1 On June 26, 1995, his holiness John Paul II bestowed the title of `Pontifical' on the Atheneum, so that it is now the `Pontifical Atheneum of the Holy Cross'.

Holiness, prayer, and sanctification of work—these were to be the three hinges on which the symposium would turn; and it was going to devote a day to each. It was decided not to hold the meeting exactly a year after the beatification, because of ordinary academic pressures in the months of May and June, but to put it off until the autumn (October 12–14, to be exact).

The general content of the symposium having been established, and an organizing committee appointed,[2] other elements of the plan could be worked out. The chancellor of the Atheneum, who supported the project at every step, agreed to open it. Joseph Cardinal Ratzinger very kindly agreed to take part by giving an inaugural address. It was thought a good idea to invite speakers from different countries and different areas of scholarship, thereby reflecting the universality typical of what Blessed Josemaría preached. In fact the eight speakers came from six different countries (France, Italy, German, Spain, USA) and, even though most of them were theologians, they also included people in the field of philosophy, canon law and the social sciences.

A highpoint of the symposium was the audience granted by John Paul II on October 14. His words, which are included in the preliminary papers of this book, were warmly greeted. He received us with fatherly affection and encouraged us in our work of studying the teaching of Blessed Josemaría, confident that theological thought must benefit from his message.

When thanking Dr. Alvaro del Portillo for his presence at the opening of the symposium, the organizing committee, conscious in particular of how close he was to Monsignor Escrivá, requested him to write something for the Proceedings; he was good enough to do just that and we feel that his contribution does us special honor.

In this book citations of books by Blessed Josemaría refer to numbered 'points' rather than pages, where the text is numbered in that way.

José-Luis Illanes,
President of the Organizing Committee
Rome, March 11, 1994

---

[2] The committee members were Reverend Professors Manuel Belda, José Escudero, Paul O'Callaghan and myself; the Reverend Ignasi Durany was the secretary.

Papal Audience

Address by his holiness John Paul II

Dear Brothers and Sisters,

1. I am pleased to welcome you on the occasion of the theological symposium on the teachings of Blessed Josemaría Escrivá, which has been taking place these past days at the Roman Atheneum of the Holy Cross, a little more than a year since his beatification.

I greet the chancellor, Bishop Alvaro del Portillo, and the rector of the Atheneum, Ignacio Carrasco de Paula; my greetings go also to the organizing committee, the speakers and all of you who took part in this important study event.

2. The history of the Church and of the world unfolds through the action of the Holy Spirit who, with the free cooperation of men, directs all things toward the fulfilllment of God the Father's saving plan. A clear manifestation of this divine Providence is the constant presence down the centuries of men and women faithful to Christ, who, with their life and their message, shed light on various periods of history. Among these distinguished figures, Blessed Josemaría Escrivá has an eminent place, for as I had occasion to stress on the solemn day of his beatification, he reminded the contemporary world of the universal call to holiness and of the Christian value which professional work can have in the ordinary life of each person.

In addition to the sanctification of souls, the action of the Holy Spirit has as its goal the constant renewal of the Church, so that she may effectively carry out the task entrusted to her by Christ. In the recent history of the Church's life, this process of renewal has a fundamental reference point—the Second Vatican Council, during which the Church, assembled together in the person of her bishops, reflected anew on the essence of her mystery, so as to be able to proclaim the Gospel to the world in a way that would have a decisive influence on the life of individuals, on cultures and on peoples. The conciliar texts and the documents that followed them had as a common characteristic the full awareness of the salvation accomplished for us by Christ. From this awareness stems the sense of mission which the texts of the Ecumenical Council and the whole subsequent Magisterium emphasize—that sense of mission to which I myself recently referred in the Encyclical Letter *Veritatis splendor*.

3. The deep awareness with which the Church today is conscious of serving a redemption that concerns every aspect of human existence was prepared, under the guidance of the Holy Spirit, by a process of gradual intellectual and spiritual development. The message of Blessed Josemaría, to which you devoted the work of your congress, is one of the most significant charismatic impulses in this direction, stemming from a unique grasp of the radiant, universal force of the Redeemer's grace. In one of his homilies, the founder of Opus Dei observed: 'There is nothing that is outside of the concern of Christ. Speaking with theological precision [. . .] one cannot say that there are realities—good, noble or even indifferent—which are exclusively profane; for the Word of God has made his dwelling among the sons of men, he was hungry and thirsty, worked with his hands, knew friendship and obedience, experienced sorrow and death.'[1]

On the basis of this deep conviction, Blessed Josemaría invited men and women from the most varied social conditions to sanctify themselves and to cooperate in the sanctification of others by sanctifying ordinary life. In his priestly activity, he was deeply aware of the value every soul has and of the Gospel's power to enlighten consciences and to awaken a serious and active Christian commitment to defending the person and his

---

[1] Bl. Josemaría Escrivá, *Christ Is Passing By*, Dublin, 1974, 112.

or her dignity. In *The Way*, Blessed Josemaría wrote: 'These world crises are crises of saints. God wants a handful of men "of his own" in every human activity. Then . . . "*pax Christi in regno Christi*"—the peace of Christ in the kingdom of Christ.'[2]

4. How much power this doctrine has in terms of the arduous and at the same time appealing work of the new evangelization, to which the entire Church is called! In your congress you have had the opportunity to reflect on various aspects of this spiritual teaching. I invite you to continue in this work, because Josemaría Escrivá de Balaguer, like other great figures in modern Church history, can also be a source of inspiration for theological thought. In fact, theological research, which has an irreplaceable role of mediation in the relationship between faith and culture, progresses and is enriched by drawing on the Gospel, under the impulse of the experience of Christianity's great witnesses. Blessed Josemaría, without a doubt, should be included among them.

We cannot forget, however, that the importance of the figure of Blessed Josemaría Escrivá derives not only from his message but also from the apostolic undertaking which he brought into being. In the 65 years since its foundation, the prelature of Opus Dei, an indissoluble unity of priests and lay people, has contributed to making Christ's saving message resound in many walks of life. As Pastor of the universal Church, echoes of this apostolate reach me. I encourage all the members of the Opus Dei prelature to persevere in this work, in faithful continuity with the spirit of service to the Church which always inspired the life of your founder.

With these sentiments, I invoke on all an abundance of heavenly gifts, in pledge of which I most cordially impart my Blessing to you and to all who are inspired by the teachings and example of Blessed Josemaría Escrivá de Balaguer.

Vatican City, October 14, 1993

---

2 Bl. Josemaría Escrivá, *The Way*, Dublin, 1985, 301.

Papal Audience

Greeting by Bishop Alvaro del Portillo

Holy Father, one and a half years ago the Prelature of Opus Dei and with it countless faithful the world over had the immense joy of hearing your holiness proclaim the solemn formula of beatification of its founder, Josemaría Escrivá.

As part of the ceremonies to commemorate that ecclesial event, the Roman Atheneum of the Holy Cross, which owes its existence to the prayer and zeal of Blessed Josemaría, decided to hold a theological symposium on the subject of his teachings.

In the course of the conference itself, after the cordial inaugural greeting from his eminence, the cardinal prefect of the Congregation for the Doctrine of the Faith, scholars from different countries read papers on the three main aspects of Blessed Josemaría's teaching—the call to holiness and apostolate in everyday life; the spiritual life, as an intimate relationship with God based on a sense of divine filiation; and the Christian as the life of the world.

These papers and the discussions which followed them showed the richness of the spiritual message of the founder of Opus Dei, which throws so much light helpful to a theological understanding of the Christian calling; as also on the call which every Christian receives to sanctify his own life, conscious of his gift of divine filiation and in a spirit of generous dedication to all mankind, especially those most needy, materially or spiritually. Through the spread of this generous exercise of

Christian solidarity, Blessed Josemaría's message and example reach further and further to the benefit of all: and those who are experiencing suffering continue to be (as was the case when Opus Dei was starting) the column on which the apostolic work of the prelature rests.

The symposium papers in their final form confirm us in our conviction about the historical importance of the founder of Opus Dei, and give us new encouragement to continue to spread throughout the Church the fruit of a foundational charism whose effectiveness is already to be seen in so many places all over the world and in all walks of life.

The members of the Prelature of Opus Dei, priests and lay people, learned from Blessed Josemaría to love and serve the Church with all their heart, with their entire life, always keeping very close to the Pope and the bishops. Faithful to his example, I want to assure Your Holiness of our most filial and full attachment, and today we should like to add a special word of thanks for your recent Encyclical *Veritatis splendor*. We are all so very pleased that this meeting is being held so close to the fifteenth anniversary of election of Your Holiness to the see of Peter. It makes me very happy to be able to assure the Pope, from so close to hand, that our prayer for him and for his intentions, always an assiduous and active prayer, will today be even more fervent and happy (if that be possible). Greetings, Holy Father: *ad multos annos, semper feliciores*. Finally, Holy Father, allow me to request on behalf of myself and all those taking part in the symposium your apostolic blessing.

Opening Ceremony

Address by Bishop Alvaro del Portillo

Your eminences, your excellencies, distinguished academics, ladies and gentlemen.

These words of mine have a double purpose – to open the theological symposium on the teachings of Blessed Josemaría Escrivá, and to inaugurate the academic year of the Roman Atheneum of the Holy Cross.

In this connection, I am pleased to recall something his holiness John Paul II said in his homily during the solemn mass of beatification of the founder of Opus Dei: 'With supernatural intuition, Blessed Josemaría untiringly preached the universal call to holiness and apostolate. [...] In a society in which an unbridled craving for material things turns them into idols and a cause of separation from God, the new beatus reminds us that these same things, creatures of God and of human industry, if used correctly for the glory of the Creator and the service of one's brothers and sisters, can be a way for men and women to meet Christ'.

The Holy Father was drawing attention here to the core of the spiritual message of the founder of Opus Dei, and stressing its pastoral and theological importance. In the months that have gone by since May 17, 1992, as is normal in the year following a beatification, many liturgical ceremonies of thanksgiving were held. Following on the beatification, devotion to Blessed Josemaría Escrivá, which was already world-wide, has been steadily on the increase. During the same period special lectures have been given in many countries which have also helped show the ecclesial and social signification of Blessed Josemaría's life and work.

That is also the purpose of the symposium starting today, and which marks the opening of the Atheneum's academic year. Nine years ago now, in October 1984, in the homily of the Mass which inaugurated the activities of the then Centro Academico, and now the Roman Atheneum, I used the occasion to recall the care with which Monsignor Escrivá de Balaguer for years prepared the ground for the establishment of this institution, through his prayer and personal effort. You can imagine how pleased and happy it makes me today to open a new academic year and, along with it, a symposium which brings together students and teachers from a number of different countries, to study some aspects of Blessed Josemaría's rich teachings.

In one of his Letters, Monsignor Escrivá wrote an idea about the history of the Church, which can also be applied to the history of Opus Dei: 'First comes life, the lived pastoral phenomenon. And then law, which usually develops out of custom. And last of all, theological doctrine, which develops step by step with the lived phenomenon.'[1] This idea reflects not only his personal experience as a founder, but also his profound and lively faith. For the words I have just read point, above all, to the primary role of the action of God: the life he is speaking about is not human life *per se*, much less mere vitality, but life as it develops in the Church as the fruit of the grace won by Christ on the Cross and made operative thanks to the action of the Holy Spirit which is something constant and always new and surprising. This life, this Christian life, is something basic and fundamental to everything else.

But Christian life is life in the Church. The Holy Spirit, sent by the Father and the Son, enables us to understand the truth that Christ has entrusted to his Church and he stirs us to live in the unity of ecclesial communion. This life set in motion by the Holy Spirit develops in the bosom of the Christian community, in union with the entire Body of the Church, and in filial adhesion to those who exercise the ministry of Pastors in that Body. And that is why law (and along with it approval and recognition by ecclesiastical authority) comes immediately after the lived phenomenon.

---

1 Letter, March 19, 1954, 9.

However, the process does not stop there, because life and law go back to the truth of the Gospel, on which everything that is genuinely Christian is grounded. It is at this point that theology comes into play, theology being that effort-in-faith to understand more deeply the life of the Church and of its institutions. This stage, then, is the fruit that maturity brings—'last of all', Blessed Josemaría said in the passage which I am discussing; we are, therefore, in the presence of a fully developed life, which makes it possible and necessary for theology to do its serene work of reflection and analysis.

In recent years many studies by theologians and canon lawyers have been published on the spirituality of Opus Dei and the teachings of its founder. And yet it is only natural that his beatification, and the considerable ecclesial effects it has had, should give rise to renewed interest in this subject, as evidenced by this symposium. Sixty years have already gone by since the foundation of Opus Dei, and almost twenty since its founder went to heaven. A long time, in terms of the life of man; and yet not a long time at all if we look at it in historical terms or in terms of the process of understanding the intellectual and theological implications of a spiritual message. Even though many essays have appeared which study the person and teaching of Blessed Josemaría, there is much, very much, still to be done.

Monsignor Josemaría Escrivá's central teachings are now very well known, and some of them have been incorporated into solemn declarations of the Magisterium of the Church. But most of them fall into areas which theology has scarcely begun to explore. The symposium which begins today aims to make a contribution in this regard, focusing its attention on three general points of special importance – the vocation to holiness, the spiritual life and the sanctification of work. When these three days of study have been concluded, and in response to the wishes of the organizing committee, I shall be very happy to write a commentary for inclusion in the Proceedings which will later be published, in order to offer my own thoughts on the themes of the symposium.

However, I should like to say at this point that the more I study and meditate in prayer on the teachings of Blessed Josemaría, the more I am convinced that I am only beginning to explore something indescribably rich, which seems to be constantly inviting me to make fascinating and ever-new discoveries. And like so many who approach his thought, his life, I always feel ever more impelled to praise the superabundance of divine Goodness, which shines out so dazzlingly from those gifts the Trinity has given the Church in its saints and beatified members.

I do not wish to conclude without expressing my gratitude to his eminence Joseph Cardinal Ratzinger for his Inaugural Message to the symposium, and also to greet all the speakers and those who take part in the round-tall discussions, as also the organizing committee and all those present.

As I pointed out, this occasion also marks the opening of a new academic year at the Roman Atheneum of the Holy Cross. The work of its teachers and of its non-teaching personnel, and also the interest taken and study done by its students, has enabled a university institution begun scarcely nine years ago to acquire a distinguished personality and look forward to a bright future. At this point, not without emotion, I should like to recall one of those who have contributed decisively to the consolidation of the Atheneum; I refer, as you must realize, to its Secretary General, the very reverend Monsignor Guiseppe Molteni, whom God called into his presence last August, in a way unforeseen by us, but foreseen by his infinite and fatherly Mercy. For me, and for all the academic staff, it is consoling to think that from heaven, beside Blessed Josemaría, he will continue to look after the Atheneum and encourage its scholarly activities, and be a particular help to the new Secretary General.

To conclude these words of greeting to all those taking part in this symposium, I also declare inaugurated the 1993–94 academic year of the Roman Atheneum of the Holy Cross.

Opening Ceremony

Message from Joseph Cardinal Ratzinger

'A song of praise to God arises from this vale of tears. Around God's throne there is a growing choir of the redeemed, whose lives are now a selfless progress of love and glorification. Not only in heaven are these voices heard; they rise from us too, for a call comes to us from the throne, from the seat of God: "Praise our God, all you his servants, you who fear him, small and great" (Rev 19:5). It is an appeal to us too, here and now, to join in this eternal liturgy.'

I spoke these words a little over a year ago, in May 1992, in the homily at one of the Masses celebrated in thanksgiving for the beatification of Josemaría Escrivá.

It was only logical that, on such an occasion, I should evoke the heavenly liturgy: every beatification is an act whereby the Church, recognizing that one of its children has merited to enter the intimacy of God, should proclaim the convocation of heaven and earth. The Christian people, making its pilgrim way on earth, sometimes through great difficulties and bitter experiences, knows that it is part of something much bigger—the City of the saints which, begun and shaped on earth, will fill heaven.

It was logical, I say again, that in the thanksgiving Mass for a beatification, these essential perspectives of the Christian faith should be evoked and remembered: is not the eucharistic celebration the point at which the Church confesses and shares more deeply in that union between earth and heaven that beatifications and canonizations speak to us about? But is it also logical to evoke similar perspectives on the present occasion, at the start of a scholarly meeting? A symposium: is that the proper place to make mystical and pious observations? Is it not rather the moment to allow scholarship to do its work, whether the scholarship that works on the data of history, subjecting the texts of the past to critical analysis, or that which engages in more abstract analysis, dealing in concepts and seeking proofs?

Theology, which is science in the fullest sense of the word, undoubtedly does produce some results when scholarship is applied to it. Despite that, it is not out of order to evoke in this context what goes on in heaven; indeed, one needs to do that, because theology only makes sense when viewed from that perspective. Thomas Aquinas coined a formula to describe this, a justly famous one and widely repeated: theology is a form of knowledge subordinate to the knowledge that God has and the knowledge that saints have. This statement is couched in Aristotelian terms and reflects those texts in which Aristotle showed that the sciences are not unconnected intellectual worlds, but bodies of knowledge which are connected with one another, in such a way that some are based on others and therefore are subordinate to others. These ideas about the interconnections between the sciences were worked out by Thomas Aquinas when he was establishing the bases of theology. The Christian is a wayfarer, someone who does not see God, although the word of revelation gives him some insight into the mystery. Therefore, he does have knowledge, but for it he is dependent on the knowledge of another. Theology, which is born of faith, is, then, subordinate to the knowledge that God has of himself and in which the saints now partake in a direct and definitive way.

In describing things in this way, St. Thomas wanted to stress that the human heart's yearning for truth, and more so the Christian's, a yearning which is the origin of theology, is not the result of some illusion, is not some desire fated always to remain unfulfillled; it in fact represents a capacity God has inscribed on our spirit and a desire he will one day quell. Theology will find its ultimate outlet in vision, in that vision which is already a reality for the saints.

But to consider theology as a branch of knowledge subordinate to God's knowledge and that of the saints, not only implies a tension towards eschatology, towards the final consumation, that moment when the truth, already glimpsed, made known through words, is fully revealed and we have that ultimate knowledge that belongs to the saints. It also applies, given the very nature of theology, a reference to that living union with God which is attainable, even on earth, by those who, putting their faith in the word of God, make that word their own and give their heart entirely to it. For God is at one and the same time, and inseparably, truth, goodness and beauty, and the unitive force of love not only leads one to let oneself be pierced by his love; it also leads one to study his truth.

The theologian should be a man of scholarship; but he should also, precisely because he is a theologian, be a man of prayer. He must pay attention to the developments in history and scholarship, but, even more than that, he needs to listen to the testimony of those who, having gone the full way on the path of prayer, have, even in this life, attained the highest reaches of divine intimacy; that is, the testimony of those who, in ordinary language, we call saints. As we have already pointed out elsewhere,[1] the knowledge of God, saints tell us, is 'the reference-point for theological history; it is what keeps it right. In this sense, the work of theologians is always "secondary" to the real experience of saints. Without this point of reference, without being firmly anchored in such experiences, theology ceases to be real.' Practicing theology, devoting oneself to theological research and teaching, does not mean carrying out

---

1 J. Ratzinger, *To look on Christ: Exercises in Faith, Hope and Love* (New York, 1991), p. 33.

a cold, disembodied work; it means concerning oneself with a God who is love, and who is reached by love.

Now that the cleavage between 'theologians' and 'spirituals' which developed at the start of the modern age is a thing of the past, as is also the severe intellectualism which is one of the extremes of the Enlightenment stance, contemporary theology proclaims that there is indeed a close connection between theology and spirituality, thereby inviting spirituality back into the great Christian tradition. Therefore, it makes eminent sense to organize—as the culmination of a year designed to celebrate a beatification—a symposium; and it also makes sense that the words which open this session should evoke the heavenly liturgy, the choir of angels and saints who have attained the vision of God: for theology draws its nourishment from that vision and from anticipation of it in contemplative prayer.

So, it is appropriate and even necessary for us as theologians to listen to what the saints have to say, in order to discover what their message means: it is a multifaceted message, for there are many saints, and each has been given his or her own charism; and at the same time it is only one message because the saints refer us to the one and only Christ, to whom they are joined and whose richness they help us to see. In this diverse yet unique symphony that is, as Möhler would say, the Christian tradition, what particular emphasis does Blessed Josemaría Escrivá bring? What impulse does he give theology? It is not for me to answer these questions: the speakers at this congress will tell us what they think, and to what they have to say will be added the thoughts of those who, sharing the spirit of Blessed Josemaría Escrivá and on account of his message, will devote themselves, as time goes by, to teaching and theological research.

However, there is something which one immediately notices when one comes in contact with the life of Mon-

---

2 *The Way*, 584.

signor Escrivá de Balaguer or with his writings—a very vivid sense of the presence of Christ. 'Stir up that fire of faith. Christ is not a figure that has passed. He is not a memory that is lost in history. He lives! *"Jesus Christus heri et hodie, ipse et in saecula"*, says Saint Paul,—"Jesus Christ is the same today as he was yesterday and as he will be for ever",' he writes in *The Way*.² This Christ who is alive is also a Christ who is near, a Christ in whom the power and majesty of God make themselves present through ordinary, simple, human things.

One can, then, speak of Blessed Josemaría Escrivá having a marked and special type of Christ-centerdness, in which contemplation of Jesus' life on earth and contemplation of his living presence in the Eucharist lead one to discover God; and from God they throw light onto the circumstances of our everyday life. 'The fact that Jesus grew up and lived just like us shows us that human existence and all the ordinary activity of men have a divine meaning. No matter how much we may have reflected on this', he goes on, 'we should always be surprised when we think of the thirty years of obscurity which made up the greater part of Jesus' life among men. He lived in obscurity, but, for us, that period is full of light. It illuminates our days and fills them with meaning, for we are ordinary Christians who lead an ordinary life, just like millions of other people all over the world.'³

There are two things we can learn from these reflections on the life of Jesus, from the deep mystery of the fact that a God not only became man but also took on the human condition, making himself the same as us, except for sin (Heb 4:15). First of all is the universal call to holiness, to whose proclamation Blessed Josemaría made such a contribution, as John Paul II recalled in his homily during the beatification Mass. But also, to give body to this call, there is the recognition that holiness is reached, under the influence of the Holy Spirit, through

---

3 *Christ Is Passing By*, 14.

ordinary life. Holiness consists in this – living our daily life with our sights fixed on God; shaping all our actions to accord with the Gospel and the spirit of Faith. Each and every theological understanding of the world and of history derives from this core reality, as many passages in the writings of Blessed Josemaría so clearly and incisively show. 'This world of ours,' he proclaimed in a homily, 'is good, for so it came from God's hands. It was Adam's offence, the sin of human pride, which broke the divine harmony of creation. But God the Father, in the fullness of time, sent his only-begotten Son to take flesh in Mary ever Virgin, through the Holy Spirit, and re-establish peace. In this way, by redeeming man from sin, "we receive adoption as sons" (Gal 4:5). We become capable of sharing the intimacy of God. In this way the new man, the new line of the children of God (cf. Rom 6:4–5), is enabled to free the whole universe from disorder, restoring all things in Christ (cf. Eph 1:9–10), as they have been reconciled with God (cf. Col 1:20).'[4]

In this splendid passage, the great truths of the Christian faith (the infinite love of God the Father, his goodness which is responsible for creation, the redemptive work of Jesus Christ, divine filiation, identification of the Christian with Christ . . .), are linked up to shed light on the life of the Christian, particularly the Christian living in the midst of the world, with all his complex secular involvements. Underlying dogmatic insights are projected onto everyday life, and that life is encouraged to rethink, to really take to heart, the Christian message in its entirety; a spiral movement is set in motion, which involves and supports theological reflection.

But, as I said before, it is not for me to do that work, but simply to launch this symposium. I hope that what I have said, and my desire that your study of Blessed Josemaría Escrivá's spiritual message, will contribute to the development of theology to the benefit of the whole Church.

---

4 *Christ Is Passing By*, 183.

PART I: HOLINESS

The vocation to holiness in Christ and in the Church

Fernando Ocáriz, Pontifical Roman Atheneum of the Holy Cross

This paper, naturally, is tailored to the general theme of this symposium: it seeks to provide an over-view of that theme, a framework into which the papers that follow will fit harmoniously, aiming as they do to explore theologically the teachings of Blessed Josemaría Escrivá. However, given the originality and depth of the teachings of the founder of Opus Dei on the universal call to holiness, this paper will contain many references to his writings, and key references at that.[1]

My contribution will be structured around four points:

1. the call to holiness as a vocation to be and to live *in Christo*;
2. the fact that this divine call is addressed to all men and women;
3. the ecclesial dimension of this vocation and of holiness;
4. the vocation to holiness and the mission to reconcile creation to God.

I. Calls to holiness in Christ

Even nowadays the concept of holiness, as far as man is concerned, tends to be associated with that area of theology known as Spiritual Theology. Therefore, before

---

[1] At certain points I shall elaborate on ideas contained in my article in P. Rodríguez, F. Ocáriz and J.L. Illanes, *Opus Dei in the Church* (Dublin and Princeton, 1994), ch. 2, pp. 77–120.

looking at the subject from the ascetical and mystical point of view, I think it is important to remember that the concept of holiness is a basic concept of theology, one that has to do with the very essence of divine Revelation in history. Thus in the Dogmatic Constitution *Dei Verbum* we read that 'the invisible God, from the fullness of his love, addresses men as his friends, and moves among them in order to invite and receive them into communion with him'. This economy of Revelation is realized by deeds and words, which are intrinsically bound up with each other. As a result, the works performed by God in the history of salvation show forth and bear out the doctrine and realities signified by the words; and the words, for their part, proclaim the works, and bring to light the mystery they contain. The most intimate truth which this revelation gives us about God and the salvation of man shines forth in Christ, who is himself both the mediator and the sum total of Revelation.[2]

This communion with God, in which the holiness of man consists, has taken different forms of expression over the course of salvation history. In the Old Testament the Covenant between God and Israel was central, involving God's presence alongside his people.[3] The communion established by the Covenant involves Israel's *belonging* in a special way to the transcendent God (the Holy One). Israel is a holy people, in the sense that it belongs in a special way to the Holy One, which in turn means that it is divided off from other nations. This holiness also makes moral demands on the members of the Holy People, as expressly stated in the solemn words of Leviticus: 'You shall be holy, for I the Lord your God am holy.'[4]

In the New Covenant established in Christ, this divine place for holiness is extended explicitly to all nations, to all men and women, in line with the eternal will

---

[2] Second Vatican Council, Const. *Dei Verbum*, 20.
[3] Cf., for example, L. Bouyer, *La Bible et l'Evangile* (Paris, 1951), pp. 11–18.
[4] Lev 19:2; cf. 11:44.

of God, already revealed in the promise made to Abraham: 'by your descendants shall all the nations of the earth bless themselves'.[5] And so St. Paul can say not only to Jews but also to Gentiles: 'This is the will of God, your sanctification.'[6] This sanctification involves primarily, so to speak, a commitment on God's part: what he wants to bring about is the sanctification of man. But, because the human person is a free agent, St. Paul's assertion also makes moral demands on man; this moral dimension of the call to holiness is expressed very categorically in Jesus' words: 'You must be perfect, as your heavenly Father is perfect.'[7]

I shall come back later to the connection between the concept of perfection and that of holiness. But first I think it is useful to stress that the invitation to communion with Him, which God makes to man, shows us that it is God's will that all should be saved. Leaving to one side their semantic differences, the terms *salvation* and *sanctity* (holiness) mean in fact the same thing. As St. Paul writes to Timothy, God 'desires all men to be saved and to come to the knowledge of the truth;'[8] that is, to attain personal and not just intellectual union with that Truth, which is also the Way and the Life;[9]—union with Christ, and in Him with the Father and with the Holy Spirit.[10] 'This is the great boldness of the Christian faith', we read in one of Blessed Josemaría's homilies, 'to proclaim the value and dignity of human nature and to affirm that we have been created to achieve the dignity of children of God, through the grace that raises us up to a supernatural level. An incredible boldness it would be, were it not founded on the promise of salvation given

---

5 Gen 22:18. Cf. Gal 3:16; 26–29.

6 1 Tit 4:3.

7 Mt 5:48.

8 1 Tim 2:4. Cf. 2 Tim 2:25; Heb 10:26; Col 3:10.

9 Cf. H. Zimmerman, 'Knowledge of God' and J.B. Bauer, 'Truth', in J.B. Bauer (ed.), *Sacramentum verbi; an encyclopedia of Biblical theology* (New York, 1970), pp. 472–8 and 927–33.

10 Cf. Jn 14:6.

us by God the Father, confirmed by the blood of Christ, and reaffirmed and made possible by the constant action of the Holy Spirit.'[11]

Holiness, in the sense of communion with God, means that the created person shares in the uncreated holiness of God;[12] more specifically, it is a communion-participation by men in the inner life of the Trinity,[13] as 'sons in the Son'.[14] Consequently, as the founder of Opus Dei so profoundly puts it, holiness is 'the fullness of divine filiation',[15] and therefore complete identification with Jesus Christ, the Only-begotten Son of the Father.[16] So we have to say that God's universal salvific will, insofar as it is a call to holiness, is a *Christian calling*: God has so designed things that every human being is conceived and loved in Christ, that is, as a Christian.[17]

In its turn, calling involves a choosing: as we read in the Letter to the Ephesians, God has chosen us in Christ 'before the foundation of the world, that we should be holy';[18] and so we can say with St. Clement of Rome that 'God chose our Lord Jesus Christ, and (chose) us with Him'.[19] In other words, 'Jesus Christ, who is the Chosen One *par excellence*, epitomizes the entirety of God's election, and Christians will therefore be men and

---

11 *Christ Is Passing By*, op. cit., 133.

12 Cf. L. Scheffczyk, 'La santidad de Dios, fin y forma de la vida cristiana', in *Scripta theologica* 11 (1979), pp 1021–36; J.L. Illanes, *Mundo y santidad* (Madrid, 1984), pp. 21–36.

13 Cf. 2 Pet 1:4; 1 Jn 1:3.

14 Cf. John Paul II, Enc. *Dominum et vivificantem*, 18 May 1986, 32.

15 Letter, 2 February 1945, 8.

16 Cf. Rom 8:29–30. Cf. F. Ocáriz, 'La filiación divina, realidad central en la vida y en la enseñanza de Mons. Josemaría Escrivá de Balaguer', in F. Ocáriz and I. de Celaya, *Vivir como hijos de Dios* (Pamplona, 1993), pp. 15–89.

17 Cf. A. Pigna, *La vocación: teología y discernimiento*, 2nd ed. (Madrid, 1988), p. 15.

18 Eph 1:4.

19 St. Clement of Rome, *Epist. ad Corint.*, c. 64 (Funk 1, 182). Cf. St. Augustine, *Sermon* 304, 1–4.

women in Christ.'[20] This helps us see the depth of that passage in the Constitution *Gaudium et spes* which says that only in Christ does the mystery of man truly become clear; only in the mystery of the Word made flesh does one find *ab aeterno* the origin, meaning and purpose of the existence of any human being, the sublimity of his calling.[21]

Complete identification with Christ is inseparable from the perfection of Charity, because charity, as St. Thomas Aquinas explains, is 'a certain participation in that infinite love which is the Holy Spirit';[22] and it is the Holy Spirit that is entrusted with the task to 're-generate us as children in the Son'.[23] Therefore, charity constitutes, in the scale of virtues, the fullness of the law,[24] the essence of holiness.

We come to the same conclusion when we study *holiness* as man's *perfection*, in line with Christ's precept which calls us to be perfect as the heavenly Father is perfect. As we are well aware, the etymological meaning of the words *perfection* and *perfect*, in both Latin (*perfectio, perfectus*) and Greek (*teletes, téleios*) involves the notion of attainment of the aim, of a process of becoming, or of maturation. Therefore, obviously, that meaning can be applied to God only in an improper analogous sense. However, the concept of perfection as *fullness of being, and therefore of goodness*, can be applied to God in a proper analogous sense. Because the human person is a substantial unity of matter and spirit, per-

---

20 J. Morales, 'La vocación en el Antiguo Testamento', in *Scripta theologica*, 19 (1987), p. 61.

21 Cf. Second Vatican Council, Const. *Gaudium et spes*, 22.

22 St. Thomas Aquinas, *Summa theologiae*, I–II, q. 24, a. 7, c. On holiness as the perfection of charity, cf. ibid., q. 184, a. 3.

23 John Paul II, Apos. Exhort. *Christifideles laici*, 30 December 1988, 12; cf. 11. Therefore, the dynamic of the Christian life can be summarized as follows: 'to the Father—in the Son—through the Holy Spirit' (John Paul II, Enc. *Dominum et vivificantem*, 32). For more on this see F. Ocáriz, *Hijos de Dios en Cristo. Introducción a una teología de la participación sobrenatural* (Pamplona, 1972).

24 Rom 13:10. Cf. 1 Cor 13:1–3.

fection, so to speak, breaks down into a variety of different 'perfections'. However, as St. Thomas Aquinas explains, man is good *simpliciter et totaliter* thanks to his good will, whereas every other perfection, every intellectual perfection, makes him good only *secundum quid*; and the reason why this is so is that free will is the faculty which governs the entire person.[25] Consequently, in the supernatural order charity constitutes the higher goodness of the will and therefore it is what makes man *simpliciter et totaliter bonus*: man's supernatural perfection, his holiness, is brought about by charity.

But this perfection is never fully achieved, for it is always capable of further perfection: on the natural level, by the unlimited openness of the spirit; and on the supernatural level, by the (also unlimited) nature of charity. And so we read in the book of Revelation: 'let him who is holy be holier still.'[26] Hence our reflection on holiness *qua* perfection leads us to another definition of holiness: holiness is communion with God in Christ, identification with Christ. Thus, Christ alone is the *perfect man*, in the full sense: only that human nature which is hypostatically joined to the divine Person has non-perfectible communion with God, and only the human nature of the incarnate Word, thanks to that very hypostatic union, has the fullness of grace and of charity in the absolute sense.

From all this (shrouded in the luminous darkness of the Trinitarian and Christological mystery) stem important theological consequences for the spiritual life of human beings. And, as Monsignor Alvaro del Portillo has pointed out, in the life and writings of Blessed Josemaría we discover a spirituality which is strongly rooted in the 'profound perfection of the richness contained in the mystery

---

25 Cf. St. Thomas Aquinas, *De virtutibus in communi*, a. 9 ad 16. See also C. Fabro, 'El primado existencial de la libertad', in various authors, *Mons. Josemaría Escrivá de Balaguer y el Opus Dei*, 2nd ed. (Pamplona, 1985), p. 344.

26 Rev 22:11: interpreted in this sense by Council of Trent, Decr. *De iustificatione*, chap. 10 (DS 1535).

of the incarnate Word'.[27] But we should pause here, in order to move on to the second part of this paper.

II. The vocation to holiness is addressed to all

From what we have seen so far, God's call to holiness *in Christ*, that is, the Christian vocation, is clearly addressed to all. The most obvious meaning of this *universal* call is what we might term its *subjective* dimension, in the sense that all men and women personally receive this call. So, this 'universality' should not be interpreted as something counterpoised to 'particularity': it is not simply a *general* call, for the Lord says to all individually as he said to Israel: 'I have called you by name, you are mine.'[28] But there is also an *objective* dimension to the universality of this call; this lies in the fact that all the circumstances of each person's life can be the *place* and *means of* sanctification; and at every point in every person's existence the word of this God who calls is present and active; we might term this the *all-embracing* nature of God's call.

From the beginning of his mission as founder, Blessed Josemaría Escrivá never ceased to preach the universal call to holiness in the sense of the two dimensions I have termed *subjective* and *objective*.[29] Take, for example, this passage in a Letter of March 24, 1930: 'We have come to say, with the humility of one who knows he is a sinner and not worth much—*homo peccator sum* (Lk 5:8), we say with Peter —but with the faith of someone who lets himself be guided by the hand of God—that holiness is not something for a privileged few: the Lord calls all of us, Love awaits all of us: everyone, wherever he may

---

27 A. del Portillo, *Intervista sul fondatore dell'Opus Dei*, conducted by C. Cavallieri (Milan, 1992), p. 70. Cf. also T. Gutiérrez Calzada, 'Teología, cultura y amor a la Iglesia, en el beato Josemaría Escrivá de Balaguer', in *Scripta theologica* 25 (1993), esp. pp. 176–84.

28 Is 43:1.

29 Cf. A. del Portillo, *Una vida para Dios: reflexiones en torno a la figura de Josemaría Escrivá de Balaguer* (Madrid, 1992), pp. 69–73.

be; everyone, whatever his state-in-life, his job or his occupation. For that ordinary, everyday life, apparently unimportant, can be a means to holiness: you do not need to give up your own particular place in the world, to seek God, unless the Lord gives you a vocation to the religious life, for all the ways of the earth can give you the opportunity to meet Christ.'[30]

At that time, and for many years later, teaching of this sort was uncommon in Catholic circles. The *subjective dimension* of the universality of vocation (that is, of the fact that all are called to holiness) could be found more or less explicitly in the preaching and writings of many saints and masters of spirituality throughout the history of the Church;[31] but it did not come across very forcefully, for holiness was regarded only as a very remote possibility for *all* Christians only some of whom were *in fact* able to set out on the path to sanctity.

Even less widespread was an awareness of what we have termed the *objective dimension* of the universal call to holiness, that is, of the fact that all situations and circumstances in ordinary life can and should be the place and the way to attain communion with God. It was not realized that the great majority of Christians, being immersed in temporal activities, are called to holiness not 'in spite of' their ordinary circumstances but indeed precisely *in* and *through* those circumstances. The founder of Opus Dei wrote: 'How clear, to those who could read the Gospel, was that universal call to holiness in ordinary life, in one's work, without leaving one's place! However, for centuries, most Christians didn't realize this: it was not possible to have the ascetical phenomenon of many people seeking holiness in that way, without leaving their place, sanctifying their profession and sanctifying themselves by means of their profession.

---

30 Letter, March 24, 1930, 2. Cf. *Christ Is Passing By*, 20.
31 A partial, but useful, summary is to be found in J. Daujat, *La vita soprannaturale* (Rome, 1958), pp. 561–73.

And, very soon, by dint of its not being practiced, this doctrine was forgotten'.[32]

Nowadays, especially through the teachings of the Second Vatican Council,[33] this doctrine has become widespread; it is explicitly stated in the *Catechism of the Catholic Church*,[34] and it has been spelt out once again by John Paul II in his recent Encyclical *Veritatis splendor*, in the context of a commentary on a Gospel passage—the one about the rich young man—which, at first sight might seem to establish a distinction between the call to eternal life and the call to perfection.[35] However, a mentality persists that sees holiness as something accessible only to a few. As Joseph Cardinal Ratzinger has put it, 'The word "saint" has, unfortunately, undergone a narrowing over the years, and even today it leads us to think of sermonized saints, miracles and heroic virtues, things which are all very well for the chosen few, but not for us. Holiness then becomes a matter for this mysterious elite, while we carry on as we were. Josemaría Escrivá shook people out of this spiritual apathy: no, holiness is not unusual, it is expected from every baptized person. It does not consist in extraordinary deeds, but has thousands of facets. It can be practiced in all sorts of situations and occupations.'[36]

Thus, the perfection of charity, the fullness of divine filiation, is not perforce linked to exceptional deeds or actions atypical of everyday life; in fact, it can and should affect everything one does, including actions which seem quite insignificant; in those very actions a

---

32 Letter, January 9, 1932, 91; cf. J.L. Illanes' profound historical summary, 'Dos de octubre de 1928: alcance y significado de una fecha', in various authors, Mons. Josemaría Escrivá de Balaguer, op. cit., esp. pp. 96–101. Cf. also Illanes, *Mundo y santidad*, op. cit., pp. 65–79.

33 Cf. Second Vatican Council, Const. *Lumen gentium*, 11 and 39–41.

34 Cf. *Catechism of the Church*, 825.

35 Cf. Enc. *Veritatis splendor*, 6 August 1993, 18.

36 'Hombre', May 19, 1992, in various authors, *17 Maggio 1992. La beatificanzione di Josemaría Escrivá de Balaguer, fondatore dell'Opus Dei* (Milan, 1992), p. 113.

person has to live in communion with God. We read in the first Letter to the Corinthians: 'Every one should remain in the state [the original Greek uses the word *klesis*, calling] in which he was called.'[37] Clearly this means that the Christian vocation *per se* (except in special instances) does not involve a change in one's situation in the world; in fact, one could even say that, insofar as it asks the ordinary faithful to stay where they are, it confirms the full value of ordinary life in the midst of the world, as the place and means for attaining the aim of vocation, which is none other than holiness.[38]

This leads us to reflect on what is termed *human vocation* as an integral part of man's vocation to holiness. By *human vocation*, I mean those natural abilities, enriched by formation and developed through the circumstances of a person's life and previous decisions, which incline him to give a particular orientation to his life. In the light of faith, a Christian discovers in his or her leanings a providential plan and therefore a call from God. In one of his homilies Blessed Josemaría explained the role of human vocation in the context of divine vocation in these words: 'Your human vocation is a part—and an important part—of your divine vocation. That is the reason why you must strive for holiness, giving a particular character to your human personality, a certain stamp to your life; contributing at the same time to the sanctification of others, your fellow men; sanctifying your work and your environment— the profession or job that fills your day; your home and family; and the country where you were born and which you love.'[39]

---

37 1 Cor 7:20.

38 On this exegesis of 1 Cor 7:20, see A. García Suárez, 'El misterio de la Parusía y el apostolado de San Pablo,' in *Misiones extranjeras* 11 (1964), pp. 144–6; P. Rodriguez, *Vocación, trabajo, contemplación*, 2nd ed. (Pamplona, 1987), pp. 37–42; M.A. Tábet, 'La santificazione nella propria condizione di vita (commento esegetico di 1 Cor 7:17–24', in *Romana* 4 (1988), pp. 169–76.

39 *Christ Is Passing By*, 46. Cf. Bl. Josemaría Escrivá, *Friends of God* (Dublin, London and New York, 1981), 60.

Any honorable human activity can be the place and means for practicing Christian love, which is the fullness of the law. This is something Blessed Josemaría asserted very vigorously, convinced as he was that it was the core of his message; and he spoke of it, above all, apropos of work, which is a basic human reality: 'This is why man ought not to limit himself to material production. Work is born of love; it is a manifestation of love and is directed toward love. We see the hand of God, not only in the wonders of nature, but also in our experience of work and effort. Work thus becomes prayer and thanksgiving, because we know we are placed on earth by God, that we are loved by him and made heirs to his promises. We have been rightly told, "In eating, in drinking, in all that you do, do everything for God's glory" (1 Cor 10:31).'[40]

As explained earlier, the objective universality of the call to holiness is also coupled to the *all-embracing* nature of God's call. In other words, it is a call which involves all aspects of a person's life. Furthermore, God's call is the basis of man's very existence: by one and the same Word, God calls a person into being and calls him or her to holiness. Therefore, 'Christian faith and calling affect our whole existence,' we read in one of Blessed Josemaría's homilies, 'not just a part of it. Our relations with God necessarily involve giving ourselves, giving ourselves completely.'[41] And this very connection between vocation, life and holiness is what makes vocation something constant, ongoing ('Our Lord is seeking us at every moment')[42] and definitive, even for those who are not *Christifideles*: as we read in the Letter to the Romans, 'the gifts and the call of God are irrevocable'.[43]

Be that as it may, it is worth stressing that the fact that a person's entire being is involved in the logic of vocation does not mean that every choice and action of a Christian

---

40 *Christ Is Passing By*, 48.

41 Ibid., 46.

42 *Friends of God*, 196.

43 Rom 11:29.

is univocally predetermined by God's call, as if Christian freedom were nothing more than mere acceptance of a pre-established divine will, something always knowable and univocal. What happens in reality is that all decisions, all actions, including those which God's call does not univocally and materially determine (and that means most of a person's actions) have to be formally in line with the logic of his or her calling: that is, with the logic of love for God and love for one's neighbor. It is in this sense that vocation not only affects a person's entire life, but also makes that life intrinsically unitary: and this brings us back to what Blessed Josemaría always stressed in his preaching, in his original and profound view of Christian life—the need for 'unity of life'.[44]

Linked to all these aspects of the universal dimension of the universal call to holiness is a profound contemplation of the mystery of the Incarnation—of that mystery which John Paul II sums up when he says that ' the "first-born of all creation", becoming incarnate in the individual humanity of Christ, unites himself in some way with the entire reality of man, which is also "flesh"—and in this reality with all "flesh", with the whole of creation'.[45] The world (which is something good and which is imbued with a certain logic insofar as it has been created by God through the Logos)[46] has been endowed through the redemptive Incarnation, with a new goodness and a new logic. Therefore, as Blessed Josemaría used to put it, 'We must love the world and work and all human things. For the world is good. Adam's sin destroyed the divine balance of creation; but God the Father sent his only Son to re-establish peace, so that we, his children by adoption, might free creation from disorder and reconcile all things to God.'[47]

---

[44] Cf. I. de Celaya, 'Unidad de vida y plenitud cristiana', in F. Ocáriz and I. de Celaya, *Vivir como hijos de Dios*, pp. 90–128.

[45] Enc. *Dominum et vivificantem*, 50.

[46] Cf. Jn 1:3; Col 1:16; Heb 1:2. Cf. J. Ratzinger, *'In the Beginning...' A Catholic Understanding of Creation and the Fall* (Huntington, 1990), pp. 13–15.

[47] *Christ Is Passing By*, 112.

III. A vocation in the Church

Whenever one thinks about the universality of the call to holiness, one cannot help thinking of the huge number of men and women who are quite unaware of this vocation. Is there not a contradiction in maintaining that God calls to holiness even those who are not conscious of being called? Well, first it must be said that we cannot know the infinite number of ways whereby the Word of God can reach the intimacy of people's consciousness; but then we have to look at two aspects of how the Word of God makes its presence felt in history:

— The first aspect is human mediation of the Word of God: because in order to be understood and taken to heart by man the Word needs some degree of human mediation. In fact, this mediation is something that is always present right through the history of Revelation, from the Word of the Covenant and the Prophetical Word, right up to the fullness of Revelation, when the Word became man in Christ.

— The second aspect is the at once individual and collective, that is, personal and communal, nature of the call God makes to man,[48] and of deification or sanctification, which is the purpose behind this call.[49] Thus, God availed himself of the people of Israel and then of the Church in order to make his salvific plans known to mankind.

These two aspects—human mediation and the personal *and* communal nature of the call—together establish the *ecclesiality* of Christian vocation, in the sense that God calls man to form part of the Church, and calls him, moreover, through the Church. The call to holiness is

---

[48] On this point cf., for example, J. Morales, 'La vocación en el Antiguo Testamento', op. cit., esp. pp. 33–5.

[49] Cf. International Theological Commission, 'Teologia, cristologia, antropologia', I, E, 5, in *Documenta-Documenti* (Vatican City, 1988), p. 333.

indeed universal, but God wants it to be recognized as truly a call from God through the human and communal mediation of the Church.[50] In other words, the Church is not only the addressee of God's election and call (prefigured by that made to Israel): the Church is also endowed with the mission of making that same call known to all men through the effectiveness that belongs to the Word of God, which not only calls to holiness but in fact also makes us holy.

This church is the convocation (*ekklesía*) of the saints,[51] who are precisely the chosen (*ekklektoí*)[52] and the called (*kletoí*).[53] Baptism itself is an effective call to holiness: as Tertullian wrote, Christians are 'called through water [*aqua vocati*]',[54] to communion with the Father, with the Son and with the Holy Spirit; and they are not just called: they are inserted into this communion, which is the essence of holiness. Thus, we read in *Lumen gentium*: 'They have been made sons of God in the baptism of faith and partakers of the divine nature and so are truly sanctified.'[55] For that very reason one can speak of a 'baptismal vocation' which, insofar as it is to be found inside a vocation to the Church,[56] is a calling not only to holiness but also to apostolate;[57] thus, the entire Church is called to proclaim, make real and spread the mystery of communion which is what constitutes its very self—that is, to reunite everything and all in

---

50 E. Ancilli, 'Santità cristiana', in *Dizionario enciclopedico di spiritualità* (ed. E. Ancilli), III (Rome, 1990), pp. 2246–9.

51 Cf. Acts 9:13, 32; 26:10; Rom 12:13; 2 Cor 13:12; Rev 5:8; etc.

52 Cf. Rom 8:33; Col 3:12; 2 Tim 2:10.

53 Cf. Rom 1:6f; 1 Cor 1:24; Rev 17:14.

54 Tertullian, *De Baptismo*, 16. Cf. J. Morales, 'La vocación cristiana en la primera patrística', in *Scripta theologica* 23 (1991), pp. 837–89.

55 Vatican Council II, Const. *Lumen gentium*, 40.

56 See J.L. Illanes, 'Vocación', in *Gran Enciclopedia Rialp*, XXIII, p. 661; S. Bisignano, 'Vocazione', in *Dizionario enciclopedico di spiritualità*, III, p. 2672.

57 Cf. Second Vatican Council, Decr. *Apostolicam actuositatem*, 2.

Christ.[58] As Blessed Josemaría Escrivá put it, 'It is the task of the millions of Christian men and women who fill the earth to bring Christ into all human activities and to announce through their lives the fact that God loves everyone and wants to save everyone.'[59]

So, one thing is perfectly clear: the fact that countless people are unaware of the call to holiness (or, at least, do not think about it), in no way takes from the universality of that call; rather, it reminds us that, in addition to God's own mysterious ways of speaking to the conscience of every human being, the economy of the Incarnation and Redemption is still active in the mystery of the Church. And therefore the divine Word which calls to holiness wants to make itself heard by all mankind through the word of the Church, through the word of the Lord's disciples.

When we were examining holiness as the fullness of charity we saw, there too, the 'ecclesial dimension' of the Christian vocation: for that vocation is a call to holiness which, by taking the form of communion with God in Christ, is thereby, perforce, communion with *all the saints* (that is, with the universal Church), and it in fact takes the form of communion in charity; in that charity which 'binds everything together'[60] and which, together with the Eucharist which is its ongoing source of nourishment, is the source of the Church's unity.[61] Therefore, any true appreciation of Christian vocation in any of its personal and particular forms rules out individualism and isolation, because it necessarily brings

---

58 Cf. S. Cong. for the Doctrine of the Faith, Letter *Communionis notio*, May 28, 1992, 4. It is a question of the *sacramentality* of the Church; on this subject see B. Gherardini, *La Chiesa è sacramento. Saggio di teologia positiva* (Rome, 1976).

59 Bl. J. Escrivá, *Conversations with Monsignor Escrivá de Balaguer* (Dublin, 1968), 112.

60 Col 3:14.

61 'Ecclesia est una [...] ex unitate caritatis, quia omnes connectuntur in amore Dei, et ad invicem in amore mutuo' (St. Thomas Aquinas, *Expositio in Symbolum Apost.*, a. 9).

with it openness to the communion of the universal Church and, through the Church, to communions with all mankind.

This ecclesial dimension of the call to holiness does not rule out there being great diversity within the people of God: in other words, ecclesial communion is not uniformity, but unity in diversity.[62] 'As there is in heaven', Blessed Josemaría wrote, 'so there is in the Holy Church, which is God's family on earth, room for everyone, for all kinds of apostolic activity, each of which has its own particular characteristics: *unusquisque proprium donum habet ex Deo: alius quidem sic, alius vero sic* (1 Cor 7:7). Each has his own special gift from God, one of one kind and one of another.'[63]

More specifically, we might briefly recall here that Christian vocation does not mean that that call should be identically the same for all. On the contrary, the call reaches each person in a personalized way: it is a call made to all, in the sense that all are called to the same goal and all the ways that lead to that goal have certain essential features in common, which is why one can say that the Christian calling is the same for all. Yet it always structured as a personal call, so that each is called to full communion with God in Christ in the Church, via that personal route along which Providence is guiding him or her.[64] As John Paul II has written, all personal vocations 'share in a deeply basic meaning—that of living out the commonly shared Christian dignity and the universal call to holiness in the perfection of love'.[65]

As we know, among the various forms taken by the Christian vocation common to all (Christian vocation is

---

[62] Cf. S. Cong. for the Doctrine of the Faith, Letter *Communionis notio*, 15–16; for a commentary on this, cf. F. Ocáriz, 'Unità e diversità nella communione ecclesiale', in *L'Osservatore Romano*, June 21, 1992.

[63] Letter, August 15, 1953, 15. See John Paul II, Apos. Exhort. *Christifideles laici*, 55–60.

[64] Cf. *Christ Is Passing By*, 112.

[65] John Paul II, *Christifideles laici*, 55. Cf. A. Pigna, 'La vocacíon', op. cit., p. 106.

never to be found in the abstract), there are some which are not just designed by the divine Providence which guides the freedom of all, but which are the outcome of a divine initiative which precedes any awareness or decision on that person's part,[66] and which leads him or her to live in some special way the spirit of Christ and his or her form of participation in the mission of the Church. We shall not stop here to study the fact, nature and diversity of vocations of that kind (what are called *specific vocations*, of which vocation to the priesthood is one), nor can we examine here what we mean by their *preceding* men's free choice, in the context of the mystery of the connections between eternity and time, between grace and freedom.[67] But it is useful here to stress once more the universality of vocation, because it would be a mistake to think that someone whose personal calling takes the form of a specific vocation (in the sense referred to) is 'more called' to communion with God and to building up the Church than those whose personal vocation, so to say, takes the direct form of the common Christian vocation.

IV. The vocation to holiness and the mission to reconcile creation to God

The divine call to holiness, in its objective universality, implies not only a requirement of personal sanctification but also the duty to set creation free from disorder and to reconcile all things to God: this means sanctifying the world. We have here what we might term the *cosmic dimension* of Christian vocation: 'All the things of the earth', Blessed Josemaría wrote, 'including material things and all the earthly and temporal activities of men, need to be raised up to God—and now, after sin, redeemed and reconciled—each in keeping with its own

---

[66] See, for example, M. Adinolfi, *L'apostolato dei Dodici nella vita di Gesù* (Milan and Turin, 1985), p. 55.

[67] On this, cf., for example, F. Ocáriz, 'Vocation to Opus Dei as a vocation in the Church', in Rodríguez, Ocáriz and Illanes, *Opus Dei in the Church*, in fn. 5, esp. pp. 145ff.

nature, in line with the immediate purpose God has given it, but not losing sight of its ultimate supernatural destiny in Jesus Christ: "for in him all the fullness of God was pleased to dwell, and through him to reconcile to himself all things, whether on earth or in heaven, making peace by the blood of the Cross" (Col 1:19–20). We must put Christ at the peak of all human activities.'[68] Therefore, the sanctification of the world and of all temporal activities and structures calls for prior recognition of the nature and proper end of each of these realities, of their creaturely value and therefore of their divine origin—hence the need first to understand their 'ultimate supernatural destiny in Jesus Christ'.

The mission to sanctify the world is one that belongs to the whole Church and, therefore, to all the faithful, to each in the way most suited to his or her personal vocation. Hence the *secular dimension* is proper and essential to the whole Church. But, as the Second Vatican Council has reminded us, it is for lay people to sanctify the world from within the activities of temporal structures:[69] this is what is called the secular 'nature' of Christian lay people. Those whose particular vocation involves distancing themselves in some way from the ordinary conditions of human life also fulfilll a very effective role in sanctifying the world; this is the case of the religious state or, more generally, of consecrated life, which belongs undeniably to the life and holiness of the Church.[70]

Clearly, the universality of the call to holiness is an assertion of the positive value of earthly things, and of work

---

[68] Letter, March 19, 1954, 7. On the expression 'to put Christ at the peak of all human acitivites', which occurs so frequently in the founder of Opus Dei's preaching and writing, see P. Rodríguez, 'Omnia traham ad meipsum. Il significato di Giovanni 12, 32 nell'esperienza spirituale di Mons. Escrivá de Balaguer', in *Annales theologici* 6 (1992), pp. 5–34.

[69] Cf. Vatican Council II, Const. *Lumen gentium*, 31, 33 and 36; Decr. *Apostolicam actuositatem*, 2 and 5; John Paul II, Apost. Exhort. *Christifideles laici*, 15. Cf. also A. del Portillo, *Fieles y laicos en la Iglesia*, 2nd ed. (Pamplona, 1981), pp. 191–7.

[70] Cf. Vatican Council II, Const. *Lumen gentium*, 44.

in particular; but that value is a theological one: we are poles apart here from any sort of naturalism. In fact, it is essential to have a theoretical and practical grasp of the primacy of grace, because it is not our strength that sanctifies the world: it is a strength given us by Christ in the Holy Spirit. In this connection it is helpful to recall what St. Mark tells us about Jesus' calling of the Apostles: he 'appointed twelve, to be with him, and to be sent out to preach and have authority to cast out demons'.[71] *Being in Christ* is, then, the indispensable premise for any effectiveness of the Apostles and, after them, of all Christians, who are called to share actively in the apostolic mission of spreading the Gospel, not just as teaching but in all its fullness as 'the power of God for salvation to every one that has faith';[72] a power which cures each and every form of illness affecting the human spirit and which sets the world free from the power of the evil one. This *being in Christ* is pre-eminently brought about in the Eucharist, 'in which the Lord gives us his Body and changes us into one single Body',[73] from which we can see that the Eucharist is 'the center and root'.[74] And it is from this eucharistic root, no less, that the mystery of the Church takes shape and is manifested in its most essential form,[75] as the entire life of the Christian becomes life in the Church and, therefore, the sign and instrument of the salvation of the world.[76]

If, on coming to the end of this paper, we look at the past and present history of the world and of the Church, we might still be tempted to think that the teaching on the universal call to holiness is, indeed, a nice theory, but it is a fairly Utopian one. This is not the place to explore the theology of history, hidden as it is in the mystery of

---

[71] Mk 3:14–15.

[72] Rom 1:16.

[73] S. Cong. for the Doctrine of the Faith, Letter *Communionis notio*, 5. On the eucharistic nature of the Church, cf. J. Ratzinger, *Il nuovo Popolo de Dio*, 4th ed. (Brescia, 1992).

[74] *Christ Is Passing By*, 87.

[75] Cf. S. Cong. Doct. Faith, Letter *Communionis notio*, 5.

[76] Cf. Second Vatican Council, Const. *Lumen gentium*, 1.

God and of his work in man and in the world. However, we should not forget that holiness is undoubtedly the goal of the personal effort of everyone, but it is also and above all *God's gift* not only to individual persons but also to the Church and to the world, insofar as the solidarity each human being has with Christ means that the holiness *in Christo* of some works mysteriously in favor of the salvation (final holiness) of many.

Having reached this point, I should like to conclude what I have to say by reading a very beautiful passage, a well-known one, from the writings of Blessed Josemaría Escrivá. Here it is:

'If we look at the history of mankind or at the present situation of the world, it makes us sad to see that after twenty centuries there are so few who claim to be Christians and fewer still who are faithful to their calling.

'Many years ago, a man with a good heart but who had no faith, said to me, pointing to a map of the world: "Look how Christ has failed! So many centuries of trying to give his teaching to men, and there you have the result: there are no Christians." There are many people nowadays who still think that way. But Christ has not failed. His word and his life continue to enrich the world. Christ's work, which his Father entrusted to him, is being carried out. His power runs right through history, bringing true life with it, and "when all things are subjected to him, then the Son himself will also be subjected to him who put all things under him, that God may be everything to every one (1 Cor 15:28)."

'God wants us to cooperate with him in this task which he is carrying out in the world. He *takes a risk with our freedom* [. . .]. Christian optimism is not something sugary, nor is it a human optimism that things will "work out well". No, its deep roots are awareness of freedom, and faith in grace. It is an optimism which makes us be demanding with ourselves. It gets us to make a real effort to respond to God's call.'[77]

---

77 *Christ Is Passing By*, 113–14.

Holiness and ordinary life in the teaching of Blessed Josemaría Escrivá

Prof. William E. May, John Paul II Institute for the Study of Marriage and the Family, Washington, D.C.

Today, some twenty-nine years after the promulgation of the Dogmatic Constitution *Lumen gentium* of Vatican Council II, one of the great truths central to that document, namely, that *all* men are called to be saints,[1] is better known by Catholics, although, unfortunately, far too many are still ignorant of it.

This great truth was, of course, at the heart of the teaching of Blessed Josemaría Escrivá from the moment he founded Opus Dei on October 2, 1928, thirty-seven years prior to *Lumen gentium*, until his death on June 26, 1975. He ceaselessly preached this truth at a time when it was commonly thought, within the Catholic world, that the call to holiness was reserved for a privileged few. This point is emphasized by numerous commentators,[2] and it was underscored by Blessed Josemaría himself in a letter written in 1954:

---

1 On this see Vatican Council II, Dogmatic Constitution *Lumen gentium*, ch. 4, 'De universali vocatione ad Sanctitatem in Ecclesia'.

2 Thus, for example, Alvaro del Portillo has insisted that the underlying spirit of the Work is, first of all, 'la santificación en la vida ordinaria, de no admitir ningún tipo de disociación entre lo humano y lo sobrenatural. La llamada a la plenitud de la vida cristiana es universal, está dirigida a todos'. 'El Camino del Opus Dei', in *Mons. Josemaría Escrivá de Balaguer y el Opus Dei en el 50 aniversario de su fundación* (2nd ed., Pamplona, 1985), pp. 35–6. And Pedro Rodríguez writes: 'Esta invitación universal a la santidad ... ha sido tema incesante de la actividad pastoral del autor de *Camino*'. See Rodríguez, *Vocación, trabajo, contemplación* (Pamplona, 1986), p. 93.

With the beginning of the Work in 1928, my preaching has been that *holiness is not something for the privileged few*. We have said that all the ways of the earth, all states of life, all the professions, all honest tasks can be divine ... we tell each one—all women and all men—that there where you are you can acquire Christian perfection.[3]

The purpose of this paper is to present systematically and examine theologically the teaching of Blessed Josemaría on ordinary life as the place and means of sanctification or holiness, giving particular attention to the sanctification of work and of the family and to the value of 'little things'.

I will begin by considering the ultimate basis for the universal call to holiness inasmuch as it is absolutely necessary for us to understand *why* we are called to be saints. I will then examine the meaning of 'sanctification' or 'holiness'—in what does it consist and what makes its attainment possible? Blessed Josemaría's insistence that ordinary or everyday life is indeed for laypeople the 'place' and 'means' of their sanctification will then be put into its context and examined, giving particular attention to the meaning of work, the value of 'little things', and the Christian meaning of marriage and family.

I. The ultimate basis for the universal call to holiness: Baptism and our divine filiation

A biblical passage frequently on the lips of Blessed Josemaría was St. Paul's insistent reminder to the Thessalonians that 'this is the Will of God, your sancti-

---

[3] Bl. Josemaría Escrivá, Rome, March, 19 1954, cited by Rodríguez, op. cit., pp. 93-4. 'Ever since the beginning of the Work in 1928, I have been preaching that *holiness is not something for a privileged few*. We have come to say that all the ways of the earth can be divine—all states-in-life, all occupations, all noble human tasks ... we tell everyone—women and men—that that is where they can attain Christian perfection.'

fication' (1 Thess 4:3).[4] We are called to be saints because of *who* we are. God made us to be the kind of things we are precisely because he willed to create beings to whom he could give his own life, his inner Triune life. 'We do not exist,' Blessed Josemaría says, 'in order to pursue just any happiness. We have been called to penetrate the intimacy of God's own life, to know and love God the Father, God the Son, and God the Holy Spirit, and to love also—in that same love of the one God in three divine Persons—the angels and all men.'[5] Indeed, the ultimate *why* and *wherefore* of our existence—the reason our nature is endowed with intelligence and freedom—is that god made us to be not only creatures, but his *children*, members of the divine family: 'Men have not been created just to build the best possible world. We have been put here on earth for a further purpose: to enter into communion with God himself.'[6] The sense of divine filiation, as Alvaro del Portillo, among others, has emphasized, is at the core of Blessed Josemaría's teaching and preaching.[7]

---

4 See, for example *Friends of God*, Homilies by Bl. Josemaría Escrivá de Balaguer (New York, 1986), 2, 177, 294.

5 *Christ Is Passing By*, Homilies by Bl. Josemaría Escrivá de Balaguer (New York, 1985), 133. See also ibid., 64, 65.

6 Ibid., 100. On this topic see Fernando Ocáriz, 'La filiación divina, realidad central en la vida y en la enseñanza de Mons. Escrivá de Balaguer', in *Mons. Josemaría Escrivá de Balaguer y el Opus Dei en el 50 aniversario de su fundación* (2nd ed., Pamplona, 1985), pp. 173–213, esp. 178–9.

7 Alvaro del Portillo, 'Foreword' to *Christ Is Passing By*, pp. 11–12: At the core of the preaching of Josemaría Escrivá 'is a sense of divine filiation ... He continually echoes St. Paul's message: 'For all who are led by the Spirit of God are sons of God. For you did not receive the spirit of slavery to fall back into fear, but you have received the spirit of sonship. When we cry 'Abba! Father!' it is the Spirit himself bearing witness with our spirit that we are children of God, and if children, then heirs, heirs of God and fellow heirs with Christ, provided we suffer with him in order that we may also be glorified with him' (Rom 8:14–17).' Cf., Bl. Josemaría's appeal to this text from St. Paul in ibid., 64, 118, 135, 136. As another commentator, Fernando Ocáriz, has observed: it is essential that the sense of divine filiation be 'understood not as just one among many theoretical truths: it should be seen and practiced as something basic, as the foundation of all Christian living': op. cit., p. 174.

We become God's children when, in baptism, 'our Father God takes possession of our lives, makes us share in the life of Christ, and gives us the Holy Spirit'.[8] Through baptism, indeed, 'we are made bearers of the word of Christ'[9] and take upon ourselves the responsibility of shaping our lives according to its demands,[10] of which the most central is that we seek earnestly the holiness to which we are called by the simple fact that we are in truth baptized persons, sealed with its sacramental character, and summoned to participate in the redemptive work of Christ.[11] In short, it is in and through baptism that we become children of God, brothers and sisters of Jesus Christ. 'God the Father ... sent to the world his only-begotten Son, to reestablish peace; so that by his redeeming men from sin, "we might become sons of God" (Gal 4:5), freed from the yoke of sin, capable of sharing in the divine intimacy of the Trinity ... It is God who has the last word—and it is a word of his saving and merciful love and, therefore, the word of our divine filiation. Therefore, I repeat ... today, with St. John: "See how greatly the Father has loved us; that we should be counted as God's children, should be indeed his children" (1 Jn 3:1). Children of God, brothers of the Word made flesh, of him of whom it was said, "In him was life, and that life was the light of man" (Jn 1:4). Children of the light: that is what we are. We bear the only flame capable of setting fire to hearts made of flesh.'[12]

Our divine filiation, which literally *divinizes* us,[13] is the ultimate basis for our vocation to holiness, to the holiness that God wills us to attain precisely in and through our living union with his only-begotten Son. In

---

8 *Christ Is Passing By*, 128. Here I have changed the tenses of the verbs from 'has taken' to 'takes', 'has made' to 'makes', and 'has given' to 'gives'.

9 *Friends of God*, 210.

10 See *Conversations with Monsignor Escrivá* (Dublin, 1969), 22.

11 Cf. ibid., 24, 44.

12 *Christ Is Passing By*, 65, 66.

13 See ibid., 103: 'Our faith teaches us that man, in the state of grace, is divinized—filled with God.'

and through our baptism we commit ourselves to holiness and to participate in the redemptive work of Jesus Christ, for Christ 'calls us to identify ourselves with him and carry out his divine mission'.[14] Jesus' work of salvation as Blessed Josemaría says, 'is still going on, and each one of us has a part in it. It is Christ's will, St. Paul tells us in impressive words, that we should fulfilll in our flesh, in our life, what is lacking in his passion, 'for the good of his body, which is the Church' (Col 1:24).'[15] Our divine filiation and thus our vocation to be saints, in other words, has an *ecclesial* dimension, precisely because the Church is, as Fernando Ocáriz so well puts it, 'the *place* of the Christian vocation'.[16] As God's children we are members of his Church, Christ's body, the holy people whom he has chosen to cooperate with him in redeeming all things in Christ, and we can cooperate in this mission only if we *become what we are*, God's very own children, whose 'work', like that of our brother Jesus, is to do the Father's will.

I believe that we can come to a deeper understanding of the meaning of our divine filiation and the crucial significance of baptism if we reflect on the relationship between nature and grace and the existential and baptismal import of free choice.

That human beings differ radically in kind, and not merely in degree, from other animals is a truth that can be philosophically demonstrated,[17] and is a truth central to Catholic faith. Alone of all his material creatures, God made man in his own image and likeness (Gen 1:28), endowing him with intelligence and free choice. He made man to be *this kind* of creature, to have this *nature*, precisely because he willed to create a being to whom he

---

14 *Christ Is Passing By*, 110.

15 Ibid., 129.

16 Fernando Ocáriz, 'Vocation to Opus Dei is a vocation in the Church' in *Opus Dei in the Church* (Dublin and Princeton, 1993), p. 80. See all of pp 77–116, and in particular pp. 77–89. 'Vocation to holiness in the Church', for a development of this idea.

17 An illuminating presentation of this issue is Mortimer Adler, *The Difference of Man and the Difference it Makes* (New York, 1968).

could give his very own life. By nature human beings are inwardly receptive of this life; they are the kind of beings who are inwardly capable, because of their nature, of being divinized. It is absurd to think that God could become incarnate in a pig or dog or chimpanzee or dolphin, and it is absurd to think this way because these creatures of his, who lack intelligence and the power of free choice, are not inwardly open, by reason of their nature, to receiving God's very own life. But God has indeed become incarnate in his creature man—he has become 'flesh' (*sarx egeneto*: Jn 1:14). He has shared our nature so that we can share his. And free choice is central to this.

In giving men the nature they have, God created persons who have the power to make or break their lives by their own free choices. Persons are of themselves, *sui iuris*, i.e., in their own power or dominion. Their choices and actions are their own, not the choices and actions of others. If God's gift of his own life and friendship is to be in truth a *gift*, it must be freely received; it cannot be forced on men or settled by anything other than the free choices of the God who gives and the persons to whom it is given. Nature, in other words, is for grace; creation is for covenant.

This truth about human persons - that they are free to determine *themselves* through their free choices—is a matter of Catholic faith. It is central to the Scriptures (cf. Sir 15:11–20), to the teaching of the Fathers and all the scholastics,[18] and is the defined teaching of the

---

[18] See St. Augustine, *De libero arbitrio*. The apostolic Fathers, such as Justin Martyr, stressed free choice in the face of pagan determinism. Early in the history of Christianity, Justin developed a line of reasoning that was to be used over and over again by such writers as Augustine, John Damascene, and Aquinas. He wrote: 'We have learned from the prophets and we hold it as true that punishments and chastisements and good rewards are distributed according to the merit of each man's actions. Were this not the case, and were all things to happen according to the decree of fate, there could be nothing at all in our power. If fate decrees that this man is to be good, and that one wicked, then neither is the former to be praised not the latter to be blamed. Furthermore, if the human race does

Church.[19] Free choice is indeed the existential principle of our lives.[20]

Moreover, free choice is central to the reality of baptism, in and through which, as we have seen, we become 'new' creatures in Christ, members of the divine family, children of God called to be holy as our heavenly Father is holy. For at the heart of baptism is a free, self-determining choice whereby one renounces a life of sin—the 'old', Adamic existence—and commits oneself to live henceforward worthily as a child of God, as one who has been divinized. Most of us were baptized as infants, and at that time, could not actually make free choices for ourselves. But others, our godparents, stood as our proxies, responding in *our name* to the call to die to sin and live in a way worthy of God's own children. And, as we grew in the household of the faith, we renewed our baptismal commitment when we received the sacrament of confirmation; and we are given the opportunity to reaffirm this commitment frequently during our lives, particularly during the liturgy of the Easter vigil. In baptism God freely gives his life to us, and, moved by his grace, we freely accept this gift.

Baptism entails the kind of choice rightly called a commitment. Indeed, as Germain Grisez has so rightly noted, baptism is *the fundamental option* of the Christian[21] whereby the Christian freely commits himself to a life in union with Jesus and to share in his redemptive work.

---

not have the power of a freely deliberated choice in fleeing evil and in choosing good, then men are not accountable for their actions.' *The First Apology* 43; trans. W.A. Jurgen, *The Faith of the Early Fathers* (Collegeville, 1970), i, n. 123. See also St. Thomas Aquinas, *Summa theologiae*, 1–2, Prologue.

19 The Council of Trent solemnly defined the truth that humn beings, even after the fall, are endowed with free will. See DS 1555. See also the Vatican II Pastoral Constitution *Gaudium et spes*, 17, where the council fathers stressed that the ability to choose freely 'is an exceptional sign of the divine image in man'.

20 This truth is emphasized by Karol Wojtyla, *The Acting Person*, trans. Andrzej Potocki (Dordrecht and Boston, 1979), pp. 121–8. The centrality of free choice is developed systematically and masterfully by Germain Grisez, *The Way of the Lord Jesus*, i, *Christian Moral Principles* (Chicago, 1983), pp. 41–72.

21 Grisez, op. cit., p. 551.

II. In what does sanctification consist? The primacy of grace

All men are called to holiness by God through Christ and in the Spirit. This is, in essence, the meaning of our divine filiation. Essentially, then, holiness or sanctification is, as Alvaro del Portillo has said, 'nothing other than the perfection of the Christian life, nothing other than the fullness of divine filiation'.[22]

The work of sanctification, of becoming holy, is first and foremost something that pertains to the supernatural order. *God* takes the initiative. Sanctification, holiness, is possible only if one is intimately united to and abandons oneself to the One whom Scripture calls the Holy One: 'Be holy because I am holy' (Lev 11:44).[23] Sanctification is possible only because of the grace of God, freely given to his children through his only-begotten Son, and it consists essentially in an intimate, loving union with Jesus, our Redeemer and Saviour.

This truth is absolutely central to the spirituality of Blessed Josemaría. With St. Paul he was acutely aware of the tension within human hearts between the 'old', Adamic man, the man wounded by sin and concupiscence, and the 'new' man in Christ. Of ourselves we are nothing. Blessed Josemaría expresses this truth vividly and unforgettably in many of his writings, particularly in the section of *The Way* dedicated to considerations on the virtue of humility. There he tells us that of ourselves we are 'trashcans',[24] 'dust, fallen, and dirty',[25]

---

[22] Alvaro del Portillo: 'holiness ... is nothing other than the perfection of the Christian life, which is the fullness of divine filiation'. 'Mons. Escrivá de Balaguer, testigo del amor a la Iglesia', in *Palabra*, 130 (June, 1976), p. 9. Cited by Ocáriz, 'La filiación divina...,' p. 177.

[23] This matter is discussed masterfully by Pedro Rodríguez, *Vocación, Trabajo, Contemplación*, pp. 105–11. I will rely extensively on his treatment of this issue in what follows.

[24] *The Way* (New York, 1985), 592.

[25] Ibid., 599.

'beggars',[26] etc. Indeed, were we to follow the impulses of our hearts and the dictates of our reason we would lie flat on the ground, prostrate, vile worms, ugly and miserable in the sight of God.[27] But God is our Father, our Redeemer, our Sanctifier, and his grace, as St. Paul tells us (2 Cor 12:9) and as Blessed Josemaría never tires of repeating, is enough for us.[28] Above all, Jesus, in union with whom we are truly God's children, is not only our God, our Lord and Saviour, our Redeemer, but is above all our *personal friend*. Long ago St. Thomas Aquinas rightly said that 'Christ is our best and wisest friend',[29] and this magnificent truth is set forth time and time again by Blessed Josemaría.[30] Precisely because Jesus is our best and wisest friend, we must get to know him intimately by meditating on the Scriptures, in particular on the passion, in order to love him passionately, and to love all persons in him if we are to cooperate with God's grace in the work of sanctification.[31]

Holiness, the plenitude or fullness of our divine filiation, thus consists in a life of intimate union with Jesus and, through him, with the Blessed Trinity. God is love, and he pours his love into our hearts, we open ourselves to his offer of divine life. Consequently, sanctity or holi-

---

26 *The Way*, 608.

27 Cf. ibid., 597.

28 See, for example, *The Way*, 707, 729, 733. Rodríguez, in *Vocación, Trabajo, Contemplación*, p. 106, cites a significant passage from a letter of Bl. Josemaría—Letter,Rome, May, 31 1954—in which he says: 'And if experience of our weakness, of our personal shortcomings, causes a feeling of powerlessness ("If I am like this, how can I consecrate the world") You have to hear, in your mind and in your heart, a resounding "yes": "*sufficit tibi gratia mea*, my grace is sufficient for you".'

29 St. Thomas Aquinas, *Summa theologiae*, 1–2, q. 108, a. 4, sed contra: 'Christus est maxime sapiens et amicus".

30 See, for example: *The Way*, 88, 91, 421, 806 and especially 422; *Christ Is Passing By*, especially 162–63, 169; *Friends of God*, especially 222–5, 228–31, 234–7.

31 See, for example, *Christ Is Passing By*, in particular the homilies 'The Eucharist, mystery of faith and love', 'Christ's presence in Christians', especially 107–9; *Friends of God*, 299–305.

ness consists in loving perfectly, in loving even as we have been and are loved by God in Christ. As Blessed Josemaría says, 'The main thing we are asked to do, which is so much in keeping with our nature, is to love: 'charity is the bond of perfection' (Col 3:14); a charity that is to be practiced exactly as Our Lord himself commands: 'Thou shalt love the Lord thy God, with thy whole heart, and with thy whole soul, and with thy whole mind' (Mt 22:37), holding back nothing for ourselves. This is what sanctity is all about.'[32] This loving union with God and, in him, with him, and through him, with our neighbors, is ultimately the work of God's grace and of free, human cooperation with this grace.

Blessed Josemaría's teaching on this matter, with its insistence on the primacy *of grace*, is rooted in the Catholic tradition. Thus in his teaching on the meaning of the 'new law' given men through Jesus, the 'gospel law' or 'law of love', St. Thomas emphasized that what is 'most powerful in the law of the new covenant, and in which its whole power consists, is the grace of the Holy Spirit, which is given through faith'. Therefore, he continued, 'the new law is first and foremost the very grace of the Holy Spirit, which is given to Christ's faithful'.[33] Indeed, it seems to me that the teaching of Blessed Josemaría on this matter can be synthesized beautifully in a passage from St. Thomas, where the Common Doctor describes the *new life* given to us through our incorporation into Christ in baptism, when we indeed become God's children and receive the call to holiness. St. Thomas wrote

---

32 *Friends of God*, 6.

33 St. Thomas Aquinas, *Summa theologiae*, 1–2, q. 106, a. 1: 'Id autem quod est potissimum in lege novi testamenti, et in quo tota virtus eius consistit, est gratia Spiritus Sancti, quae datur per fidem Christi. Et ideo principaliter lex nova est ipsa gratia Spiritus Sancti, quae datur Christi fidelibus'. An excellent commentary on St. Thomas' teaching on the new law, the pinnacle of his moral thought, can be found in Servais Pinckaers, O.P., *Les sources de la morale chretienne: sa methode, son contenu, son histoire* (Freiburg and Paris, 1985), pp. 174–95. See also Ramon García de Haro, *La vida cristiana* (Pamplona, 1992), pp. 457-86.

as follows: 'Through baptism a person is reborn to a spiritual life, one proper to Christ's faithful, as the Apostle says (Gal 2:20), "the life I now live in the flesh I live by faith in the Son of God [who loved me and gave himself for me].' But this life belongs only to the members who are united to the head, from whom they receive sense and movement. And therefore it is necessary that through baptism a person is incorporated into Christ as his member. For just as sense and movement flow from the natural head to its [bodily] members, so from the spiritual head, who is Christ, flow to his members both a spiritual sense, which consists in the knowledge of the truth, and a spiritual movement, which operates through the inspiration of grace. Hence John says (1:14, 16), "we have seen him full of grace and truth, and of his fullness we have all received". And therefore it follows that the baptized are enlightened by Christ regarding the knowledge of the truth, and they are impregnated by him with an abundance of good works through the infusion of faith".[34]

---

34 St. Thomas Aquinas, *Summa theologiae*, 3, 1. 69, a. 5: 'Per baptismum aliquis regeneratur in spiritualem vitam, quae est propria fidelium Christi; sicut Apostolus dicit (Gal 2:20), "Quod autem nunc vivo in carne, in fide vivo Filii Dei.' Vita autem non est nisi membrorum capiti unitorum, a quo sensum et motum suscipiunt. Et ideo necesse est quod per baptismum aliquis incorporetur Christo quasi membrum ipsius. Sicut autem a capite naturali derivatur ad membra sensus et motus, ita a capite spirituali, quod est Christus, derivatur ad membra eius sensus spiritualis, qui consistit in cognitione veritatis, et motus spiritualis, qui est per gratiae instinctum. Unde Joan. 1 (14) dicitur, "Vidimus eum plenum gratiae et veritatis, et de plenitudine eius omnes accipimus.' Et ideo consequens est quod baptizati illuminentur a Christo circa cognitionem veritatis, et fecundentur ab eo fecunditate bonorum operum per gratiae infusionem.'

III. Ordinary life as the place and means of sanctification

1. The centrality of this truth, its context, and the dynamic unity of Blessed Josemaría's thought

Throughout his life Blessed Josemaría energetically combatted the idea—unfortunately still quite common—that sanctity is for a select few and that one can become a saint only by withdrawing from the world in which one lives. First of all, Blessed Josemaría clearly understood the *unity* of a Christian's life. 'We cannot,' he said in a homily that he gave at a Mass on the campus of the University of Navarre on October 8, 1967, 'lead a double life. We cannot be like schizophrenics, if we want to be Christians. There is just one life, made of flesh and spirit. And it is this life which has to become, in both soul and body, holy and filled with God.'[35] Blessed Josemaría considered it madness to want to change one's place in the world, as if simply by doing so one could then become holy.[36] Here he was simply following the advice given to Christians long ago by St. Paul to the Corinthians, namely, that 'each one should lead the life the Lord has assigned him, continuing as he was when the Lord called him' (1 Cor 7:17).

As Pedro Rodriquez has noted, the madness driving some to change their position in life 'is a consequence of what Monsignor Escrivá de Balaguer has called hu-

---

[35] This homily, under the title 'Passionately loving the world', is found in *Conversations with Monsignor Escrivá*, 113–23. Of all the many texts in which Bl. Josemaría expounded the doctrine that our ordinary, everyday life is *the* place where we are to sanctify ourselves, this homily is perhaps the text that sets this teaching forth most fully and comprehensively. The finest commentary that I have seen on this text is Pedro Rodríguez, 'Santità nella vita quotidiana,' *Studi cattolici*, 381, 36 (November 1992), 717–29. In what follows I will draw extensively on this excellent article.

[36] See, for instance, *The Way*, 832, 837.

morously a "mystical wishful thinking" '.[37] Moreover, as José Luis Illanes observes, 'the expression "mystical wishful thinking" has two sides to it: on the one hand, it denounces escapism which leads a person to elude the real demands of the Christian vocation; on the other it affirms the Christian vocation can and therefore should be followed in the middle of the world'.[38] Blessed Josemaría thus insisted that we are to find holiness here and now in the ordinary lives that we live in the world. This indeed is his central message.

Before citing representative texts of Blessed Josemaría on this matter, it will help, I believe, to note the context in which he proclaimed this truth. The widespread notion that sanctity is only for a privileged few has already been noted. Another widespread notion that Blessed Josemaría combatted throughout his life was a perverse misunderstanding of what the Christian life is all about. Blessed Josemaría described this view, overly spiritualistic and clericalistic, as the claim that 'being a Christian means going to church, taking part in sacred ceremonies, being taken up with ecclesiastical matters, in a kind of segregated "world" which is considered to be the ante-chamber of heaven, while the ordinary world follows its own separate path '.[39] To this false spiritual-

---

37 Rodríguez, *Vocación, Trabajo, Contemplación*, p. 98: 'The "madness of changing one's place" is something that follows logically from what Monsignor Escrivá has humorously called "mystical wishful thinking".' Rodríguez then goes on, pp. 98–9, to cite at length from a letter of Bl. Josemaría—Letter, Rome, March 19, 1954—in which the Founder of Opus Dei speaks at length of this foolishness, a madness that he had encountered time and time again in his apostolic labors. On this see, for example, Bl. Josemaría's homily, 'Passionately loving the world', 116: 'Stop dreaming, leave behind false idealisms, fantasies, and what I usually call mystical wishful thinking: If only I hadn't married, If only I hadn't this profession, If only I were healthier, If only I were young, If only I were old.' In a note the English translator observes that in the Spanish text there is 'a play on words between *ojalá* ('would that', 'if only') and *jojalata* ('tin plate'). *Mística ojalatera* is 'tin-can mysticism' as well as 'mystical wishful thinking".'

38 José-Luis Illanes, *On the Theology of Work: Aspects of the Teaching of the Founder of Opus Dei*, trans., Michael Adams (Dublin and New York, 1982), p. 41.

39 'Passionately loving the world', 113.

ism Blessed Josemaría opposed what he was audacious enough to call a 'christian materialism', a materialism 'boldly opposed to those materialisms which are blind to the spirit',[40] but nonetheless a materialism. He did so precisely because Christianity, 'which professes the resurrection of all flesh, has always quite logically opposed "dis-incarnation" '.[41] This perverse understanding of Christianity leads to the schizophrenia which, as we have already seen, Blessed Josemaría roundly repudiated. He saw clearly that 'we discover the invisible God in the most visible and material things', and that 'a man who knows that the world, and not just the Church, is the place where man finds Christ, loves that world'.[42]

Blessed Josemaría ceaselessly proclaimed that ordinary life is indeed the place and means of our sanctification, and this truth was perhaps most vigorously set forth by him in his homily on the campus of the University of Navarre, as the following citations indicate:

> Everyday life is the true setting [place, *lugar* in Spanish] for your lives as Christians. Your ordinary contact with God takes place where your fellow men, your yearnings, your work and your affections are. There you have your daily encounter with Christ. It is in the midst of the most material things of the earth that we must sanctify ourselves, serving God and all mankind.[43]

> You must understand now more clearly that God is calling you to serve him *here and from* the ordinary, material and secular activities of human life.[44]

> Either we learn to find our Lord in ordinary, everyday life, or else we shall never find him.[45]

---

40 'Passionately loving the world', 115.
41 Ibid., 115.
42 Ibid., 114, 116. On this point, see Rodríguez, 'Santità nella vita quotidiana', op. cit., 723–5.
43 'Passionately loving the world', 113.
44 Ibid., 114.
45 Ibid., 114.

A holy life in the midst of secular reality, lived without fuss, with simplicity, with truthfulness. Is not this the most moving manifestation of the *magnalia Dei*, of those prodigious mercies which God has always worked, and does not cease to work, in order to save the world?[46]

The same message is found in countless talks and other writings of Blessed Josemaría.[47]

Indeed, as Rodríguez has noted, 'the expression *place* has here [in the campus homily], as in other writings of the Founder of Opus Dei, a technical meaning: it is an anthropological and theological category, which serves to indicate the historical coordinates of our encounter with Christ and, therefore, of human existence in its concreteness.'[48] And our ordinary life is lived *in the world*; it is immersed in the secular, the material. Blessed Josemaría had a truly Catholic appreciation of the intrinsic goodness of the material world. Rodríguez accurately sums this up when he says that the 'metaphysical and theological position of matter' in the thought of Blessed Josemaría 'is rooted in its relationship to the spirit, in its

---

46 'Passionately loving the world', 123.

47 See, for instance, the following: *Christ Is Passing By*, 9: 'In order to reach sanctity, an ordinary Christian ... has no reason to abandon the world, since that is precisely where he is to find Christ.' Ibid., 105: Jesus 'wants the vast majority to stay right where they are, in all earthly occupations in which they work.' Ibid., 110: 'The ordinary life of a man among his fellows is not something dull and uninteresting. It is there that the Lord wants the vast majority of his children to achieve sanctity.' Ibid., 198: 'Mary sanctifies the ordinary, everyday things—what some people wrongly regard as unimportant and insignificant: everyday work, looking after those closest to you, visits to friends and relatives. What a a blessed ordinariness, that can be so full of love of God.' *Friends of God*, 18: 'Sanctity in our ordinary tasks, sanctity in the little things we do, sanctity in our professional work, in our daily cares.' Ibid., 60: 'The Lord wants you to be holy in the place where you are.' Ibid., 312: 'When faith is really alive in the soul, one discovers ... that to follow Christ one does not have to step aside from the ordinary pattern of everyday life, and ... that the great holiness which God expects of us is to be found here and now in the little things of each day.'

48 Rodríguez, 'Santità nella vita quotidiana', 723.

capacity to serve the spirit and to be penetrated by it, finding in this service its own true destiny.'[49] Moreover, as is now well known, the Fathers of Vatican II made their own the teaching of Blessed Josemaría on this matter, namely, that it is in the material world, in the midst of one's everyday life, that ordinary men and women are called to be saints. Thus in the Dogmatic Constitution *Lumen gentium* we read:

> A secular quality is proper and special to laymen... the laity, by their very vocation, seek the kingdom of God by engaging in temporal affairs and by ordering them according to the plan of God. They live in the world, that is, in each and all of the secular professions and occupations. They live in the ordinary circumstances of family and social life, from which the very web of their existence is woven. They are called there by God so that by exercising their proper function and being led by the spirit of the gospel they can work for the sanctification of the world from within, in the manner of leaven. In this way they can make Christ known to others, especially by the testimony of a life resplendent in faith, hope, and charity.[50]

Moreover, as John Paul II notes in his Apostolic Exhortation *Christifideles laici*, the Council considers the secular condition of the laity 'not simply an external and environmental framework, but as a reality *destined to find in Jesus Christ the fullness of its meaning... . The 'world' thus becomes the place and means for the lay faithful to fulfill their Christian vocation.*'[51]

Here it is important to note that, as John Paul II insists in *Christifideles laici*, there is a proper secular 'dimension' to the *whole* Church, common to all the faithful, whether lay, clergy, or religious.[52] But what charac-

---

49 Rodríguez, 'Santità nella vita quotidiana', 725.

50 Vatican Council II, Dogmatic Constitution *Lumen gentium*, 31.

51 John Paul II, Apostolic Exhortation *Christifideles laici*, 15. Emphasis in the original.

52 Cf. ibid.

terizes Christian lay people is their secular 'character' (*indoles*). Commenting on this distinction between the secular 'dimension' proper to the Church as a whole and to *all* the faithful and the secular 'character' definitive of Christian lay people, José-Luis Illanes points out that the affirmations of both *Lumen gentium* and *Christifideles laici* and the teaching of Blessed Josemaría on the condition of the 'ordinary Christian' 'mutually enlighten one another' and enable us to understand that the purpose of the 'Work' Blessed Josemaría founded on October 2, 1928 'is precisely to promote among lay people or ordinary Christians of the most diverse social conditions and professions the consciousness of their Christian vocation, of God's call directing them to sanctify themselves and to sanctify others *in* and *by means of* the circumstances and realities of their life *in the world*'.[53]

Ordinary life, the *place* where we are to sanctify ourselves, is the life of men and women in the world; it is made up of their lives within their families, at their work, in the thousand and one things that they 'do' each day. But before examining the meaning of work, marriage and family life, and the value of little things, I want first to summarize the *dynamic unity* of Blessed Josemaría's thought and then, in the following section, to attempt a theological understanding of the reason why ordinary life is indeed the place and means of sanctification.

First, let us look at the dynamic unity of Blessed Josemaría's classic thought. From what has been said

---

[53] José-Luis Illanes, 'Iglesia en el mundo: la secularidad de los miembros del Opus Dei', in *El Opus Dei en la Iglesia* (Madrid, 1993), pp. 227–8 (emphasis added): 'One could even go so far as to say that *Lumen gentium* and *Christifideles laici*'s statements about their secular character being proper to lay people, and Monsignor Escrivá's teachings about the condition of the ordinary Christian and about naturalness, throw light on one another ... any attempt to understand Opus Dei needs to start out from the figure of the lay person, for what Opus Dei aspires to (in line with its foundational charism, as articulated on October 2, 1928) is nothing other than to foster among lay people or ordinary Christians of all sorts of solid condition and professional background an awareness of their Christian vocation, of the call that God addresses to them to sanctify themselves and others in and through the circumstances of their life in the world.'

thus far, and particularly from a reading of Blessed Josemaría's classic work in spirituality, *The Way* (which, unfortunately, has not figured prominently in these pages) we can begin to grasp the dynamic unity of his thought. In my opinion, Pedro Rodríguez has accurately summarized this in a study devoted to the spirituality of *The Way*. He believes that there are three major lines of thought forming the backbone of this work. Two run through it as a refrain, and the third flows from their convergence. The first is the secular or worldly character of man, above all, his creative dynamism as a worker—all viewed from the perspective of the economy of grace. The second is, as it were, the supernatural axis of the vocation to holiness—the primacy of grace, of prayer, of interiority, expressed above all as the living out of one's divine filiation, one's 'baptismal spirituality'. The third, springing from these two, is the apostolic character of the layperson's vocation, i.e., his calling to participate in the redemptive work of Jesus.[54]

2. Why is ordinary life the place and means of sanctification?

Ordinary life is the place and means of sanctification because it is in our ordinary, everyday life that we make ourselves *to be* the persons we are. This life is made up of what we 'do' throughout the day. Human persons are 'acting persons', and the actions in which they engage

---

54 Rodríguez, 'La espiritualidad de "Camino"', ch. 4 of his *Vocación, Trabajo, Contemplación*, pp. 94–5: 'As I see it, there are two great lines running through this great little book which make it a "handbook for the holiness of lay people": the first line is the world, the worldly situation of man and in particular its creative dynamic—work—which are positively affirmed and viewed in the context of the economy of grace; the second line is, as it were, the supernatural hinge of the sanctifying process—what we might term the "primacy of grace", of prayer, of interiority, which the book conveys, primarily, as a living experience of divine filiation: this is what makes the spirituality of lay people a "baptismal spirituality". These two structural lives converge to produce a third one, which confers on the Christian vocation of lay people the features of an essentially apostolic vocation.'

are not simply physical events in the material world that come and go, like the falling of rain or the turning of leaves. Human actions, moreover, are not something that 'happen' to a person. They are, rather, the outward expressions of a person's choice. For at the core of an action, as human and personal, is a free, self-determining choice, which, as we saw earlier in considering the relationship between baptism and free choice, is the existential principle of our lives.

The Scriptures, particulary the New Testament, are very clear about this. Jesus taught that it is not what enters a person that defiles him; rather, it is what flows from the person, from his heart, from the core of his being, from his choice (cf. Mt 15:10–20; Mk 7:14–23). The core of an action is the free, self-determining choice that abides in the person, making him the kind of person he is. The actions we freely choose to do, as St. Thomas reminds us, abide within us, giving to us our identity as moral and spiritual beings.[55]

In other words, it is in and through the actions we freely choose to do each day that we give to ourselves an identity, for weal or woe. This identity abides in us as a disposition to further choices and actions until we make other, contradictory kinds of choices. Thus, if I choose to commit adultery, I make myself an adulterer and I remain an adulterer until, by another free and self-determining choice, I have a change of heart (*metanoia*) and repent of my deed. Even then I remain an adulterer, for I have, unfortunately, given myself that identity, but now I am a *repentant* adulterer, one who has, through free choice and God's grace, given to himself a new kind of identity, the identity of one who repudiates his freely chosen adultery, repents of it, and is now determined, through free choice and with the help of God's never-failing grace, to amend his life and *to be* a faithful, loving spouse.

---

55 Cf. St. Thomas Aquinas, *Summa theologiae*, 1–2, q. 57, a. 4: 'agere est actio permanens in ipso agente'.

How does all of this help us understand why ordinary life is the place and means of our sanctification? Recall that the *fundamental option*, the overarching choice of the Christian is his or her baptismal commitment to live worthily as a child of God and to participate in Jesus' redemptive work—to live out his or her divine filiation. As Blessed Josemaría said, 'Christian faith and calling affect our whole existence, not just a part of it.'[56] By reason of our divine filiation, our common vocation to holiness, and our *personal vocation* to fulfilll in our own flesh 'what is lacking in the sufferings of Christ for the sake of his body, the Church' (Col 1:24),[57] our mission is to integrate our lives, to bring our whole life, all our choices and actions, into conformity with out baptismal commitment. Just as a husband is summoned and obliged to see to it that his everyday life, made up of the things he freely chooses to do, is in perfect harmony with his freely chosen identity as a husband, so each one of us is summoned and obligated to make every action of our daily life one that conforms to our identity as God's children, co-heirs with Christ, whose only will is to do what is pleasing to the Father.[58]

---

56 'In Joseph's workshop', in *Christ Is Passing By*, 46.

57 Each one of us, as Bl. Josemaría frequently stressed, has his or her own unique, personal vocation, his or her own unique and indispensable role to play in carrying on Jesus' redemptive work of sanctification. A particularly illuminating text, I believe, is found in his homily, 'Freedom, a gift from God', in *Friends of God*, 28–30. Another is a brief passage in his homily. 'The Great Unknown', in *Christ Is Passing By*, 129: 'God does not want slaves, but children. He respects our freedom. The work of salvation is still going on, and *each one of us has a part in it.*' The truth that each of us has a personal vocation is central to the teaching of Vatican Council II: see for instance, Dogmatic Constitution *Lumen gentium*, 11, 46; Pastoral Constitution *Gaudium et spes*, 31, 43, 75). It is also developed by Pope John Paul II. See his Encyclical *Redemptor hominis*, 71 *AAS* (1979) 317 and his homily at Miraflores Park (Cuenca, Ecuador), 7, in *Insegnamenti di Giovanni Paolo II*, 8.1 (1985), 309. On the question of personal vocation see Grisez, *Christian Moral Principles*, pp. 559–62, 663–4, 753–5, and *Living a Christian Life*, vol. 2 of his *The Way of the Lord Jesus* (Quincy, 1993), pp. 113–29.

58 The truth I have attempted to summarize briefly here is developed at length and magnificently, I believe, by Grisez in *Christian Moral Principles*, especially in chapters 25, 26, and 27, pp. 599–682.

As Blessed Josemaría has said, 'conversation is the task of a moment; sanctification is the work of a lifetime.'[59] It is the work of a lifetime because it consists in endeavoring, each day, in everything that we do, to make our own lives a true imitation of Christ.

3. Work, the value of little things, marriage and family life

We are to become saints—to attain the fullness of our divine filiation—and through our 'ordinary, everyday life.' But in what does the 'ordinary, everyday life' of the lay person, the 'ordinary Christian', consist? It consists principally in the daily interactions one has with the members of one's own family—if one is married, particularly with one's spouse and children—with the persons with whom one comes into contact in his or her own work, in the 'work' one does, and in the myriad of 'little things' that one does from the time one rises in the morning until one retires at night. The 'ordinary, everyday life' in the world in and through which we are to sanctify ourselves and others, consequently, consists principally in our life within our own families, the work we do in collaboration with others, and the 'little things' of every day. Hence we shall now consider the meaning of work, the value of 'little things', and marriage and family life.

a. The meaning of work

Throughout his apostolic life Blessed Josemaría unceasingly reminded all with whom he came into contact of the dignity, the value, and supreme importance of work in the Christian's life.[60] Indeed, one's ordinary work is, in Blessed

---

[59] 'The conversion of the children of God', in *Christ Is Passing By*, 58.
[60] Among the many, many places in which Bl. Josemaría proclaims this teaching are the following: *The Way*, 162, 306, 334, 348, 373, 697, 933; *Furrow*, 482–531; *The Forge*, 618, 684, 698, 700, 702, 705, 713, 725, 735, 980; *Christ Is Passing By*, 'In Joseph's workshop', especially 45–51; *Friends of God*, 'Working for God', especially 57, 58, 60, 61, 62, 64, 65; 'Opus Dei: an institution which fosters the search for holiness in the world', *Conversations with Monsignor Escrivá*, 55, 59, 70; Letter, Rome, May 31, 1954.

Josemaría's mind, 'the hinge on which our calling to holiness is fixed and turns.'[61] In a celebrated saying, which Pope John Paul II, while still Cardinal Karol Wojtyla, called a 'happy expression',[62] Blessed Josemaría put the matter this way: 'you have to sanctify your work, be sanctified in your work, and sanctify through your work.'[63] Ordinary work, for Blessed Josemaría, 'is not only the context in which [the majority of men] should become holy; it is the *raw material* of their holiness.'[64] It is by sanctifying our work, sanctifying ourselves in our work and sanctifying others through our work that, as Blessed Josemaría said, we can succeed in making 'heroic verse out of the prose of each day'.[65] In fact, he wrote, 'the miracle' which God asks of you is to persevere in your Christian and divine vocation, sanctifying each day's work: the miracle of turning the prose of each day into heroic verse by the love which you put into your ordinary work.'[66]

---

61 *Friends of God*, 62. Here I have used the translation of this passage as found in José-Luis Illanes, *On the Theology of Work*, p. 49.

62 Cardinal Karol Wojtyla, in a lecture he gave in 1974 on the subject of 'Evangelization and the inner man', wrote as follows: 'How can man, in his effort to impose himself on the face of the earth, put his spiritual stamp on the world? ... We can reply with a happy expression—which everyone knows so well —which Monsignor Escrivá de Balaguer has been using for so many years: 'by each person sanctifying his own work, sanctifying himself in his work, and sanctifying others through his work'. This lecture is published in *La fe de la Iglesia: textos del Card. Karol Wojtyla* (Pamplona, 1979), pp. 94–5. The text is cited by Illanes, *On the Theology of Work*, p. 101, note 95.

63 This particular form of this saying is given in Letter, Rome, May 31, 1954, and is cited in this way by Illanes, *On the Theology of Work*, p. 49. The same thought is expressed in slightly different ways in many places by Bl. Josemaría. Thus, in *Conversations with Monsignor Escrivá*, 55, we read: 'Sanctity, for the vast majority of men, implies sanctifying their work, sanctifying themselves through it, and sanctifying others through it. Thus they can encounter God in the course of their daily lives.' And in ibid., 70: 'Those who want to live their faith perfectly and do apostolate ... must sanctify themselves with their work, must sanctify their work, and sanctify others through their work.' See also *Christ Is Passing By*, 46; *Friends of God*, 9.

64 *Conversations with Monsignor Escrivá*, 70.

65 Ibid., 116.

66 *Christ Is Passing By*, 50.

Blessed Josemaría frequently prefixed the adjective 'professional' to the substantive 'work'.[67] But it is most important, indeed absolutely crucial, to realize that 'professional work' does *not* mean 'the work of people of the "professional class"'—doctors, lawyers, teachers—'but professional work in the sense of work undertaken as a stable condition of one's life, work by which one is involved in everyday society.'[68] By 'work' Blessed Josemaría means 'every job that is not opposed to the divine law', for every job of this kind is 'good and noble, and capable of being raised to the supernatural plane, that is, inserted into the constant flow of Love which defines the life of a child of God'.[69] In fact, as Blessed Josemaría rightly insisted, 'It is time for us Christians to shout from the rooftops that work is a gift from God and that it makes no sense to classify men differently, according to their occupation, as if some jobs were nobler than others. Work, all work, bears witness to the dignity of man, to his dominion over creation. It is an opportunity to develop one's personality. It is a bond of union with others, the way to support one's family, a means of aiding in the improvement of the society in which we live and in the progress of all humanity.'[70]

It is evident that what makes work of such importance in the mind of Blessed Josemaría is the fact that it is the free, responsible activity of the human person, as the one who is called by God to participate in both his *creative* and *redemptive* activity: 'work is a participation in the creative work of God ... Moreover, since Christ took it into his hands, work has become for us a redeemed and redemptive reality.'[71] Blessed Josemaría frequently meditated on and asked others to meditate on the passage in the gospel according to St. John in which our Lord says: 'And when I am lifted up from the earth, I shall draw all things to my-

---

67 See, for instance, *Christ Is Passing By*, 45, 49, 50.
68 Illanes, *On the Theology of Work*, p. 9.
69 *Friends of God*, 60.
70 *Christ Is Passing By*, 47.
71 Ibid.

self' (Jn 12:32). Reflecting on this passage he said: 'By his death on the Cross, Christ has drawn all creation to himself. Now it is the task of Christians, in his name, to reconcile all things with God, placing Christ, *by means of their work in the middle of the world*, at the summit of all human activities.'[72]

Man can sanctify himself in his work—and is called to do so—precisely because, as Rodríguez says, 'when man works, he not only transforms things but also, at the same time and above all, he realizes and develops his own being as a Christian. And realizing our being as Christian is what is meant by saying that 'one is to sanctify oneself' in one's work.[73] Work, in other words, has an 'immanent' aspect as a human activity—as something that man freely *chooses* to do—and precisely as such it is in and through his work that a human person 'fulfillls' or 'realizes' himself and that, as a Christian, he can 'fulfill' his baptismal commitment, his divine filiation. John Paul II brings out this aspect of work—what he terms its 'subjective' aspect—magnificently in his Encyclical *Laborem exercens*. The Holy Father, in passages that express well what Blessed Josemaría meant when he said that we are to sanctify ourselves in our work, emphasizes that 'as a person, man is the subject of work ... Independently of their objective content, these actions [i.e. the actions that go to make up work] must all serve to realize his humanity, to fulfilll the calling to be a person that is his by reason of his very humanity [*vocationi, ex qua est persona quaeque vi ipsius humanitatis eius est propria*].'[74] Continuing, the Holy Father says, in words reminiscent of Rodríguez' comment, that 'through work man not only transforms nature, adapting it to his own

---

72 *Conversations with Monsignor Escrivá*, 59. See *Christ Is Passing By*, 183.

73 Rodríguez, *Vocación, Tranajo, Contemplación*, p. 80: 'Man, when he is at work, not only transforms (material) things: at the very same time, and above all, he builds his own being and, if he is a Christian, when he works he builds and unfolds his Christian being. And this building of our Christian being is what "sanctifying oneself" means.'

74 Pope John Paul II, Encyclical *Laborem exercens*, 6.

needs, but he also achieves fulfilllment as a human being [*se ipsum ut hominem perficit*] and indeed, in a sense, becomes 'more human" '.[75]

We sanctify ourselves in our work by uniting our work with the redemptive work of Jesus himself. We do so by putting love into our work. As Blessed Josemaría said, 'the dignity of work is based on Love. Man's great privilege is to be able to love and to transcend what is fleeting and ephemeral ... Work is born of love; it is a manifestation of love and directed toward love ... Work ... becomes prayer and thanksgiving because we know we are placed on earth by God, that we are loved by him and made heirs to his promises ... [it provides us with the opportunity] to give ourselves to others, to reveal Christ to them and lead them to God the Father—all of which is the overflow of the charity which the Holy Spirit pours into our hearts.'[76]

We can sanctify ourselves in our work precisely because of our divine filiation and the love that God pours into our hearts when he makes us to be his children. In fact, as Ocáriz has observed, it is the 'reality of divine filiation that prevents slavery from entering into our work, since "in the midst of the limitations that accompany our present life, in which sin is still present to us to some extent at least, we Christians perceive with particular clearness all the wealth of our divine filiation, when we realize that we are fully free because we are doing our Father's work." '[77]

But we can sanctify ourselves in our work only if we sanctify our work. Here we must recall that work, in addition to having the intransitive or *subjective* aspect considered above, also has a transitive or *objective* aspect; it

---

[75] Ibid., 70. An excellent commentary on *Laborem exercens* is provided by John Finnis, 'Fundamental Themes of John Paul II's *Laborem exercens* (1982)', in *The Church's Social Teaching: Proceedings of the Fifth Annual Convention of the Fellowship of Catholic Scholars* (Scranton, 1983).

[76] *Christ Is Passing By*, 48, 49.

[77] Ocáriz, 'La filiación divina...', op. cit., p. 198, with an internal citation from *Christ Is Passing By*, 138.

has an effect on the material things of this world, on human culture and civilization. There is indeed, as Rodríguez brings out very well, an intimate unity between the intransitive (subjective) and transitive (objective) aspects of work. If, in one's work, one seeks only one's own self-realization, one falls into a false individualistic understanding both of human existence and of our call to holiness as God's children, as members of his family. God calls us, through our work, to 'care' for the earth, to 'humanize' it. Indeed, as Rodríguez notes, 'culture, in truth, is nothing else than nature *humanized*', and it is humanized through our work.[78]

And we can sanctify our work only if we do it well—a point that Blessed Josemaría emphasized again and again in his preaching and writing. A representative and eloquent passage illustrating this aspect of his teaching is the following: 'do your work perfectly ... love God and mankind by putting love in the little things of everyday life, and discovering that divine something which is hidden in small details. The words of a Castilian poet are especially appropriate here: "Write slowly and with a careful hand, for doing things well is more important than doing them" [Despacio, y buena letra; el hacer las cosas bien importa mas que el hacerlas].[79] This passage—and countless passages throughout the works of Blessed Josemaría convey the same message—brings out also the value of little things.[80] Blessed Josemaría delighted in speaking of the example of medieval stonemasons, whose beautiful craftsmanship at the top of cathedrals could not even be seen by those below but only by God. Their work was sanctifying because it was done for God, out of love, and hence it was *done well*.[81] Sloppy, careless work cannot be sanctified be-

---

78 Rodríguez, *Vocación, Trabajo, Contemplación*, p. 81, emphasis added: 'This culture is nothing other than humanized Nature.'
79 *Conversations with Monsignor Escrivá*, 116.
80 On the value of little things, see in particular the section entitled 'Little things' in *The Way*, 813–30. See Letter, May 31, 1954.
81 See the text, for instance, in *Friends of God*, 65.

cause it is not the proper raw material for sanctification. It cannot contribute to the 'humanization' and 'redemption' of the world in which we live. If work is to be sanctified it must be done well: 'as a motto for your work,' Blessed Josemaría said, 'I can give you this one: *if you want to be useful, serve.* For, in the first place, in order to do things properly, you must know *how* to do them. I cannot see the integrity of a person who does not strive to attain professional skills and to carry out properly the task entrusted to his care. It's not enough to want to do good; we must know how to do it. And, if our desire is real, it will show itself in the effort we make to use the right methods, finishing things well, achieving human perfection.'[82]

Not only are we called to sanctify ourselves in our work and to sanctify our work, but we are called to sanctify others through our work. By reason of our divine filiation and our baptismal commitment to participate in Christ's redemptive work, our own work, our own freely chosen activities in the material world of everyday life, has an apostolic character. The apostolate of the laity, Blessed Josemaría insisted (as did Vatican Council II after him), is not an 'ecclesiastical' activity, something 'juxtaposed' to their workaday world. Rather our work 'is also an apostolate, an opportunity to give ourselves to others, to reveal Christ to them and lead them to God the Father'.[83] Indeed, in a particularly picturesque passage Blessed Josemaría called one's 'professional prestige' in one's job—no matter what the job might be—one's 'bait' as a 'fisher of men'.[84] Our work, in other words, forms our apostolate. It provides us with the occasion to bring to others the redeeming love of Christ.

---

82 *Christ Is Passing By*, 50.

83 Ibid., 75.

84 *The Way*, 372: 'You stray from your apostolic way if the occasions—or the excuse—of a work of zeal makes you leave the duties of your office unfulfilled. For you will lose your professional prestige, which is exactly your "bait" as a fisher of men.' Cf. ibid., 347.

b. The value of 'little things'

This has been touched on briefly above, in considering work. But the 'little things' that constitute so much a part of our daily lives include far more than the 'little things' so central to our 'work' understood as a 'stable condition of one's life, the work by which one is involved in everyday society'.[85] By the 'little things' that form the warp and woof of our ordinary daily lives Blessed Josemaría had in mind the countless 'trifling opportunities that come our way'[86]—the way we greet others, cope with the frustrations we encounter (traffic, rude clerks, what have you). All these 'trifling opportunities' must be turned into occasions for sanctifying ourselves and others. A cardinal teaching of Blessed Josemaría was that we must 'be faithful, very faithful, in all the little things'.[87] Indeed, as the Founder of Opus Dei put it, the 'little things' of daily life, the 'trifles', are the 'oil, the fuel we need to keep our flame alive and light shining'.[88] So true is this that one of the greatest dangers to our lives as Christians lies in imagining that 'God cannot be here, in the things of each instant, because they are so simple and ordinary'.[89]

So important are 'little things' to our ordinary, daily life in the world—the 'place' where we are called to sanctify ourselves and others—that Blessed Josemaría devoted a special section of *The Way* to a consideration of their crucial significance for us as children of God, called to make him and his love efficaciously present in the ordinary world in which we live.[90] Two brief reflections included early in this section of *The Way* sum

---

85 Illanes, *On the Theology of Work*, p. 9. See above, under the discussion of work.

86 See Bl. Josemaría's homily, 'The richness of everyday life' in *Friends of God*, 9.

87 Cf. ibid., 18 and 20.

88 Ibid., 41.

89 Bl. Josemaría Escrivá, homily 'Towards holiness', in *Friends of God*, 313.

90 Cf. *The Way*, 813-30.

matters up quite clearly: 'You have mistaken the way if you scorn the little things',[91] and 'Great holiness consists in carrying out the "little" duties of each moment'.[92]

Indeed, it is precisely because she valued 'little things' and their crucial importance in living out faithfully God's call to holiness that Mary is our model and the cause of our joy. As Blessed Josemaría said in meditating on Mary and the model she offers us, 'the supernatural value of our life does not depend on accomplishing great undertakings suggested to us by our overactive imagination. Rather it is to be found in the faithful acceptance of God's will, in welcoming generously the *opportunities for small, daily sacrifice*', in 'accepting from God our condition as ordinary men and sanctifying its apparent worthlessness. Thus did Mary live.'[93]

c. *Marriage and family life*

'Do you laugh because I tell you that you have a vocation to marriage? Well, you have just that—a vocation'.[94] Blessed Josemaría clearly understood marriage as a divine vocation throughout his life—this passage is found in the first edition of *The Way*, written in 1939, when the idea that marriage is indeed a divine vocation was not well understood by many Catholics. That Christian marriage is a vocation and a means of holiness is central to the teaching of Blessed Josemaría: 'For a Christian,' he wrote, 'marriage is not just a social institution, much less a mere remedy for human weakness. It is a real supernatural calling.'[95]

The ordinary life of most laypeople is spent working and in the midst of their families. If they are ever going to sanctify themselves and others—and carry out faithfully the vocation entrusted to them of becoming holy

---

91 *The Way*, 816.
92 Ibid., 817.
93 Bl. Josemaría, homily, 'The Blessed Virgin, cause of our joy', in *Christ Is Passing By*, 172.
94 *The Way*, 27.
95 *Christ Is Passing By*, 23.

and of participating in Christ's redemptive work—they will do so only by sanctifying their work (as we have seen) and by sanctifying their married and family life.

The great truth here—one clearly recognized by Blessed Josemaría—and magnificently developed by Vatican Council II and, in a pre-eminent way, by Pope John Paul II—is that the beautiful human reality of marriage, which has God as its author and came into being with the creation of the first man and woman—is itself, like the man and woman who marry, inwardly capable of being divinized and incorporated into God's covenant of grace and love. This has been the constant teaching of the Church, for the marriages of Christian men and women are sacraments of the new law of grace.[96] Indeed, the marriages of Christian men and women not only point to but inwardly participate in the life-giving, grace-giving spousal union of Christ with his bride, the Church (Eph 5:31–33). Inasmuch as the sanctifying mission of marriage and family, so dear to the heart of Blessed Josemaría, has been developed so magnificently by Pope John Paul II in his Apostolic Exhortation *Familiaris consortio*, in what follows I will, on the whole, simply seek to summarize and comment on the teaching set forth in that document.[97]

When Christian men and women marry they do so as persons who are already, through baptism, united with Christ and with his spotless bride, the Church, his

---

[96] This was solemnly defined as a truth of faith by the Council of Trent at its 24th session, November 1563. For text see DS, 1797–1800, with accompanying canons, 1801–1812. It has been constantly reaffirmed by the Magisterium: e.g., Leo XIII, Encyclical *Arcanum divinae sapientiae*, Pius XI, Encyclical *Casti connubii*, Vatican Council II, Pastoral Constitution *Gaudium et spes*, 47–52, Paul VI, Encyclical *Humanae vitae*, John Paul II, Apostolic Exhortation *Familiaris consortio*.

[97] A superb text devoted to the presentation and analysis of the Church's teaching on marriage and family is Ramón García de Harol, *Matrimonio e Famiglia nei Documenti del Magistero* (Milan, 1988), English translation by William E. May, *Marriage and Family in the Documents of the Magisterium* (San Francisco, 1993). Chapter eight of this masterful work is devoted to an analysis of the abundant teaching of John Paul II on marriage and family, in particular the teaching found in *Familiaris consortio*.

body (cf. 1 Cor 6:15–20). By means of their baptism, as Pope John Paul II states, 'men and women are definitively placed within the new and eternal covenant, in the spousal covenant of Christ with the Church. And it is because of this indestructible insertion that the intimate community of conjugal life and love, founded by the Creator, is elevated and assumed into the spousal charity of Christ sustained and enriched by his redeeming power.'[98] As a result their marriage 'is a real symbol of that new and eternal covenant sanctioned in the blood of Christ. The Spirit which the Lord pours forth gives a new heart, and renders man and woman capable of loving one another as Christ has loved us. Conjugal love reaches that fullness to which it is interiorly ordained, conjugal charity, which is the proper and specific way in which the spouses participate in and are called to live the very charity of Christ, who gave himself on the cross.'[99] Christian spouses are thus called upon, John Paul II continues, *to be what they are!*,[100] that is, spouses who can, in and through their married lives, mediate to their families and to the world in which they live the saving grace of Christ and his Church and to reflect in their marital and family life the redemptive love that Christ bears for his spotless bride, the Church.

John Paul II assigns four major tasks to Christian husbands and wives. They are:

- to form a community of persons,
- to serve life by welcoming from God the gift of human life, nourishing it and educating it in the love of God and neighbor,
- to participate in the development of society, and
- to participate in life and mission of the Church.[101]

The Christian family, rooted in the sacramental

---

98 Pope John Paul II, Apostolic Exhortation *Familiaris consortio*, 13.
99 Ibid.
100 Ibid., 17.
101 Ibid., Part III.

marriage of Christian husbands and wives, is sin truth, as the Fathers of the Church, Vatican Council II, and John Paul II remind us, a 'church in miniature', the 'domestic church'.[102] It thus has a specific and original ecclesial role as a believing and evangelizing community and as a community in dialogue with God.[103] Christian married couples 'not only *receive* the love of Christ and become a *saved* community, but they are also called upon to *communicate* Christ's love to their brethren, thus becoming a *saving community*'[104]

In the context of our contemporary culture, characterized by the banal slogan of those who advocate contraception and abortion to the effect that 'no unwanted baby ought ever to be born', it seems to me that one of the crucially important sanctifying missions of Christian marriage and family is to enlighten human minds and open human hearts to the sublime truth that 'no human person, including unborn children, ought ever to be unwanted, i.e., unloved'. And the only way in which society can be developed in which all human persons are indeed wanted is for men and women to shape their choices in accord with the truth. The truth demands that they recognize the precious goods of human sexuality, the goods of marriage: absolute fidelity to one's spouse and an openness to the goodness of human life.

---

102 Vatican Council II, Dogmatic Constitution *Lumen gentium*, 11; cf. Decree on the laity, *Apostolicam actuositatem*, 11; John Paul II, Apostolic Exhortation *Familiaris consortio*, 49. Helpful theological studies: Domenico Sartore, C.S.I., 'La famiglia, chiesa domestica', *Lateranum* 45 (1979) 282–303; Jean Beyer, S.J., 'Ecclesia domestica', *Periodica de re morali, canonica, liturgica* 79 (199) 293–326; Vigen Guroian, 'Family and Christian virtue in a post-Christendom world: reflections on the ecclesial vision of John Chrysostom', *St. Vladimir's Theological Quarterly* 35 (1991) 327–50.

103 John Paul II, Apostolic Exhortation *Familiaris consortio*, 50–62.

104 Ibid., 49.

IV. Conclusion

Because we make ourselves to be the persons we are in and through the deeds we freely choose to do in our everyday, ordinary life at home and at work, we can only live out our vocation as God's children and attain, with God's grace, the plenitude of our divine filiation by sanctifying ordinary life. It is indeed the place and means of our sanctification. But, Blessed Josemaría reminds us, 'sanctification is the work of a lifetime'.[105] As he likewise noted, 'people are not born holy'. Rather, 'holiness is forged through a constant interplay of God's grace and the correspondence of man'.[106] It is possible only with God's help, with his grace. As a result, we must make use of the means needed to ensure that our vocation to holiness can take root and develop. According to Blessed Josemaría, the two most indispensable means, 'which are like living supports of Christian conduct', are 'interior life and doctrinal formation, the deep knowledge of our faith'.[107] Without a deep, mature knowledge of the truths that God has so graciously made known to us through the mediation of his Son and of his Son's bride the Church, we can never fulfilll our vocation as his children. Nor can we do so unless we develop an interior life, one of constant prayer rooted in personal familiarity with our best and wisest friend, Jesus. What we must do is 'foster deep down in our hearts a burning desire, an intense eagerness to achieve sanctity, even though we see ourselves full of failings. Do not be afraid ... Speak now from the bottom of your heart: 'Lord, I really do want to be a saint. I really do want to be a worthy disciple of yours and to follow you unconditionally.'[108]

---

105 *Christ Is Passing By*, 8.
106 *Friends of God*, 7.
107 *Christ Is Passing By*, 8.
108 *Friends of God*, 20.

PART II : SPIRITUAL LIFE

Prayer and the basic structure of faith

Georges Cottier, Theologian of the Papal Household

In these years which lead us to the end of the second millenium, the Church is called to the great undertaking of a *new evangelization*. The Holy Spirit is impelling us along a route beset by challenges: the Gospel needs to be proclaimed not only to those who do not know it, but also to those who try to forget it or have already managed to do so. It has to be proclaimed tirelessly, in order to deepen our attachment to Christ. For this new evangelization to take place, evangelizers themselves have to be evangelized. The encounter with Christ and full attachment to his Person are grounded on faith, the *initium salutis*. Though faith is a gift from God, it can be prepared for, and doubts which prevent people from receiving it can be dispelled; once they adhere to that faith, they need God's help to ensure that they do not fail to grow in it.

Such being the case, as we prepare ourselves for the undertakings which lie before us, examples of living faith and examples of holiness are an indispensable help. And one of these examples is a saint of our time, Blessed Josemaría Escrivá. Reflecting on some aspects of his spirituality, we shall try to draw some conclusions applicable to the apostolate of faith in the framework of the new evangelization.

'Resignation? ... Conformity? Love for the will of God!'[1] And, before that: 'Stages—to be resigned to the will of God; to conform to the will of God; to want the

---

1 *The Way*, 774.

will of God; to love the will of God.'[2] To reflect faith in the spirituality of Blessed Josemaría, we can begin with this thought, which, in a few lapidary phrases, describes the path to holiness which he himself followed and which he taught to his sons and daughters. In other words, his own life constitutes an example of constant openness to the will of God, which he sought with his whole soul. When this will of God takes the form of the Cross and draws from him laments which might seem to be a reproach, immediately, by a kind of spontaneous reflection, he responds by total acceptance, with the result that the profound peace which dwells in his soul is never destroyed.

In line with the great spiritual tradition rooted in the heart of the Gospel and to be seen particularly in St. Teresa of Avila's *Way of Perfection*, *love for the Father* finds its concrete and daily expression in the search for the will of God, the object of the third petition in the Our Father: *thy will be done on earth as it is in heaven.*

And, indeed, the will of God is communicated to us through moral conscience enlightened by faith and through impulses of the Holy Spirit. The judgments that conscience makes direct us either to do specific things or to avoid doing them. However, if we widen the word 'action' to include interior attitudes, conscience asks us often for a reaction, an acceptance of events which form the fabric of our lives, and which we have chosen or, on the contrary, which we would have preferred to have rejected. Everyone comes up against events or demands external to him which he finds repugnant or which take a lot out of him. All these circumstances which are beyond our control and which go to make up our life should be appreciated with the help of faith.

This leads us to a threefold certainty: the Providence of God is omnipotent, it embraces all things; everything works for the good of those who love God (cf. Rom 8:28); the will of the Father is a will which loves us.

---

2 *The Way*, 757.

'For this is the will of God, your sanctification' (cf. 1 Thess 4:3). Sanctification, in turn, involves a sharing in the cross of Jesus.

Union with God our Father is a relationship of filiation with the Only Son; and Christian prayer, which expresses this relationship with the Father, has its most intimate source in the Holy Spirit himself, according to the disconcerting words of St. Paul to the Romans and the Galatians, 'For all who are led by the Spirit of God are sons of God. For you did not receive the spirit of slavery to fall back into fear, but you have received the spirit of sonship. When we cry, "Abba! Father!" it is the Spirit himself bearing witness with our spirit that we are children of God, and if children, then heirs, heirs of God and fellow heirs with Christ, provided we suffer with him in order that we may also be glorified with him' (Rom 8:14–17; cf. Rom 8:26–30; Gal 4:4–7).

What we have been discussing finds its fullest dimension in the light of this great Pauline passage.

The mystery of filiation through grace, which shapes the identity of the baptized, is to be found at the very center of Josemaría Escrivá's spirituality. This filiation, which is above all ontological in character, should become part and parcel of a person's life; it should be lived through the practice of the Christian virtues, outstanding among which are the theological virtues. And it becomes alive fully when there exists a perfect union between a person's will and the will of the Father. Union or fusion of wills defines love and, in our case, supernatural love, charity. But this same love presupposes that each person guides his life by the light of faith.

It does sometimes happen that life offers us contradictions, illness, things that go wrong, suffering, tests, or that it calls for sacrifices which seem to be beyond our strength. How are we to see in all this the mark of the goodness of our Father in heaven?

Perhaps it is then that we come to grasp why loving the will of God is an expression of holiness; but we need also to understand that, in order to reach that level of identification, there is a long road to travel.

Being resigned to the will of God: This phrase has been used before to indicate acceptance of the divine will. But resignation is only a first step, and yet only a very imperfect one. It means that one has countered an initial tendency to rebel; but a person who is resigned adopts an external attitude towards God's will. His will is not given over to God; rather, it endures, it gives in the way that someone who is weak yields to someone who is strong. It is an attitude more servile than filial. If the person had it his way, he would arrange things differently; his desire is still focused in a different direction. However, he has overcome his interior rebellion. And this may be progress.

Conforming to the will of God: This is an advance. There is submission to the will of God, given that the soul adopts a religious attitude, inspired by the virtue of religion or devotion to God. One accepts God's lordship, puts oneself in the position of servant to Master. This conformity to the will of God can be a great and noble attitude. But human will and divine will are still not perfectly united. The human will does not allow itself to be entirely won over; it still keeps its distance to some degree. The divine will is seen in terms of fate, as something inescapable; but it is not seen as the will of the Father.

We might locate the great school of the Stoics here; and in fact people have spoken of a Christian stoicism. However, it is an advance, insofar as what we have here is an essentially religious attitude.

Wanting the will of God: This step is a more perfect one, because it implies that the human will is active and positive, and goes out to meet the will of God. But, this attitude, like the preceding one, may derive from the virtue of religion, as a kind of fulfilllment of that natural virtue. The virtue of religion is the most perfect of the moral virtues, but it is not a theological virtue.

Loving the will of God: True, loving is a kind of wanting or desiring. But not every sort of desire for the will of God fits in with love in the sense used here, which is the *supernatural love of charity*. Loving the will of God applies to a person who lives the grace of divine filiation and who advances with his whole being, with the ardent flame of his love, to meet the God he loves: because this will of God is the will of the Father and, therefore, a supremely lovable will. In this sort of love for the will of the Father, the *sequela Christi* is being fully put into practice: one is making one's own the offering Jesus made in the garden of Gethsemane: 'nevertheless, not as I will, but as thou wilt' (cf. Mt 26:39). This kind of love, as revealed in Jesus' offering, can be heroic; it can even go as far as self-immolation, the sacrifice of one's very life.

Therefore, if *loving the will of God* is nothing less than the expression of theological charity, then the life of charity obviously presupposes and at the same time nourishes the life of faith. It gives rise, then, to the *faith that works through love* (Gal 5:6). Otherwise, how could we know that the Providence of God, of him who is our Father, covers history in its entirety, whether the history of mankind or the history of each individual? God is interested in everything we do, everything that happens, every one of our encounters. He is present in the most ordinary of everyday things, which constitute the place of our sanctification and an encounter with Christ. Josemaría Escrivá used to say to his sons and daughters: 'everyday life is the true setting of your lives as Christians'.[3]

And so, in training people for holiness one needs to lay stress on those things that have to do with faith and with the solidity of that faith. And to stress, too, the active power of faith. I have extracted a few key texts in this connection: 'Some describe faith and trust in God as being imprudent and rash.'[4] Trust in God has to do

---

3 *Conversations with Monsignor Escrivá de Balaguer*, 113.
4 *Furrow* (London and New York, 1987), 43.

with faith and hope. Radically, it is an attitude of faith in the loving Providence of the Father and in his salvific action. This sort of trust in the presence and action of the Father lies at the very basis of apostolic action: 'A keen and living faith. Like Peter's. When you have it— our Lord has said so— you will move the mountains, the humanly insuperable obstacles that rise up against your apostolic undertakings.'[5]

Throughout his life, Josemaría Escrivá bore witness to this sort of love for the will of God. I recall a few episodes of this type. At the beginning of the Work in Madrid, he was getting very valuable help from a young priest, José Maria Somoane, who suddenly became ill and died on June 17, 1932. It was a hard blow for Escrivá: 'Lord, why have you taken him? Why have you deprived yourself of a faithful servant, who could have been so effective in the service of the Work? But you know best, and you are doing what is best for him and for us.'[6] He really felt resentful about this blow he had received, but he immediately reacted with faith.

In the spring of 1941, his mother, from whom he had asked so much by involving her in the apostolate of the Work, fell ill. He had promised to preach a retreat to the priests of the diocese of Lérida, in Catalonia. Having heard the doctor's rather optimistic report, he left Madrid, entrusting his mother to our Lord. Two days later, during the retreat, he was told that his mother had died. His sorrow and pain was such that he could not but make a filial complaint to God; but he followed this by immediately accepting the divine will: 'Lord, how can you do this to me? There I was, looking after your priests, and you do this to me?' But a little later on, he added: 'May the most just and most lovable Will of God be done, be fulfillled, be praised and extolled for ever. Amen. Amen.'

---

5 *The Way*, 489.
6 *Registro Histórico del Fundador* (henceforth RHF), 20165, pp. 1635–6.

When he got back to Madrid, he went to the oratory where his mother's body lay. And here again, just as when he heard the news, he began to cry. When he got off his knees, he asked for a stole and said the *Te Deum*. And yet he could not suppress a lament: 'My God, my God, what have you done? You have taken everything from me: you take it all away. I thought that my mother was much needed by these daughters of mine, and now you leave me with nothing ..., with nothing!' But he was heard to make this prayer: 'Lord, I am content, because I know that you love her and you have shown me a mark of confidence. . . . We must try to ensure that all my sons manage to be with their parents when their parents die, but sometimes it just won't be possible. And you have so arranged things, Lord, that in this I should set them an example.'[7]

I shall recall here his reaction to the death in a car accident of three of his sons in 1960. His anguished question to God: Why?, was immediately followed by an act of abandonment to divine Providence.[8] We meet the same attitude, again and again, all through the course of a life in which he does encounter trials, especially when the Work itself was under fire.[9]

If he was being treated in this way, there must have been a reason for it: Blessed Josemaría had such profound experience of the mystery of the Cross, that he went as far as to write: 'Accepting the will of God wholeheartedly is a sure way of finding joy and peace—happiness in the Cross. Then we realize that Christ's yoke is sweet and that his burden is not heavy.'[10]

One needs to be able to recognize the Cross of Christ in the difficulties that arise. Discovering the Cross 'means discovering happiness, joy [...]; it means becoming identified with Christ, it means being Christ, and

---

7 RHF, 4417.

8 Cf. F. Gondrand, *At God's Pace* (London and New York, 1989), p. 264.

9 Cf. ibid., pp. 243ff.

10 *The Way*, 758.

therefore being a son of God.' And he adds: 'The basis of the spiritual life of the members of Opus Dei is their sense of divine filiation.'[11]

Blessed Josemaría asks his sons and daughters to be apostles in ordinary, everyday life; work well done, with all the demands it entails, honest work, is where they are to sanctify themselves. One can then understand the aspects of the life of faith which he particularly valued: 'a humble, lively and operative faith,'[12] for faith expresses itself in humility;[13] a faith 'full of sacrifice',[14] appropriate to someone who strives to be a saint.[15]

An apostle's faith should root out any kind of doubt, and when temptations beset him, a person who wants souls to be saved should cry out, taking his cue from the father of the sick child in the Gospel: 'Lord, help my unbelief.'[16]

There is a term that often crops up in his writings— the word *supernatural*. Faith gives us a 'supernatural way of seeing things'.[17] When speaking about his Work, Monsignor Escrivá used to tell his children that they are not here to carry out 'a human undertaking, but a great supernatural undertaking, which from the very start had all the hallmarks necessary for allowing it to be called, without boasting, the Work of God'.[18]

What the founder is doing here is identifying the principle, the soul, of his Work: it is a *supernatural work*. By describing that Work in this way, he is at the same time establishing a high standard. If faithfulness to this standard were to flag, the Work would cease to exist.

---

11 RHF, 20119, p. 13.
12 Cf. Bl. J. Escrivá, *The Forge* (London and New York, 1988), no. 257.
13 Cf. ibid., 324.
14 Cf. ibid., 155.
15 Cf. ibid., 111.
16 Cf. ibid., 257.
17 Cf. ibid., 657.
18 RHF 21500, p. 1.

This calling is addressed, above all, to lay people. It is the lay people who are called to strive, with the help of grace, for their own sanctification and to do apostolate in ordinary life; and work, done competently and taken seriously, plays a key role in this.

Inevitably this brings up a very important question. What connection is there between this calling and the commitment in temporal affairs which, as the Second Vatican Council stressed so forcefully, is a part of the vocation of the lay person? We are well aware that, despite the specific guidelines laid down by the Council, there has been a good deal of uncertainty in this regard—the two equally disastrous ends of the scale being to confuse both fields (Christian vocation, and commitment to temporal affairs) and to divide them radically from each other.

Josemaría Escrivá's guidelines in this regard have a clarity that is all the more remarkable because he discovered them at a time when party strife seemed to be drawing everything else. The young people around him at the time (we are in Madrid, in early 1936) were impressed by the fact that he never got involved in political discussion. He simply reminded them of what the Church's teaching was and of the duty every Christian has to fulfill all his or her social obligations. Over and above everything, he never ceased to stress the 'new' commandment of brotherly love.[19]

Later, in 1939, addressing a group of students, he would put them on their guard against an overly human way of acting, even when they were inspired by noble patriotic ideals: 'But do not forget that there is something much higher—the kingdom of Christ, which has no end. And for Christ to reign in the world, he must first reign in your heart. Does he truly reign there? Is yours a heart that is for Jesus Christ?'[20]

---

19 Cf. RHF 21500, pp. 108-9.
20 Ibid., p. 144.

Monsignor Escrivá will never cease to assert the autonomy of lay people in the temporal sphere:[21] 'I love freedom, because if we didn't have freedom we couldn't serve God: we truly should be pitied. Catholics need to be taught to live, not by calling themselves Catholics, but by being citizens who bear personal responsibility for their personal, free actions.' He will go so far as to say, using a form of words which needs to be interpreted properly, because it involves a kind of paradox: 'the sons of God in Opus Dei make their way in spite of being Catholics'.[22]

For the same reason, a similar freedom applies in the area of political choice and involvement. 'What attitude should members of Opus Dei adopt in the political life of their country? 'Whatever they feel like!, it is entirely up to them. I take no interest in what position anyone takes; I defend his freedom. If I did not, then I would not be able to protect my own freedom. And I come from a region where we reject any type of imposition...'[23] Leaving to one side the humour in these last lines, the position the founder of Opus Dei takes derives from two essential reasons. The first has in fact to do with the strictly supernatural nature of a vocation to Opus Dei, which must be protected from any tendency towards a goal other than the Kingdom of God. This does not mean that Blessed Josemaría is denying the evangelical inspiration which should be behind commitment to temporal affairs. But what he is emphasizing is that it is up to each person, on his own, to discover and activate the particular form his social involvement takes (Gospel-inspired as it is).

The second reason is dictated by the supernatural plane on which the Work is set. 'Do not forget that the world is something that belongs to us, the world is our home, the world is a work of God and we have to love it,

---

21 Cf. RHF 21500, pp. 162, 234.
22 RHF 20565, pp. 36-9.
23 Ibid., p. 40.

just as we have to love those who live in it. It is up to us to consecrate the world, through this dedication to the service of God, each one in the exercise of his ordinary work, so as to bear witness to Jesus Christ and also serve the Church, the Pope and all souls. Therefore, we have to understand the world, we have to lift it up, we have to divinize it, we have to purify it, we have to redeem it with Christ, because we are co-redeemers with him.'[24]

Let us also quote these very clear statements from 1967: 'The purpose of Opus Dei is to foster the search for holiness and the carrying out of the apostolate by Christians who live in the world, whatever their state in life or position in society. [...] Christ is present in any honest human activity. [...] The one and only mission of Opus Dei is the spreading of this message. [...] And to those who grasp this ideal of holiness, the Work offers the spiritual assistance and the doctrinal, ascetical, and apostolic training which they need to put it into practice.'[25] That is why the 'members of the Work do not act as a group. They act individually with personal freedom and responsibility'.[26]

Monsignor Escrivá is very much against any attempt to 'instrumentalize lay people for ends which exceed the proper limits of the hierarchical ministry'.[27] He warns against one particular way of defining the vocation of lay Catholics: it is not a matter of 'penetrating' social milieux! 'The members of the Work have no need to "penetrate" the temporal sector for the simple reason that they are ordinary citizens, the same as their fellow citizen, and so they are there already'.[28] All this, taken together, amounts to sketching out a vocation which everyone has, but a *supernatural* vocation to sanctification and apostolate.

---

24 RHF 20565, p. 45.
25 *Conversations*, 260.
26 Ibid.
27 Ibid., 12.
28 Ibid., 266.

The notion of freedom, whereby a person responds to the love of God, and a sense of the supernatural nature of vocation guide Josemaría Escrivá's view of the spiritual life. His insistence on ordinary life should not be taken as an invitation to uniformity. In fact, quite the opposite. His experience as a spiritual director taught him that God's ways are designed to suit each person individually. In a homily on the life of prayer (April 4, 1955) we read: 'There are countless ways of praying, as I have already told you. We children of God don't need a method, an artificial system, to talk with our Father. Love is inventive, it is full of initiative. If we truly love, we will discover our own intimate paths to lead us to a continuous conversation with our Lord.'[29]

And, a little before that, in a beautiful passage about mental prayer, we find this: 'Each day without fail we should devote some time especially to God, raising our minds to him, without any need for the words to come to our lips, for they are sung in our heart. [...] Each one of you, if he wants, can find his own way to converse with God. I do not like to talk about methods or formulas, because I have never wished to straitjacket anyone. What I have always tried to do is encourage everyone to come closer to our Lord, respecting each soul as it is, each with its own characteristics. Ask him into our lives: not only in our heads, but also into the depths of our hearts and into all our outward actions.'[30]

In this way, Monsignor Escrivá puts before his sons and daughters a way of spiritual freedom, which does not mean a way which is undemanding: 'You are contemplative souls in the middle of the world', he tells them, and he uses this beautiful formula—the 'noiseless heroism of your spiritual life'.[31] The vocation of lay people in the world requires them to have this contemplative attitude, otherwise it would lose its rightful su-

---

29 *Friends of God*, 255.
30 Ibid., 249.
31 RHF 29850, p. 3.

pernatural character and make it impossible for them to change the world: 'If not, they will change nothing; instead they themselves will be changed; instead of Christianizing the world, Christians will become worldly.'[32]

The difficulties which ordinary life involves should not be used to contradict this teaching. On the contrary, ordinary life is perfectly capable of being used as a resource in prayer life: 'The street,' we read in a Letter written in 1959, 'does not get in the way of our contemplative life; the hubbub of the world is, for us, a place for prayer.'[33]

A sense of divine filiation brings with it a sense of the presence of God. Blessed Josemaría is always at pains to stress this truth of faith and to show its spiritual effectiveness: 'We've got to be convinced that God is always near us [...] He is there like a loving Father. He loves each one of us more than all the mothers in the world can love their children—helping us, inspiring us, blessing ... and forgiving...'[34]

It is not difficult to see how much in keeping this teaching is with that of the Second Vatican Council on the holiness of all the baptized and, in particular, of the vocation of lay people.

Following on from what we have said so far, I should like at this point to outline a few ideas about the demands the life of faith makes in the context of the new evangelization.

By its very nature faith comes up against demands and obstacles which arise for every new generation. But it also meets challenges which are proper to each particular epoch. These will be the ones we shall look at first.

After the symbolic success of the fall of the Berlin Wall in 1989, there was talk of its marking the end of the 'age of the ideologies'. That slogan is only partially true. It

---

[32] *Artículos del Postulador* (Rome, 1979), 212-13.
[33] Letter, January 9, 1959.
[34] *The Way*, 267. Cf. also *The Forge*, 658.

ignores, for example, the marks that Marxist ideology has left on people's psyches; it ignores the deep wounds which are gradually coming to the surface. But, above all, it tries to make out that a system has been culturally checkmated. And—true—Marxist ideology, as one elaborate but not unique ideological model, is an attempt by the proponents of society and the State to confer an absolute value on their own particular agenda and its rationale: it is something to be imposed on all members of society. That is why totalitarian power cannot be separated from its ideological dimension. Its representatives regard themselves as, in Stalin's famous phrase, engineers of souls. Having wrested control of education and the mass media, and developed an impressive propaganda machine, they had to win over people's minds, by whatever means. Totalitarian power, which described itself as 'scientific', had to be in control of people's minds: everyone had to see things its way. The consensus obtained by this method (largely a fictitious and only apparent one) took the place of truth. Ideologies are lies or illusions which impose themselves or are imposed on the collectivity, with the result that the ideological era signified the triumph of pseudo-truth, insofar as a lie is a false statement which does its level best to pass itself off as true. It is much more than a simple mistake. And that is why the decline or downfall of ideologies, falseness of which becomes immediately manifest, brings with it a crisis as to what truth means. If what we were taught to be true was in fact false, a lie, where are we to find the truth? Is truth not an illusion? In that sort of situation, the temptation to nihilism becomes very strong. To the degree that ideologies have perverted the very notion of truth, the present-day crisis of culture is above all a crisis of truth.

For these reasons, and in view of the new evangelization, apostles have to be witnesses to the truth—witnesses, in the first instance, to the virtue of faith. It is worth recalling here what Jesus said: 'You will know the truth, and the truth will set you free' (Jn 8:32). And, given that the crisis of truth also affects the cultural sphere, a witness to the truth who has an intellectual vocation has to be present in the fields of philosophy and metaphysics.

Ideology fakes the truth. Therefore ideology's fall has the effect of weakening and clouding people's sense of truth. Other sectors of our culture can contribute to this loss of a sense of truth.

If the modern age managed to develop the very notion of ideology, then that must have been because political power had access to ways of pressuring people's minds, much more effective ways than theretofore. But another, and deeper, reason for the growth of ideology had to do with an underlying crisis about the notion of *certainty*, a crisis which existed from earlier on.

The notion of certainty is different from the notion of truth: someone has certainty of a truth. Certainty is a quality a person has of possessing, of assimilating truth. A certain truth is a truth which no argument can uproot from the mind. Thus, certainty means the property truth has whereby it can impose itself on the mind: there is no appeal. Whereas truth expresses a relationship of agreement between judgment and the thing known, certainty is the effect of truth, the way it roots itself in the knowing subject: there are truths that are certain, and truths that are probable.

Truth imposes itself with certainty when the mind sees direct or indirect *evidence* of truth. That is when the object becomes present to the mind.

Now, in modern culture the accent has been shifted in a way that should not be underestimated: against the very nature of things, certainty has taken over the front seat from evidence of truth. What people are looking for now, first and foremost, is certainty.

Two things follow from this. The first, is a typical form of rationalism. What is being sought, first of all, is the *how* of knowledge; perfect possession of the object has become the criterion of truth, thereby excluding, in the field of knowledge, any imperfect grasp of truth. And that explains why the human mind has closed in on itself.

The second consequence can be found in the opposite direction. The search for certainty first and foremost, which gives priority to the subjective aspect of knowledge, has opened the way to psychological substitutes for certainty. Now that it has no connection with truth, certainty has become a tranquillizing subjective attitude. And thereby the door is opened for ideologies to enter: they are not asked to account for themselves; people make straight for something that involves no doubt, because they find that more consoling.

All this is very relevant to someone who bears witness to the truth. Thus, theological faith involves a relationship between evidence and certainty which has no equivalent in the order of human things. As far as ordinary things go, the degree of certainty depends on the degree of evidence. In theological faith absence of evidence and perfect fixed certainty live side by side: and this is so because the act of faith is grounded on something stronger than the natural evidence of reason, that is, it is grounded on the authority of God who reveals and on the authority of his utter truthfulness. So, there is undoubtedly evidence that grounds faith, but it is an evidence which is given us through a mediator: 'No one has ever seen God; the only Son, who is in the bosom of the Father, has made him known' (Jn 1:18).

The person who witnesses to the truth needs to be fully aware of the specificity of theological faith. Blessed Josemaría Escrivá teaches: 'Faith is a supernatural virtue which disposes our mind to give assent to the truths of revelation, to say yes to Christ, who has brought us full knowledge of the Blessed Trinity's plan for our salvation.'[35] These lines throw light on the way we are expected to act.

---

35 *Friends of God*, 191 (homily preached on October 12, 1947).

The kingdom of the ideologies was one ruled by 'certainties' which no longer derive from truth. That is why ideologies have been interpreted as responses, in the individual and social sphere, to a need for a sense of security. These 'certainties', it is argued, were lies, thanks to which we were able to defend ourselves against the tragic element in our lives, subject as they are to the inexorable law of time and impermanence. Now that this recourse has failed to work, man will just have to learn to live without certainties; scepticism and relativism must become the bases of new wisdom. If society takes this sort of attitude, an attitude of resigned despair, believers will be accused of being either fanatics or else people who are quite out of date and who try to hold onto the old certainties at all costs.

This new cultural scenario calls for a special testimony of faith, and of the newness of faith. People need to be shown that the certainties that a believer has come from divine truth, the source of meaning, peace and joy. That kind of testimony will dispel prejudice and overcome obstacles if it is expressed in a truly evangelical way. In other words, the person who bears witness to faith has to avoid two pitfalls—that of the tranquillizing type of certainty which has no connection with the truth, and that of correlative rejection of certainties as illusions which man has to learn to do without.

A crisis of truth, a temptation to scepticism. There is a third challenge on the path of the new evangelization—that of syncretism. What we have seen so far does not cover all the tendencies which tempt our world. As well as the tendency towards nihilism, we also need to deal with a diffuse and rampant religiosity, and with the problems (mostly new ones) which derive from Christianity's encounter with non-Christian religions. The Second Vatican Council, in its declaration *Nostra aetate*, has opened the door to a dialogue between religions which is not confined to the missions. But when one takes a sympathetic approach to the positive elements in other religions, a strong temptation arises— that of losing sight of the specific character of Christianity and of the universality of the salvation it brings us: 'there is salvation in no one else, for there is no other name under heaven given among men by which we must be saved' (Acts 4:12).

The temptation to syncretism consists in regarding the various religious experiences as in essence identical; the actual religions are just contingent expressions of religion. Christianity then comes to be seen as just one religion among many. This kind of temptation has proved very seductive; and, although in a mild form, it has its affect also on some theologians.

Faced with this challenge, which is a very serious one for the century ahead, it is vitally necessary for the witness to faith to be convinced of the transcendence of the Christian faith, of the uniqueness of that faith. The special nature of this faith derives from the personal relationship it establishes with the person of Jesus Christ, the Son of God made man. We will recall how much Monsignor Escrivá stressed the supernatural aspect, as also the importance of the believer's living in union with Jesus. We remember too the sense he had of the Eucharist, and, through the homilies he has left us, his constant and very practical invitation to the *sequela Christ*, to follow Christ. Daily meditation on the Gospel and participation in the liturgy of the Church will lead the disciple to this familiarity with Jesus, which is at the center of our faith. The witness to the truth sees himself, in this way, impelled to deepen his awareness of the fact that he is a son of God in the only-begotten Son. It is also appropriate to recall Blessed Josemaría's deep Marian devotion, as also his love for the Church.

So, we find ourselves in the presence of a rich treasure which the artisans of the new evangelization are invited to avail themselves of in order to be up to the tasks that await them.

Awareness of divine filiation

Jutta Burggraf,
International Academic Institute for the Study of
Marriage and the Family, Medo, Rolduc, the Netherlands

'Far away—there, on the horizon—heaven and earth seem to meet,' the founder of Opus Dei wrote. 'Do not forget that where heaven and earth really meet is in the heart of a child of God.'[1] Throughout his life Blessed Josemaría spoke very movingly about the mystery of divine filiation. His words, which rang true, found an echo in people's hearts. They realized that they were being addressed by someone who had been touched and inspired by his consciousness of being a son of God.

I. Experience of divine love

The roots of Blessed Josemaría's teaching on divine filiation are to be found in an experience he had in 1931. At that time the young priest was feeling that things were beyond him, that he was unworthy of his God-given mission to help people rediscover the way to holiness in the midst of everyday duties and occupations. He had come to see that, on his own, he could never succeed in such an undertaking, despite the great need for it. Then, in this difficult situation, he experienced, as he often described it, the 'greatest grace of my life'.[2] In the midst of the bustle of the city, while he was deep in prayer on a tram, the mystery of divine filiation moved his heart most profoundly. At that moment he grasped the very essence of something about which he

---

1 *Furrow*, 309.
2 Cf. A. Aranda in *Santos en el mundo. Estudio sobre los escritos del Beato Josemaría Escrivá*, ed. by Pilar Vega (Madrid, 1993), p. 17.

already had a lively faith: God is not a cold overlord of the world; he is not 'far away, in the heavens high above'. In fact, he is our Father, 'one hundred per cent our Father'. He takes an interest in everything we do, he loves us 'more than all the mothers in the world can love their children'.[3] 'I felt the Lord acting in me', he said of that experience in the tram. 'God himself was forming in my heart and on my lips, irresistibly, the tender exclamation, "Abba! Father".'[4]

Thanks to this infusion of grace in 1931, Blessed Josemaría, at a young age, discovered the mystery of divine filiation. What he experienced that day marked him for ever and is very much in evidence in his teachings. In fact it would not be an exaggeration to say that *all* his counsels on the spiritual life are ultimately based on divine filiation.[5] It should also be said that it is very difficult to detect a steady development in his writings on this truth of faith. What we do find are different accents, and it is worth pointing out the different ways he focuses on the subject depending on the context; but all Blessed Josemaría's teaching in this connection is in the last analysis an unfolding of what he experienced in 1931. In many parts of his writings he makes reference (more or less clearly) to that central experience and, specifically, to the indescribable joy of knowing himself to be enveloped in God's paternal love: 'my life has led me to realize that I am very much a son of God,' he confesses, 'and I have experienced the joy of getting inside the heart of my Father'.[6] 'Words have yet to be invented to express all that a person feels—in his heart and will—when he realizes that he is a son of God.'[7]

---

3 *The Way*, 267. This phrase, much used by the founder of Opus Dei, also occurs in other passages in his writings; cf., for example, *The Forge*, 929.

4 Bl. J. Escrivá, in *Artículos del Postulador* (Rome, 1979), 70.

5 Cf. the homily 'The conversion of the children of God', in *Christ Is Passing By*, 64: 'Divine filiation is the basis of the spirit of Opus Dei.'

6 Homily 'Getting to know God', in *Friends of God*, 143.

7 *Furrow*, 61.

On the one hand, the writings of Blessed Josemaría do not provide us with any substantially new insights into the doctrine of divine filiation as time goes on. In fact his first books, from the thirties (*The Way* and *Holy Rosary*),[8] speak of God as Father in so intimate a way that it seems there is nothing more to be said. The same basic turns of phrase are to be found in the middle period of his life,[9] and also in his later writings, as can be seen from his homily 'The Holy Spirit, the Great Unknown'[10], in 'Christ the King'[11] or in *The Way of the Cross*.[12]

However, we can see that the way he presented this teaching could change quite a lot. Whereas his earlier writings are permeated by a spontaneous, subjective experience, his later writings are more 'reflective' in style and more objective in content.[13] What is very clear in these later writings (as I see it) is the effort the author is making to align his personal experience with the traditional spirituality of the Church, in order to enable *other people* to identify with that experience.

For the founder of Opus Dei, theoretical study of a truth of faith did not mean leaving filial piety to one side; on the contrary, it meant constantly renewing that piety. Even when, as time went by, he reflects on his original experience of divine love in more general terms, he never speaks about the mystery of divine filiation in a theoretical, detached way; no, he speaks of it with the

---

8 The first edition of *Santo Rosario* (*Holy Rosary*) dates from 1934.

9 Cf., for example, *Furrow*, *The Forge* (drafted largely in the '40s and '50s, and published posthumously); or the homilies 'Christian vocation' (1951) in *Christ Is Passing By* and 'Life of prayer' (1954) in *Friends of God*.

10 Homily 'The Holy Spirit, the Great Unknown' (1969) in *Christ Is Passing By*.

11 Homily 'Christ the King' (1970) in *Christ Is Passing By*.

12 First published in 1981.

13 The reason for this change is probably that the earlier works were largely collections of aphorisms, while the later ones consisted of homilies; but it is interesting that the author chose one literary genre to begin with and later changed to another.

vibrance of a man who recalls, even decades later, how forcefully the love of his life took hold of him, nevermore to leave him on his own. This style of reflection in his mature years was (perhaps this is how to describe it) one of conscious intensity, of solid intimacy, and, therefore, even more 'human' than in the years of his youth, as if all his specifically 'human' faculties had become perfectly integrated with one another and now he was able to explain himself better.

Blessed Josemaría's later writings differ from his earlier ones not only in style but also in the essential themes they cover. And, so, in his more considered texts the language of the Magisterium and the findings of systematic theology are more clearly to be seen.[14] What previously was taken for granted, is now dealt with explicitly. The reason for this is because he was conscious of the lack of formation of those he was addressing. From a certain point onwards (around the mid-sixties) especially doctrinal depth became increasingly more called for in preaching, to help the faithful build their own spiritual lives on the solid foundation of the doctrine of the Faith. In this Blessed Josemaría's concern for theology and for the Church played an important part: at a time when things were falling apart and when *subjective feeling* was often being used as a yardstick for everything, the founder of Opus Dei tried to put his own experience of divine love at the service of the Church—in such a way that that experience itself became strengthened (now 'objectively') by linking it to the authentic Magisterium of the Church.

---

14 Cf., for example, the commentaries on Gal 4:5 in the homilies 'The conversion of the children of God' (1952) and 'Christ the King' (1970), in *Christ Is Passing By*, 65 and 183. In the second homily (in an almost identical passage) he adds a reference to the action of the Holy Spirit in the Blessed Virgin.

II. The dogmatic basis

In Blessed Josemaría's writings on divine filiation two structural lines can be identified, in keeping with classical theology, lines which are closely interwoven and each of which, in a way, conditions the other. The first line runs from above to below, from the Trinity to the heart of man; this is what is traditionally called 'indwelling'. The second runs in the opposite direction, from human nature towards divine nature; this is called 'elevation'. We shall now go on to take a brief look at these two lines.

1. The indwelling of the Blessed Trinity

Blessed Josemaría makes it very clear that only 'God can unite us to himself; only he can sanctify us. So, the initiative comes from the Father:[15] '(God) is a Father who loves his children so much that he sends the Word, the Second Person of the most Blessed Trinity [...] to redeem us. He is the loving Father who now leads us gently to himself, through the action of the Holy Spirit who dwells in our hearts.'[16]

God the Father sends his Son to the world to seek out men and women who have gone away from God. And the Son sends the Holy Spirit to the heart of the redeemed.[17] But in the last analysis it continues to be the Father who gives us the Holy Spirit *through* Christ,[17] in order to apply the work of redemption and bring it to fruition in each human being.

The Holy Spirit is the divine gift *par excellence*,[19] the personal love of the Father and of the Son. Through him

---

15 Cf. the homily 'The strength of love', in *Friends of God*, 228.
16 Homily, 'The Eucharist, mystery of faith and love' in *Christ Is Passing By*, 84.
17 Cf. Jn 16:17; homilies 'The conversion of the children of God' and 'Christ the King' in *Christ Is Passing By*, 66, 118 and 130.
18 Cf. Tit 3:6; *Christ Is Passing By*, 85.
19 Cf. Acts 2:38ff.; 11:17; *Christ Is Passing By*, 127.

the love of God has been poured into our hearts.[20] Being possessed by the Holy Spirit means being possessed by the Love of God, who with his divine uncreated essence[21] indwells in the soul in grace. In this way man becomes the temple of God.[22] The founder of Opus Dei often reminded Christians of their sublime dignity, using St. Paul's famous words, 'Do you not know that you are God's temple and that God's Spirit dwells in you?'[23]

Given the nature of the relationship that exists between the divine Persons and their intimate, inseparable union founded on that relationship (by virtue of '*circuminsessio*'), the sending of the Holy Spirit brings with it also the presence of the Father and the Son. Blessed Josemaría speaks of the 'Blessed Trinity's love for men'.[24] The *entire* Trinity, he emphasizes, 'desires ardently to dwell in our soul':[25] 'If a man loves me, he will keep my word, and my Father will love him and we will come and make our home with him.'[26] Father, Son and Holy Spirit co-act in the soul in grace.[27] Blessed Josemaría spared no effort to get Christians to open their eyes to the wonderful thing that was taking place within them: 'Our heart now needs,' he explains, 'to distinguish and adore each one of the divine Persons. The soul is, as it were, making a discovery in the supernatural life like a little child opening his eyes to the world about him.'[28] And he gives the following (mystical) piece of advice: 'In the intimacy of your soul, you can indeed hug him tight.'[29]

---

20 Cf. Rom 5:5; Col 1:22; homily 'The Christian's hope' in *Friends of God*, 125.
21 'Inhabitatio substantialis sive personalis' (cf. DS 1678).
22 Cf. Rom 8:9; 1 Cor 6:19; Gal 4:6; homilies 'For they shall see God', in *Friends of God*, 178; 'Christ's presence in Christians', in *Christ Is Passing By*, 103.
23 1 Cor 3:16; cf. *Christ Is Passing By*, 134.
24 *Christ Is Passing By*, 85.
25 Ibid., 84; cf. *The Forge*, 15.
26 Jn 14:23; cf. also 2 Cor 6:16; cf. *Friends of God*, 306.
27 Cf. *Christ Is Passing By*, 118.
28 *Friends of God*, 306.
29 *The Forge*, 345.

This means that indwelling is not something *exclusive* to the third Person;[30] but to him is 'appropriated' the work of our sanctification. The founder of Opus Dei takes extraordinary pains to stress the singular action of the Holy Spirit on the human soul.

The Holy Spirit is the principle of our new life; and, to the extent that he establishes a personal encounter of enormous strength and intimacy between the Christian and Christ, he incorporates us in Christ.[31] This is perhaps one of the most profound mysteries of the human being who is in grace, the fact that Christ is his or her life and yet the Christian does not cease to be his or her self.[32] But what Christ brings about, he does always as the mediator between God and men. He is not alone the *Goal* but also and in a special sense the *Way*; he is not only the Revealed One but also the Revealer. His entire nature evidences a ceaseless tending towards the Father. Therefore, union with him is a true sharing in the relationship he has with the Father. And in this way the Christian is elevated in Christ to divine filiation.[33] His incorporation in Christ has as its ultimate goal an encounter with the heavenly Father, an encounter made possible by the power of the Holy Spirit. And it is enlivened and animated by the action of the third divine Person, who gives the Christian an 'awareness' of his

---

30 Some authors think that a 'special' indwelling can be attributed to the Holy Spirit in addition to the 'general' indwelling of the Blessed Trinity. According to that theory, the indwelling is not just an *appropriatum* but also a *proprium* suited to the third Person. This theory, a very debatable one, goes back to some 18th-century theologians, such as Lessius (d.1625), Petavius (d.1647), Thomassin (d. 1655) and also Matthias Joseph Scheeben, *Die Mysterien des Christentums*, II (Fribourg, 1951), pp. 518ff. Leo XIII put forward a profound teaching on the indwelling of the Holy Spirit in his encyclical *Divinum illud munus*, May 9, 1897; cf. also John Paul II, Enc. *Dominum et vivificantem* May 18, 1986, 58ff.

31 Cf. Gal 5:25; 2 Cor 13:4; cf. also J. Störh, 'La vida del cristiano según el espíritu de la filiación divina', in *Scripta theologica* 24 (1992–3), p. 885.

32 Cf. Gal 2:20; cf. St. Augustine, *Enarrationes in Ps.* 17, 51 (36, 154) *et in Ps.* 90 II, 1 (PL 37, 1159); cf. also Bl. J. Escrivá, *The Way of the Cross*, sixth station.

33 Cf. *The Forge*, 265.

divine filiation.[34] 'If we are docile to the Holy Spirit, the image of Christ will be formed more and more fully in us, and we will be brought closer everyday to God the Father,' Blessed Josemaría stresses; 'We will place ourselves in the hands of our Father God, with the same spontaneity and confidence with which a child abandons himself into his father's care.'[35]

Here, the encounter initiated by the Holy Spirit finds its goal; it focuses on the Father, the origin of all motion. In the Holy Spirit and through Christ, man in grace finds his way into the life of the Trinity.[36] This enables him to live as a son in the presence of God the Father.

2. The elevation of human nature

The Holy Spirit brings the Christian into the love of the divine Trinity. The Spirit, who is God's intimacy, enters man's heart and raises it up, submerging it in the heart of God. In other words, through grace he is made a sharer in the divine nature.[37]

When a human being receives divine grace, he is born to supernatural life,[38] born again from God in the love of freedom.[39] This rebirth is an effective action of God's which takes place in the most intimate being of man, changing him and elevating him. And therefore it can be regarded as analogous to the eternal generation of the Son. So, grace means a special way of being conformed to the *Son* of God, who becomes like us in order that we should become like Him; who abases himself in order to raise us up. Of course, our supernatural birth is infinitely

---

34 Cf. Rom 8:16; *Christ Is Passing By*, 131.

35 *Christ Is Passing By*, 135.

36 Cf. ibid., 133.

37 'Consortium divinae naturae': 2 Pet 1:4. Grace is a real and physical (even when accidental and analogous) participation in the divine nature: cf. St. Thomas Aquinas, *Summa theologiae*, III, q. 2, a. 10 ad 1.

38 Cf. *Furrow*, 317; *Christ Is Passing By*, 131.

39 Cf. Jn 1:13; 3:3–6; Jas 1:17–18; 1 Pet 1:23; homily 'Christ the King', in *Christ Is Passing By*, 180.

distinct from eternal generation; but God is our Father also through the unique and identical relationship which makes him Christ's Father. A Christian who lives in *physical communion* with his God is Christ's brother[40] and therefore a son of the Father in a most real way.[41] 'See what love the Father has given us, that we should be called Children of God; and so we are.'[42]

Blessed Josemaría never downplayed the realism of Christian thought regarding the origin of mankind. He was never afraid to assert that grace 'divinizes' man.[43] In fact, man is brought into the inner life of the Blessed Trinity, taken up into the generation of the Son and into the spiration of the Holy Spirit. On this account he belongs to the family of God in the truest sense,[44] and therefore enters into a trusting relationship with God.

The founder of Opus Dei was very fond of the words in the Gospel of John 'I have called you friends',[45] and if he stressed that friendship with God does not necessarily have to be based on filiation,[46] he also underlined the fact that supernatural filiation always includes an offer of friendship and finds its fulfillment in that friendship.[47] That is not something that often occurs in human relationships: children are not necessarily friends of their parents; they can lose their love, but that does not mean they cease to be children of their parents. Divine grace, on the contrary, makes us children of God to such a

---

40 Rom 8:29: 'in order that he might be the first-born among many brethren'. Cf. *Summa theologiae*, III, q. 23, a. 1; homily 'To Jesus through Mary' in *Christ Is Passing By*, 145.

41 *Summa theologiae*, III, q. 23, a. 3: 'Filiatio adoptionis est quaedam similitudo filiationis naturalis'.

42 1 Jn 3:1–2. Cf. Homilies 'Getting to know God' in *Friends of God*, 143, and 'The strength of love', *Friends of God*, 228.

43 Cf. *Christ Is Passing By*, 133.

44 'Domestici Dei': Eph 2:19; cf. *The Forge*, 587.

45 Jn 15:15; cf. also Eph 2:19; Rom 5:10; *Christ Is Passing By*, 93; *Friends of God*, 315; *Conversations*, 102.

46 *Christ Is Passing By*, 185.

47 Cf. *Furrow*, 750.

point that, to the degree that we continue to be his children, we are also, at one and the same time, his friends.

In relation to us, God's only desire is to be a good father: 'though he is the creator of the universe, he doesn't mind our not using high-sounding titles, nor worry about our not acknowledging his greatness.'[48] He leads man right into his personal love, brings him into the inner core of his being and confides his mysteries to him. His action has no aim other than to enable his children to attain freedom and happiness,[49] in this life as in the next. He has so ineffably arranged things that in addition to grace he even gives men (as brothers of Christ) the *right* to eternal glory.[50] This right includes everything that is His, heaven and earth complete; and this is definitively and irrevocably confirmed when a person's life reaches its term, and the Christian is taken forever into his true fatherland. 'Meanwhile,' Blessed Josemaría says, 'we have to be on our guard, alert to the call St. Ignatius of Antioch felt within his soul as the hour of his martyrdom approached. "Come to the Father," come to your Father, who anxiously awaits you.'[51]

III. Implications for Christian life

The human person has been created, if we focus on his deepest theological-religious dimension, to respond to God's call and accept the great invitation to belong to the family of God. It is a very high goal: if we think about it, it can be a stimulus and a source of joy. But it can also happen that a 'poor creature', who is conscious of his weaknesses and sees he is just a 'handful of dust',[52] becomes discouraged in the face of such a goal.

---

48 *Christ Is Passing By*, 64.

49 Cf. *The Way of the Cross*, prologue.

50 Cf. Tit 3:7; cf. DS 1528, 1545.

51 *Friends of God*, 221 (Ignatius of Antioch, *Epistola ad Romanos*, 7, 2: PG 5, 694); cf. also *Furrow*, 885.

52 Cf. Gen 2:7; *The Way of the Cross*, prologue.

How could anyone think himself worthy of sharing in the mysteries of the Blessed Trinity?

1. The 'Trinity on earth'

Blessed Josemaría knew man's heart; he knew the doubts which can beset any Christian. However, he discovered an 'easy' way to God, and, to show his sincere gratitude, he encouraged others to follow that same route. Christ himself opened up this way through his Incarnation, when he chose for himself a human mother and a human father (he was tied to St. Joseph by a spiritual and legal relationship) and in this way he founded on earth a 'divine family'. By spiritually joining that family, the founder of Opus Dei teaches, one can become gradually, and as it were automatically, involved in the inner life of God, thanks to frequent contact with Jesus, Mary and Joseph.[53]

Drawing his inspiration from Christian art, Blessed Josemaría liked to call the family of Nazareth the 'Trinity on earth', which has reference to the Trinity in heaven.[54] Of course, he was not speaking in 'dogmatic' terms. The analogy here is not ontological, because the relationships that obtain between Jesus, Mary and Joseph are completely different from those between the Father, the Son and the Holy Spirit in the eternal processions.[55] However, from the spiritual point of view this image he is using is very revealing, in the sense that it identifies an easy way to God: when a Christian enters the life of

---

53 Cf. *Friends of God*, 221.

54 This expression very probably goes back to John Gerson (1363–1429), who, for the first time, in a homily preached at the Council of Constance, gave the title of the 'Trinity on earth' to the Holy Family ('Sermo de nativitate B. Mariae Virginis' in *Ioannis Gersonii Opera Omnia*, III (Antwerp, 1706), cols. 1345–58.

55 The theory that man is the image of the Son and woman the image of the Holy Spirit is also of (limited) interest in this connection; for St. Joseph is depicted as the image of the Father thanks to his spiritual and legal relationship to Jesus. This theory is outlined in Blanca Castilla y Cortázar, '¿Fue creado el varón antes que la mujer? Reflexiones en torno a la antropología de la creación', in *Annales theologici* 6 (1992), pp. 319–66, esp. p. 361.

Jesus, he begins to imitate the Son of God made man, and establishes a living relationship with Mary and Joseph, and feels increasingly part of the family of Nazareth. Here he can learn both to have a relationship in all simplicity with God, and to approach life with serenity. He becomes accustomed to seeing everyday events from God's point of view and acquires an ever deeper inner peace. 'It is a peace that comes from knowing that our Father God loves us, and that we are made one with Christ and are under the protection of the Virgin Mary and assisted by St. Joseph,' Blessed Josemaría explains. 'This is the great light that illuminates our lives. In the midst of difficulties and of our personal failings, it encourages us to keep up our effort'.[56]

For Blessed Josemaría a trusting relationship with Mary and Joseph is part and parcel of a spiritual life based on divine filiation.[57] This relationship is founded primarily on the Christian's identification with Christ, that is, on his search for communion with Christ. And yet, from a deeper perspective, it is Mary (the Mother of the Saviour and mediatrix of all graces)[58] who gives Christ to us and has a very profound part to play in our spiritual rebirth. Because she is the Mother of Christ, she has become our mother too, thanks to our incorporation in Christ.[59] The same is true of St. Joseph, who, because he is truly Mary's husband, can be called 'father' of her first-born and of all her children.[60] This means that our relationship with Mary (and also with Joseph) is not only a *result*, but also, mysteriously, a *basis* of our communion with Christ. Both of them lead us to the Son, who then leads us to his earthly parents, so that we can learn from them how to have a more affectionate rela-

---

56 *Christ Is Passing By*, 22.
57 Cf. *The Forge*, 354.
58 Cf. address of Paul VI, November 21, 1964, during the Second Vatican Council, when the constitution on the Church was approved: *AAS* 56 (1964), pp. 1015ff. Cf. also *Lumen gentium*, 61.
59 Cf. *Christ Is Passing By*, 141 and 171.
60 Cf. *The Way*, 559.

tionship with him. 'The beginning of the way, at the end of which you will find yourself completely carried away by love for Jesus, is a trusting love for Mary'.[61]

Our connections with Mary and Joseph, on the one hand, and with Jesus on the other, are therefore reciprocal, but they are not symmetrical. Jesus brings us to his parents, so that they can in turn lead us to him, showing us how to love the Son of God in a simple way, like children, and eventually come to him and with him to our heavenly Father. Our life of Marian piety and our veneration for St. Joseph are, then, Christocentric and have a strong Trinitarian component, as Blessed Josemaría expounded in many of his writings. The ultimate goal of the interior life is to give ever more explicit expression to divine filiation.

2. The audacity of divine filiation

Through the action of the Holy Spirit (and the cooperation of Mary and Joseph), the Christian comes to find himself in a relationship of personal friendship and love with God his Father. One of the deepest needs of the human soul is to strengthen friendship, to love and be loved, to share feelings and mutually bear difficulties with one's fellows. 'Happy is he who has found a true friend.'[62] Yet all friendship involves risk, insofar as the response of others to friendship can never be foreseen. This applies also in the case of friendship between God and men, because it too is put to the test. If tests of that sort are borne and overcome, the true disinterest that derives from love is demonstrated. Because of this supernatural risk and sharing, Blessed Josemaría speaks of the wonderful 'adventure' of divine filiation.[63]

---

61 *Holy Rosary*, 'To the reader'.
62 Sir 25:12 (Vulg.); cf. also 6:14–16; homilies 'Finding peace in the heart of Christ' in *Christ Is Passing By*, 166; 'Towards holiness', in *Friends of God*, 315.
63 Cf. *Furrow*, 184.

Objectively speaking, only God really runs a risk in loving his children. He takes a risk with men, even though he knows their weaknesses and their fallen nature, even if he overlooks the fact that there is a danger that they will treat him as something to be used, or be mistreated in the way that something useless is mistreated.[64] But man also runs a risk, at least from a subjective point of view, when he abandons himself to God: he very well knows that God sends unexpected trials to his best friends.[65]

The greatest obstacle to obtaining a sense of divine filiation lies in the blindness of the human heart, which fails to discover this connection with the Cross. Everyone knows from personal experience (and from his many contacts with other people) that a Christian can refuse to regard God as a good Father, when he, in his Providence, arranges things differently from what one might wish or expect. Blessed Josemaría rejected outright this superficial view of the goodness of God, and yet he was fully conscious of human suffering in all its forms.[66] For him, divine filiation was never a kind of sentiment or something pleasant, the outcome of agreeable feelings or a passport to a comfortable life. He taught that pain and suffering are natural to the life of a son of God. Those whom the Lord calls to be close to him are called also to be nailed to the Cross: 'being with Jesus means we shall most certainly come upon his Cross.'[67] Being near the Cross means being able to live as a son of God in an especially intense way: 'God is my Father, even if he sends me suffering. He loves me tenderly, even while wounding me '[...] Can I complain if I meet suffering as my travelling companion? It will be a sure sign of my sonship, because God is treating me as he treated his own divine Son.'[68]

---

64 Cf. *Christ Is Passing By*, 93.

65 For example, in the life of Abraham: Gen 11:26–25:11. Scripture always depicts Abraham as a friend of God: cf. 2 Chron 20:7; Jud 8:25–27; Is 41:8.

66 Cf. *Furrow*, 233, 245, 251; *The Forge*, 793.

67 *Friends of God*, 301.

68 *The Way of the Cross*, first station, points for meditation, 1.

Two thousand years ago no divine intervention happened to set the cross aside (and with it the sins of mankind); similarly, pain (as a *consequence* of sin and as *sin itself*) and suffering will proclaim until the end of time the unfathomable mystery of human power, in the face of which almighty God himself chooses to yield. And just as Christ himself, in full agreement with the heavenly Father, bore the Cross in order to prove to men that God's love went all the way, so too Christians are called to bear their cross and to discover the mystery of generous love and superabundant redemption. All of which helps us see why the founder of Opus Dei encourages us to love the Cross,[69] which is a sure sign of predilection and a guarantee of true divine filiation.[70] Unless one has a deep understanding of human suffering and strives to bear it well and to do so voluntarily—and in this 'co-redeem'[71]—one cannot appreciate what it means to be an intimate friend of God.

And it is not through suffering as such that we have been redeemed but through infinite love, which made itself known through acceptance of suffering. Therefore, acceptance of suffering and privation by a Christian is not focused on suffering itself, that is, the cross as such, but on Him who was crucified. And *His* love, too, took the form of free self-giving, self-sacrifice.[72] Hence the lover (not the beloved) requires continuous and ever clearer testimonies of love. Because he does not want his lot to be better than that of Christ crucified, he wants to have the same portion as Christ. By virtue of the basic law of true friendship, he tends to have the same opinion, the same will, the same heart and the same spirit as Christ's, and to be treated as He was. 'Other

---

69 Cf. *The Way*, 873; *The Forge*, 42.
70 Cf. *Furrow*, 70.
71 Cf. *The Forge*, 4, 26, 55.
72 Cf. *The Way*, 866.

than losing you, there is no sorrow that deserves the name,'[73] Blessed Josemaría prayed. He spoke of his desire to prove he was a true son,[74] a true friend of God.[75]

Given this connection with Christ, one gradually comes to realize little by little that the heavenly Father sends his friends only what is good and useful, even when it may not seem like that from a worldly point of view, 'But, have you again forgotten that God is your Father,' Blessed Josemaría asks, 'all-powerful, infinitely wise, full of mercy? He would never send you anything bad. That thing that is worrying you, it's good for you, even though those earthbound eyes of yours may not be able to see it now.'[76] God is a friend whose closeness we enjoy the more we experience it. The longer we are friends with him, the less risk seems to be involved and the happier we are (it is an unmerited happiness). We attain a joy which becomes more and more stable because we are able to see, in everything that happens, that the paternal love of God is at work; this makes it possible for us to love divine filiation 'passionately'.[77] 'If God is for us, who can be against us? Let them be sad who are determined not to recognize that they are children of God'.[78]

3. 'Tension' between spiritual childhood and spiritual maturity

As a *son* or *child*, the Christian is in an active relationship of personal interchange with God his Father.[79] He needs to respond to this at all levels and in all circumstances. Provided he does not place obstacles in the

---

73 *The Forge*, 253.
74 Cf. *Furrow*, 175.
75 Cf. *The Way of the Cross*, thirteenth station, points for meditation, 3.
76 Ibid., ninth station, points for meditation, 4.
77 *The Forge*, 333.
78 *Friends of God*, 108.
79 Cf. *The Way*, 897.

way of grace (if he were to do that, he would be rejecting God's love), divine filiation impresses on him bit by bit the stamp of a complete personality: the profound, ontological reality of being a son to God expresses itself in the life of grace which also increasingly affects his outlook, his way of thinking and feeling, and desiring and planning the future. As long as he is on earth he is not perfect, but with the help of God he feels less and less bound by arrogance, simulation and calculation.[80] He lives like a child, with simplicity—serene, uncomplicated, docile, not worried by anything,[81] with an invincible confidence in his almighty Father,[82] and with the breadth of spiritual outlook proper to a true heir[83] who in some way owns the whole world; it is in fact in his union with God that he finds himself at his freest.[84] Because he knows that the Father has infinite love for him, he too can love infinitely; because only Jesus matters to him, he can reject everything secondary. Because he relies only on the word of the Lord, he is free with respect to the words of men; because it is divine wisdom that guides him, he does not mind if he gives the impression of being crazy with the love of God.[85] Because his fortitude is grounded on God alone, he puts no value on being great in the eyes of men.[86]

But the question does raise its head as to how this sort of attitude can fit in with tending to view holiness in the midst of the world. Can the father of a family manage to have no worries? Does he not have to plan for his children's future? Should he not try to make a success of everything he takes on? To what extent can a politician be allowed to be unconcerned about public opin-

---

80 Cf. Mt 18:1–5; Mk 9:33–37; *Christ Is Passing By*, 143; *Friends of God*, 102.
81 Cf. *The Way*, 862, 864, 868; *Furrow*, 417; *The Forge*, 226.
82 Cf. *The Way*, 857, 875; *The Forge*, 331, 348; *Christ Is Passing By*, 64.
83 Cf. *The Way*, 874; *Furrow*, 96.
84 Cf. *Christ Is Passing By*, 138; *Friends of God*, 27.
85 Cf. *The Way*, 438, 910, 916.
86 Cf. *The Way*, 869, 892; *Holy Rosary*, 'To the reader'.

ion, or a policeman be allowed to behave like someone who is out of his mind? Essentially, the question boils down to this: can a Christian who lives in the world give the impression that someone who follows Christ acts like a child? For the founder of Opus Dei this problem did not exist; he saw no contradiction at all between simple, genuine behavior towards God and men, and the mature personality of an adult. In fact he taught that both things can be obtained at one and the same time, because they are mutually connected, and support one another: when a Christian tries to be friends with Jesus, he is seeking a full human and supernatural maturity,[87] which in some way is also necessary for him if he is to accept and bear up under the tests which God sends us, on account of the trust he places in us.[88] The very fact that God is ready to make men sharers in his inner life, clearly shows the high regard he has for his creatures.[89] God does not forget man, but he counts on him and in some way regards him as an adult when he calls him to follow Christ.[90] By declaring his children to be of age, God is giving them not only the right but also the duty to work in the world responsibly and autonomously. Consequently, men should never consider themselves to be mere 'spectators' of what is going on in the world;[91] on the contrary, they should strive to pour Christian spirit into all the environments in which they find themselves.[92] Awareness of divine filiation does involve making an effort; only if one has a strong will,[93] broad knowledge,[94] and a sincere readiness to give of oneself[95]

---

87 Cf. *Furrow*, 267; *Christ Is Passing By*, 135.
88 Cf. *The Way*, 853, 877, 888.
89 Cf. ibid., 854.
90 Cf. Gal 4:1–3; 1 Cor 3:1.
91 Cf. *Furrow*, 790.
92 Cf. ibid., 311.
93 Cf. *The Way*, 856, 883, 891.
94 Cf. ibid., 857.
95 Cf. *Christ Is Passing By*, 147.

is it possible to show that one is a true friend of God in the most varied kinds of situations, and to bear witness to the love of the heavenly Father.

The life of a Christian adult is not at odds with the life of spiritual childhood; its opposite, rather, is a lack of maturity[96]—the kind of self-centered, capricious childish behavior which can be found at any age. On the contrary: a person who 'enters' into God learns there to love the world; he 'penetrates' the divine 'mission', and this leads him to apostolate and evangelization in the real world; that is why the Christian addresses himself to his fellow men with passionate zeal. As an adult son, he prays for the grace to forget himself, and he will have no second thoughts about devoting himself with all his energies to the happiness of others, not even when a cold wind hits him and he has to go against the current.[97] He is afraid neither of life nor of death,[98] because he is convinced that he is not alone; the presence of the Triune God gives him the feeling of always being *en famille*, being at home where he may happen to stop.[99] When the atmosphere which the grace of God has created in his heart reaches out into his surroundings, the human and spiritual temperature is warmed up considerably, and the son of God can sow peace and joy[100] and help others to live a life full of meaning. Normally he finds no difficulty in having solidarity with all his brothers and sisters,[101] but he gives more weight to friendship with God than to the world's friendship.

---

96 Cf. *Friends of God*, 66.
97 Cf. *Friends of God*, 228.
98 Cf. Bl. J. Escrivá, Letter, 19 March 1954.
99 Cf. F. Ocáriz, 'La filiación divina...', op. cit. (in fn. 16 on p. 36 above), p. 192.
100 Cf. *Furrow*, 59.
101 Cf. ibid., 229, 303, 317.

The Christian, *alter Christus, ipse Christus*, in the thought of Blessed Josemaría Escrivá de Balaguer

Antonio Aranda,
Dean of the Faculty of Theology at the
Pontifical Roman Atheneum of the Holy Cross

I. Introduction

A study of the type we now embark on, centered on an important theological subject, which is, however, not being examined as such but rather as it is treated in the writings of a master of the spiritual life, can be approached in two possible ways. One way involves going directly to the subject under analysis and beginning to describe the method that is to be used. The other, which is the approach we are going to take, includes in its starting-point an element which might be described as pre-theological. This element needs to be dealt with on account of the special light it sheds; it provides a degree of prior understanding of our theme, obtained not only from the author's writings but also (and earlier on) from his own life.

If one looks at how it is expressed in his spiritual and pastoral writings, Josemaría Escrivá's thought should be described as essentially Christological. The mystery of the God-Man is the main supporting framework—and, in some way, the only framework, as we shall go on to explain—of his discourse, which shows signs of always being activated, or to be more precise 'actualized', by his faith in the permanent presence of the Redeemer and his effective action over the course of history.

In fact, that mystery of faith, the redemptive Incarnation, is the underlying inspiration of Christian thought and it has been from the beginning the solid ground on which all Christian spiritual experience, in all its various forms, has developed. On this point as on all, the testimony born by the life and intellectual work of Blessed Josemaría is in line with all Catholic tradition,[1] understood in its dual dimension of received deposit and progress in understanding that deposit. From this tradition of doctrine passed on by the Fathers, the Magisterium, the Liturgy, saints, theologians ... , his thought is nourished, and there too he finds his language. Using that as his source, as a man endowed with an ecclesial charism and mission of enduring value, and at the same time one exceptionally well suited to the needs of the age, he provides specific viewpoints and accents and thereby helps advance that tradition.

Do these elements, perhaps, not reveal a new way, provided by the Holy Spirit, of orienting how Christians might follow and imitate Christ? Our reflections will turn on this question, seeking to offer a theological answer, or at least something close to it. This means that we must at the outset pose the question and tackle it from this viewpoint.

We are going to systematically structure into two sections an analysis of the formulas *alter Christus, ipse Christus* that are applied to Christians and which largely summarize the spiritual teaching of Blessed Josemaría: first we shall look at the theological basis of these terms and the meaning they tend to have in tradition, and then we will examine the special stresses put on them in the writings of the founder of Opus Dei. This will be followed by a concluding section dealing with theological reflection and perspectives.

---

[1] I shall not go into this subject in this essay, except for making a few references. I have looked at some aspects of it in an article on 'El cristocentrismo de la espiritualidad cristiana' in *Biblia, exégesis y cultura* (Pamplona, 1994).

But before setting out to do all this, I want to refer to the pre-theological factor I mentioned at the beginning, something implicit in the genesis of this study, casting its light right across it. One of the passages which most impressed me when I read biographical data on the founder of Opus Dei is something that happened in a tram in Madrid in 1931—a sublime supernatural gift, possibly the most sublime of those he received, which, in the midst of great tribulation, caused him to experience the joy and peace of being a son of God. It was a personal sort of grace and, at the same time, like so many others in his experience but particularly so, a grace foundational in character—a charismatic event and, so to say, one emblematic of his person and of his teaching; it is echoed in a veiled way in these words:

'When the Lord dealt me those blows, around the year thirty-one, I didn't understand why. And then, suddenly, in the midst of that great bitterness, (came) those words: 'you are my son' (Ps 2:7), you are Christ. And all I knew how to do was to say over and over again: Abba, Pater! Abba, Pater! Abba! Abba! Abba! Now I see it as a new light, as a new discovery: as one sees, with the passing of the years, the hand of the Lord, of divine wisdom, of the Almighty.

'You did this, Lord, to make me see that having the Cross means finding happiness, joy. And the reason—I see it now more clearly than ever—is this: having the Cross means being identified with Christ, it means being Christ, and therefore, being a son of God. [...]

'The Cross: that is where Christ is, and you have to lose yourself in Him! There will be no more suffering, no more hardship. You mustn't say: Lord, I can't go on, I'm a wretch ... No! That is not true! On the Cross you will be Christ, and you will feel like a son of God, and you will cry out: Abba, Pater! How happy to find you, Lord!'[2]

---

2 Cf. AGP, sec. RHF 20.119, p. 13.

It can be said, as historical and theological study will show in more detail, that Blessed Josemaría's life, that is, his human and priestly personality, his ecclesial activity, his foundational work, his thought, were forged from his youth onwards in the depth of this supernatural identification with the Son of God—on his Cross and in his glorification, in his daily life and in the paschal event, in his priestly ministry of self-giving and service to the Church and to all men. Josemaría lived and died as a man endowed charismatically with a very vivid sense of adoptive divine filiation and an exceptional capacity to contemplate the God-Man in the depth of his redemptive mystery.

Josemaría Escrivá lived and died intensely united to Jesus, completely in love with him, immersed in his presence, all of which led him to cultivate the Blessed Trinity. This *was* his life, as those of us who knew him could appreciate even if we found it difficult to put into words. There are certain things one can see and pick up, when someone is communicating his very life, which we cannot yet describe properly because we have not as yet made them a part of our life. The fullness of life of a saint such as Josemaría Escrivá lies hidden within the theological mystery of the fullness of Christ—which is why one can feel very close to him and yet not fully understand him.

Take, for example, something he used to say at times to a group at a formation meeting or just in informal conversation: 'I see the Blood of Christ boiling within you.'[3] He would say it very forcefully, with real conviction and joy. His attitude was that of someone who, by a few simple, spontaneous words, spoken with his lips, his eyes and his heart, conveys a deep personal conviction, a truth that he possesses and that also possesses him. That graphic reference to the Blood of Christ (his Life) running through the veins of Christians was a light which helped Josemaría Escrivá to convey the essence

---

3 Cf. RHF, 20.166, p. 12.

of a spirit of self-surrender and service to all men in the setting of ordinary life. But first and foremost (although there were those who did not at the time realize it) it was a spark sent out by his own inner, loving contemplation of Christ.

'I see the Blood of Christ boiling within you.' Spoken by a man of God, these words had the eloquence of truth. At one thrust, but not on their own, because they were spoken in a context of a personal relationship, spiritual life and in-depth formation, they provided a key to understanding Christian vocation and all the supernatural gifts. They show the grace received in Baptism to be an effective impulse, a dynamic principle, something that gives one the energy for self-surrender; they allow one to see that configuration to Christ is something that is happening all the time to a member of his Body, to a person who is in permanent communion with Him and with others.

I could give other examples of things he said which are equally evocative of his spirit. They have the special force of actual events, which, although they are in the past, remain very vivid because they are part and parcel of the person himself; they come across as so genuine. He didn't need to make an elaborate speech. He didn't need to spell it out, but what he was saying was something like so: 'If someone sees the life of Christ in me, it is because he sees Christ in me; or, to put it better, the one who can be seen all the time—in us, in our life and apostolic endeavors—is Christ: it is He who is there before us all the time.' And, undoubtedly, this intuition was completely right. With this intuition and with the help of theology we will now begin our study of what is meant by saying that a Christian is *alter Christus, ipse Christus,* a favourite description of Blessed Josemaría's.

II. Bases for a theological reflection

What is the theological basis for describing the Christian as *alter Christus, ipse Christus*? What roots does this description have in the Bible, tradition and the Magisterium? What, really, is its prevalent traditional meaning? These are the first questions we shall study.

1. Roots in New Testament revelation

The expression *alter Christus* does not occur as such in the New Testament, but its meaning has a solid biblical foundation. Thus, there are passages which view the spiritual actions of the Christian, and indirectly the Christian himself as the subject of these actions, from the perspective of supernatural conformation to the actions of Christ and, therefore, to Christ himself. We shall look for the biblical basis of our subject by following out this doctrinal line, which is to be found mainly in St. Paul's writing. To do so we shall review the content of the notions of *conformation* to Christ and *incorporation* in Christ, and also that of fullness in Christ.

St. Paul's teaching on the *Christian's conformation to Christ* occurs in his *Letters* in various wordings which are closely connected with one another. In Romans 8:29, for example, he speaks of conformation to *the image of his Son*; Philippians 3:10 refers to becoming like Christ *in his death*; in Philippians 3:21 he speaks of our body being changed to be like *his glorious body*. The commonly accepted meaning is of a spiritual transformation of the Christian into Christ, in an eschatological sense: just as in Baptism we have been conformed to his death, so too shall we be conformed to the image of the Risen One in his glory.[4]

---

4 Cf. W. Pohlmann, 'Symmorfos', in H. Balz and G. Schneider (eds.), *Exegetical dictionary of the New Testament*, III (Grand Rapids, 1990), pp. 287–8. I am including in these paragraphs some ideas found in the work cited in fn. 1 above.

'The entire history of salvation,' Spicq has written,[5] 'and also the particular existence of each of the chosen, is governed by this aim of the divine *prótesis*: to form a Christian being, with clearly defined features, the same as those of the beloved Son, in whom the fullness of the divinity dwells bodily.' In Baptism man, reborn and renewed by washing in the Holy Spirit (Tit 3:5), is clothed with the 'new nature' (cf. Rom 13:14; Gal 3:27; Col 3:10), that is, he puts on Christ and becomes *like him* (Rom 6:1-11; Col 3:1-4; Eph 2:5-6).[6] 'And given that he is conformed to his image, during his life he will suffer *with* Christ so as himself to be glorified *with* Him (Rom 8:17). That is the way the likeness will gradually come about.'[7]

This process whereby the baptized person is conformed to the glorious Humanity of Jesus, through spiritually sharing in his death and resurrection, constitutes the essence of the spiritual life of the Christian. In this context Pauline language uses certain very expressive verbal forms, such as: 'suffer with him' (*sympaschein*; e.g. Rom 8:17); to be 'crucified' with him (*synstaurosthai*; e.g. Gal 2:19); 'die' with him (*synapothnéskein*; e.g. Rom 6:8); be 'buried' with him (*synthaptesthai*; e.g. Rom 6:4); be 'raised' with him (*synegeirein*; e.g. Col 3:1); 'be glorified with him' (*syndoxazesthai*; e.g. Rom 8:17); 'reign' with him (*symbasileuein*; e.g. 2 Tim 2:12). The fullness of this oneness between the Christian and Christ takes place in heaven, understood also as living or being *syn Kyrio*, 'with the Lord' (1 Thess 4:17; Rom 6:8).

On the basis of these texts Christian spiritual life can be said to consist in a process of *Christification*—a progressive transformation to align the Christian with the

---

5 C. Spicq, *Teología moral del Nuevo Testamento*, II (Pamplona, 1973), p. 771.

6 Cf. R. Schnackenburg, *Das Heilsgeschehen bei der Taufe nach dem Apostel Paulus* (Munich, 1950).

7 C. Spicq, op. cit., p. 771.

glorious image of the God-Man, who has died and has risen, who is 'seated at the right hand of the Father'.[8]

So, the Pauline notion of *conformation* to Christ offers a solid foundation for the later doctrinal development which depicts the Christian (or, concretely, the priest) as *alter Christus*.

Similarly, the Pauline expression 'in Christ' (*en Christo*) and other analogous expressions—'in the Lord' (*en Kyrio*), 'in Him' (*en autó*)—also allow us to describe the intimate union between Christ and Christians. This can be taken to mean both 'being Christ's' (2 Cor 10:7) and, especially, Christ's influence over the baptized person (a member of his, a part of his body), to the point where one can speak of both sharing one and the same life: the Christian lives in Christ or, the other way around, it is Christ who lives in the Christian (Gal 2:20; 2 Cor 13:5; Rom 8:10; Col 1:27; Eph 3:17).[9]

If this doctrine allows us to speak of a process of identification between Christ and each Christian, St. Paul's teaching also provides a basis for there being identification between Christ and all the baptized as a whole, that is, between Christ and the Church which is his Body (Rom 12:4–5; 1 Cor 12:12–27; Eph 1:22–23; 4:1–16; Col 1:18–24; 2:19). A theological terminology in the Augustinian tradition will later speak of the 'total Christ': the Church as such, not only each Christian, is and is called to be spiritually Christ.

Following the same line we can identify a scriptural basis for describing the Christian as *alter Christus* in the doc-

---

[8] The Second Vatican Council describes this process as follows, for example: 'All the members must be formed in his likeness until Christ is formed in them (cf. Gal 4:19). For this reason we, who have been made like him, who have died and risen with him, are taken up into the mysteries of his life, until we reign together with him (cf. Phil 3:21; 2 Tim 2:11; Eph 2:6; Col 2:12, etc.). On earth, still as pilgrims in a strange land, following in trial and in oppression the paths he trod, we are associated with his sufferings as the body with its head, suffering with him, that with him we may be glorified (cf. Rom 8:17), (Const. *Lumen gentium*, 7; cf. A. Grillmeier's commentary in LTK, *Das zweite vatikanische Konzil*, I, pp. 166ff.

[9] Cf. J. Fitzmyer, *Pauline theology* (Englewood Cliffs, 1967), pp. 67–73.

trine on the *fullness of Christ* in which Christians share. The New Testament speaks of this in a number of passages using the words *pléres, plérein,* and *pléroma* (that is, the adjective *full,* the verb *to fill* and the noun *fullness*), which provide eloquent vocabulary for explaining who Christ is and that which he communicates of himself.

A very interesting, perhaps the main, passage, is provided by the Prologue in the fourth Gospel: '*Et Verbum caro factum est et habitavit in nobis; et vidimus gloriam eius, gloriam quasi unigeniti a Patre, plenum gratiae et veritatis*' (Jn 1:14), '*et de plenitudine eius nos omnes accepimus, et gratiam pro gratia*' (1:16). In v. 14 the meaning of *pléres* is specific: the glory of the incarnate Word, visible to the believer, has as its genuine content *cháris* and *alétheia*— the grace and truth of God, which through Christ have become a historical event, things manifested in his actions when he was on earth. The glory of the Son consists in the fact that in him the grace and truth of God are made present.[10] In him they are found in all their fullness and are communicated. As incarnate Son he has the fullness of grace and truth, and makes us sharers of them. In v. 16 the same idea is continued: in the incarnate Word the fullness of divine grace has been made present and active, and therefore the attitude of a person who believes in Christ can be defined as an unceasing reception of that superabundance.[11]

These two texts suffice to deduce some conclusions useful to our purpose, but there are also other passages which will help us articulate these conclusions better:[12]

— Ephesians 4:13 ('... *donec occuramus ... in virum perfectum, in mensuram aetatis plenitudinis Christi*') speaks of the maturity of those who, because they have Christ as their model, are, as it were, adults: people made 'to the measure of the full stature of Christ', that is, made to the full size of his holy hu-

---

10 Cf. G. Kittel, Italian edition, X, p. 638.
11 Cf. ibid., p. 688.
12 Cf. ibid., p. 687ff.

manity, we might say, and not like children easily exposed to all kinds of influences.

— Colossians 1:19 ('... *in ipso complacuit omnem plenitudinem inhabitare'*) shows that God so wished that the fullness of the divine nature should dwell in Christ, in the historical Christ (he who shed his blood on the cross, v. 20); also Colossians 2:9 ('*in ipso habitat omnis plenitudo divinitatis corporaliter'*) attributes to Christ crucified and glorified the fullness of deity, that is, divine power and authority. This *pléroma tes theótetos* is the most unambiguous way of referring to the complete unity of action that exists between God and Christ the man: through his absolute plenitude and perfect divinity, God brings about salvation through Christ.

In Christ, therefore, the salvific action of God has burst into history; by the historical event of the incarnate Son, God has brought to term that eschatological action which was his original purpose. In the suffering and glorified Christ, divine grace and truth have mercifully blotted out sin, and recreated the world under its original sign of the glory of God. Christians have been made sharers in the superabundance of his gifts and the efficacy of his mediation: each baptized person is, in the fullness of Christ which he sacramentally shares in, someone anointed, a bearer on earth of the Holy Spirit, a son in the Son and a mediator in the Mediator—someone in whom, to the measure of the full stature of Christ, being and role (that is, the gift of being supernaturally a son of God, and the apostolic mission that he has received) are fused into an indissoluble unity.

A Christian is in fact (and this daring assertion is supported by the indefectibility of revelation) someone called to *belong to Christ* and to be *in* Christ, and therefore called also *to be another Christ*—someone equipped by the Holy Spirit to attain full identification with the Son of God made man: even here on earth he is conformed to Christ in a real way—and yet in an imperfect way because he always needs to improve. Christian fullness is tending towards the fullness of the holy humanity of Christ.

On this central point, on this common doctrine of Christian spirituality, Blessed Josemaría's theological-spiritual thought is extraordinarily rich, nourished as it is by its contact with biblical teaching (as we have just seen) and traditional theological and spiritual teaching (as we shall go on to examine); but it also has its source in the special gifts connected with his foundational charism.

2. Roots in theological-dogmatic tradition

This section of the study needs to begin differently from the previous one. Whereas the words *alter Christus* do not occur as such in the New Testament (even though their roots and meaning is to be found there), there are, on the contrary, some explicit references in the living tradition of the Church to the Christian and the priest being another Christ. As regards the *ipse Christus*: I have not found any precedent for its use by Blessed Josemaría. Clearly, very many texts from the tradition evidence this same idea—but not in the same words.

In the traditional approach to this subject we can distinguish two main 'divisions'—one more or less catechetical and liturgical, centered on the meaning of the name of Christ and, by derivation, the name Christian, and the second more theological, found in connection with the development of the Pauline doctrine mentioned above and with the theology of priesthood. We shall look at these in short, historical sections.

a. Christ, the Anointed; the Christian, a new Christ

From the very beginning there has always been a central line running through Christian theological thought, and it is still present today, which tries to attain a deeper understanding of the mystery of the redemptive Incarnation by studying the name of Christ, the Messiah or *Christós*, a title essential to Jesus' office as well as being his proper name. Grasping the complete identity between his being and his office, and expressing it in the name Jesus Christ is a defining feature of Christian thinking on the mystery of Christ, or to put it another way, this title—along with that expressed in the title *Iesus-Kyrios*—is the most typical expression of the Church's *sensus Christi*. It is basic to traditional Christological reflection and for that very reason, it is, so to speak, an interpretative tool we need to use to explore the thought of Josemaría Escrivá.

From the Patristic period onwards, the New Testament assertion that 'Jesus is the Christ' (the Messiah, the Anointed) has been developed along the line described, in an effort to throw light on the redemptive mission of the Word incarnate—and consequently that of the Church and of each Christian, whatever ecclesial role he or she has—by looking at the mission of those anointed in the Old Testament: priests, kings, and prophets. This has given rise to a substantial body of doctrine, the reputation and weight of which is virtually unrivalled in tradition, which has produced the theology of the *munera Christi*, so influential in contemporary ecclesiology. However, that is not a subject we should stay with here; we must move on to an off-shoot of that great current.

I refer to the customary description of the Christian as a 'christ', someone anointed, by virtue of his sharing through Baptism in the Anointing of Jesus and therefore in the meaning of his name and in his condition. The Christian is the image of Christ, and can be called a *christ* because he has received in the baptismal gift of the Holy Spirit a share in the Anointing of the Humanity of Jesus. Right down the centuries this has been taught. In fact, the waters of this off-shoot of the name of the Anointed contain all the revealed knowledge about Christ and the Christian, which will later be explicated in the theology of the threefold *munus*. I rather think that in the *alter Christus* formula, used by the Church on occasions, and (along with the *ipse Christus*) so typical of Blessed Josemaría, there is a considerable percentage of the theological line we are commenting on, even though it is not its main component or the only source of its meaning. There is a certain distance between the *alter Christus* (with capital C) and the *christ* with a small c whom we are discussing; but it is also worth stressing that they both derive from a biblical trunk.

In Christian writing many instances are to be found of the Christian being described as a *christ*. I shall go on to give some examples but without making any comment because what interests us here is not so much their theological or spiritual content as the *fact* that they represent a traditional language. They come mostly from commentaries on the Creed, from baptismal catechesis, from sermons *in traditione Symboli*, etc.; as also from commentaries on particular biblical passages, such as, for example: Psalms 104:15; 1 Peter 2:9ff.; Romans 8:29; 13:14; Galatians 3:27; Revelations 5:9–10. They evidence profound pneumatological and Christological content, even though their form of expression and their direct origin (normally catechetical) looks rather unsophisticated.[13]

— *Origen*:

'If it is true to say that, though there is one Spirit, there are as many holy spirits as souls who possess the Holy Spirit, then the same can be said in reference to Christ. From the one Christ come a large number of christs of whom the Scripture speaks: do not touch my christs, do not harm my prophets (Ps 104:15). Just as there is one God, and many are called gods in whom God dwells ... so there is just one Christ who makes christs, one Spirit who is reproduced in the souls of each of the saints. Besides, if Christ makes christs by the mere

---

13 Some of these passages and many others like them are collected in P. Dabin, *Le sacerdoce royal des fidèles dans la tradition ancienne et moderne* (Paris, 1950). Others can be found in G.W.H. Lampe, *A Patristic Greek Lexicon* (Oxford, 1968) s.v. 'chrisma', III, c, p. 1529; 'christianós', B, 5, p. 1530; 'christós', J, p. 1532; 'Chrío', B. 9, pp. 1533–4. See also A. Blaise, *Dictionnaire latin-français des auteurs chrétiens* (Turnhout, 1954), s.v. 'christus', p. 1493 and his *Le vocabulaire latin des principaux thèmes liturgiques* (Turnhout, 1966), p. 472.

fact of being the Christ, then he makes children of God all whom he adopts as he is the one and true Son of God.'[14]

— *Eusebius of Caesarea*:

'Christ will walk before me every day. These are the Church's saints, those called according to the words: do not touch my christs'.[15]

— *St. Basil of Caesarea*:

'John says (1 Jn 2:20) we are anointed by the Spirit. But why us? Because this is what happened to our Lord according to the flesh ... He is Christ by the Spirit and by the anointing of the Spirit. Our Lord's anointing did not occur at all from outside the divinity. This is true both for Christ's name and that of Christians who receive their name from him.'[16]

— *St. Cyril of Jerusalem*:

'By being baptized in Christ and putting him on, you have been made according to the model of the Son of God. The God who predestined us to adoption, conformed us to Christ's body. Well then, being part of Christ, you are naturally called christs, for God has said of you: do not touch my christs. In this way you were made from Christ when you received the pledge of the Holy Spirit. All within you was made in the manner of an image since you are images of Christ.'[17]

— *The blind Didymus*:

'Aaron was anointed by Moses, and in his wake all belonging to the priestly line were consecrated by chrism. In this way now so are those who by

---

14 *Ex lib. I sup. Isaiam*: PG 13,217. The italics in these quotations are ours.
15 *Eclog. prophet.*, I, c. XIX: PG 22, 1077 BD.
16 *Adv. Eunomium*, V: PG 29, 725 C.
17 *Cat. Myst.* III: PG 33, 1088 A.

taking their name from the chrism are called christs, that is, the anointed. This chrism is a figure of the holy one we received.'[18]

— *St. Cyril of Alexandria*:

'The name of Christ is fitting not only for the Emmanuel but for all anointed with the grace of the Holy Spirit. The name, in effect, stems from the thing: we are called christs because we were anointed ... Therefore we are all christs and called by this name precisely because of the gift of anointment. However, Christ alone is the Emmanuel for he is also the true God.'[19]

— *St. John Damascene*:

'Oil is used in Baptism to indicate our anointing, which makes us anointed ones, or christs. It further promises us God's mercy through the Holy Spirit'.[20]

— *St. Jerome*:

'Christ is anointed by nature, we by grace, because he possesses the fullness of divinity and in the saints the anointing is but partial.'[21] '(The sinful woman's case) is especially relevant to you who are about to be baptized. She broke her alabaster jar so that Christ would make you christs, that is, anointed ones.'[22]

— *St. Augustine*:

'All Christians share in the anointing though in the Old Testament it was exclusive to two types of

---

18 *De Trinit.*, 1. III: PG 39, 712 A.
19 *Ep. I ad monach. Aegypti*: PG 77, 20 BCD. Cyril also points out in this passage that Christians can be called christs, but their mothers can only be called *christotókoi* and not *theótokoi*. Mary alone is both Mother of Christ (*christotókos*) and Mother of God (*theotókos*).
20 *De fide orthodoxa*, IV, c. IX: PG 94, 1125 B.
21 *Brev. in Psal.* 44: PL 26, 958B.
22 *Tract. in Marc. XIII*, in G. Morin, *Anecdota Maredsolana* (Oxford, 1895), III, part II, p. 366 (cited by P. Dabin, op. cit., p. 84, 5).

people. So it follows that we are Christ's body because we were anointed and because in him we are all both christs and one Christ, as the Head and members form the total Christ.'[23] 'All who have been anointed by his chrism we can rightly call christs and yet there is but one Christ: the whole body with its Head.'[24]

— *St. Bede*:

(The text is identical with that of Augustine just quoted.) 'All who have been anointed with his chrism are rightly called christs, even though there is but one total Christ whose body is joined to the Head'.[25] '(Habakuk) called all the elect christs; all are appropriately thus named due to being anointed with grace ... (The mediator) saved them not because he already found them christs, but because he made them christs, that is, anointed by the adoption of the Spirit.'[26]

— *St. Anselm of Canterbury*:

'All Christians are but one Christ in Christ.'[27]

—*Peter Lombard*:

'We are the body of Christ and we are christs in him because we were anointed with the fullness of his anointing, from which Christ's name comes. Christ comes from chrism.'[28]

---

23 *Enarr. in Ps XXVI, sermo* II, 2: PL 36, 200.
24 *De Civ. Dei*, XVII, c. IV: PL 41, 532. On the only Christ, Head and body, or total Christ, made up of Christ and the christs, St. Augustine's teaching is ecclesiologically rich and throws much light on the subject we are discussing. Cf. for example what he has to say in his *Sermons*. Very helpful in this regard are the excellent subject indexes to his sermons in *Obras completas*, XXVI (Madrid, 1985) s.v. 'cristiano', p. 720; 'Cuerpo místico', p. 724; 'Jesucristo y la Iglesia', p. 797; 'Jesucristo y el cristiano', p. 798.
25 *In Sam. proph. alleg. expos.*, I, c. IV: PL 91, 512 B.
26 *Super cant. Habac. alleg. exp.*, I, c. IV: PL 91, 512 B.
27 *Medit.*, I, 6: PL 158, 714 A.
28 *Comm. in Ps XXVI*: PL 191, 267 B.

— *Richard of St. Victor*:
'Do not touch my christs (Ps 104). The anointed are called christs ... However, we know that God's anointing is love itself. Those who have been anointed, those who ardently love the things of God, are God's christs and can be called christs.'[29]

What conclusions can we draw from our study of these texts? They simply illustrate that the New Testament doctrine of the Christian becoming like (*assimilazione*) Christ through the action of the Holy Spirit[30]—which is the main source Christian anthropological thought draws on—gave rise to a very significant line of theological thought. Reflection on the Anointed and on the anointed, on Christ and those who are *christs* in him—in his own anointing, which is the presence and action of the Holy Spirit in his Humanity—has developed from early on a most useful framework for understanding what being a Christian means, a framework which goes far beyond its material content.

This reflection in the intimate union between Christ and Christians, which extends over many centuries, starting out from the concept of anointing, opens the way to a theological development of the revealed truth that the Christian is in Christ and Christ is in the Christian. Moreover, it underlines not only oneness of consecration (as we would say today) but also oneness of mission. The Christian is a new *christ* because he shares in the gift and mission of the one and only Christ. In this connection, it is worth noting that the Christian is Christ through this sharing, which is not theologically very different from the statement that the Christian is *alter Christus*, or even *ipse Christus*.

---

29 *Adnot. myst. in Ps CIV*: PL 196, 336 AB.

30 I am using the term 'assimilazione' with no special theological sense but as a synonym of configuration, incorporation, identification etc.

These terms are implicitly part of the line of thought described earlier as an 'off-shoot', which derives from a richer, main current. This off-shoot of the *christós* has two noteworthy features. One of these reflects on the Christian by starting out from baptismal anointing and, therefore, its conclusions are valid for any baptized person. Every Christian is, through baptismal anointing, a *christ*; every Christian is spiritually like Christ, sharing in Jesus' being and mission in the Holy Spirit. The second feature lies in the strong priestly emphasis of that line of thought. From the passages quoted and from very many similar ones which we might have cited, it is possible to deduce an awareness in tradition of the priestly nature of baptismal anointing. Theological reflection on the subject of anointing, the Anointed and the anointed (Christians) was from the start a way of understanding the common priesthood of the faithful.

b. *From the theology of anointing to the theology of character*

It is well known that, from St. Thomas Aquinas onwards, the theology of priesthood got a new lease of life, developing largely around the notion of sacramental *character*. Theological reflection on the participation of Christians in the being and mission of Christ contributed to this development: it became the central theological category for discussing both the baptismal participation of the faithful and the ministerial participation of priests. This new theological emphasis went far beyond itself, to my way of thinking: it is in fact a new off-shoot, different from the earlier one, a new way of channelling the waters from the great biblical resource of conformation to Christ into new methodological notions and frameworks.

In sum, we move from the theology of anointing to the theology of character. That is to say, theological reflection on the relationships between Christ and Christians leaves behind the *Christós* framework and now takes its basic inspiration from the *charákter* framework; here the basic priestly theme is maintained but, obviously, with a different intellectual structure. This has, as a side effect, the fact that Christians are no longer (except very infrequently) described as *christos*. We now enter a period marked by a linguistic, but not theological, departure from formulas akin to the future *alter Christus*.

This does not mean that during this period, for example, in St. Thomas, traditional theology of anointing disappears, but rather that the basic methodological framework for developing the doctrine of the priesthood of ministers and faithful is going to rely on the notions of grace and character, rather than those of anointing and the triple *munus* (though these latter are not entirely abandoned). There are certain passages in St. Thomas which are a sort of paradigm for this new theological climate—for example, in question 63 of the *tertia pars*. Here the capacity of the individual member of the faithful to engage in worship, the *deputatio ad cultum Dei* (in the sense of expressing how he participates in the priesthood of Christ) is described in terms of the character sacramentally stamped on him: 'manifestum est quod sacramentalis specialiter est character Christi, cuius sacerdotio configurantur fideles secundum sacramentales characteres, qui nihil aliud sunt quam quaedam participationes sacerdotii Christi, ab ipso Christo derivatae.'[31] [...] Character sacramentalis est quaedam participatio sacerdotii Christi in fidelibus':[32] 'It is manifest that sacramental character is specifically the character of Christ, seeing that a configuration to his priesthood is imparted to the faithful through sacramental characters which are nothing else than certain kinds of participation in the priesthood of Christ deriving from Christ himself.[32] [...] Sacramental character consists in a certain participation in Christ's priesthood present in his faithful.'

One cannot criticize—quite the contrary—the intellectual richness of this new theological approach. I only

---

31 St. Thomas Aquinas, *Summa theologiae*, III, q. 63, a. 3c.
32 Ibid., a. 5c.

want to draw attention to the immense effect it had on later thought and, secondarily, on terminology, on the subject we are discussing. It marks a transition from a more Trinitarian and pre-pneumatological idea of what a Christian is (someone anointed in the Anointed) to a form of thinking more proper to sacramental theology, to different and intellectually more exact modes of approach, which will eventually take over completely.[33]

As far as our own topic is concerned, it is only reasonable to expect that in this new theological and doctrinal way of looking at things it is less likely that the Christian will be described as another Christ, though it is not surprising that the description of the *priest* as *alter Christus* should come to the fore—which is what happens subsequently, as we shall now examine briefly.

c. *The anti-Lutheran controversy of priesthood*

Clearly, if, in the context we are discussing, there is this move from the theology of anointing to the theology of character, and if this is developed with reference to divine worship, the danger arises that the notion of priesthood will be linked too closely to the latter. If, moreover, in Christian worship the accent is placed too sharply on the liturgical expression of that worship it might lead (at least methodologically) to an over-valuation of priestly ministry and a parallel undervaluation of baptismal priesthood. That could well happen, given the right intellectual input. My own view is that that did in fact happen in Catholic thought in reaction to what the Reformers had to say on these very subjects.

One can detect in the anti-Lutheran controversy a marked stress in Catholic theology on the distinction be-

---

[33] Cf. the following passage from the *Catechism of the Council of Trent*, where it teaches that it is the sacramental character that causes Christians to share in Christ's anointing: 'The second effect of the sacraments is not common to them all, but belongs only to three of them—baptism, confirmation and order. That effect is the character which they mark on the soul. When the Apostle says, "God has anointed us, he has sealed us...those words clearly point to a character' (Part II, c.I).

tween an 'inner priesthood' of all the baptized and an 'outer priesthood' of those who are ordained.[34] We need not discuss this in detail; it is enough to point out that this sort of language is to be found not only in such great theologians as Soto and Cajetan,[35] but also in magisterial texts such as the Roman Catechism.[36] The distinction referred to (in itself, valid and legitimate), if established in a theological climate in which the Christian priesthood tends to be viewed more from the angle of the liturgical role of a person rather than from that of the consecration-mission given the person, could lead to an impoverished view of baptismal priesthood and a degree of divorce between being and role. Therefore, returning to our subject, this would explain why, as we have said, there is talk more of a *sacerdos alter Christus* than of a *Christianus alter Christus*.

I think that this tendency has in fact existed in Catholic theology from the 17th century onwards. Worthy and influential authors, such as for example Suárez and Bellarmine, tend to speak on occasion of baptismal priesthood as just a spiritual or metaphorical priesthood, different from the priesthood of the ordained, which would be the true priesthood in the proper sense. As Dabin has written apropos of Bellarmine: 'in the area of anti-Protestant controversy it is natural that the royal priesthood should be reduced to a purely spiritual view of the same: it is not set in relation either to the anointing of Christ [...] or even to the participation of the faithful in the sacrifice of the Mass, although earlier tradi-

---

[34] There are references, too, in less reliable language to an 'improper' or 'metaphorical' priesthood (that of the baptized) and a 'true' and 'proper' priesthood (that of ministers). This language, which is not in line with the traditional balance found in Catholic statements, can only be explained in the context of the controversy against the Lutheran theses.

[35] Cf. D. Soto, *In IV Sent.*, d. 1, q. 4, a. 3, which talks, for example, about a priesthood in the general sense and a priesthood *par excellence*; cf. Cajetan, *Tertium jentaculum de sacerdotio*, ed. by Coquelle and Menasce, in *Nova et vetera* 14 (1939), pp. 274-83.

[36] Cf. Part II, c. VII, 44-8.

tion and even other authors of the Counter-Reformation period often did use and stress such relationships.'[37]

So, summing up what we have been saying, if one moves on from traditional theological reflection on conformation to Christ stemming from the theology of anointing, to reflection based on the theology of character, the description of the Christian as a new Christ insofar as he is anointed, would now tend to be applied to someone who shares through 'character' in the priestly role of Christ. But if one then moved on, for historical and doctrinal reasons, to a notion of baptismal priesthood as something purely spiritual and metaphorical, one would be pushing into the background of the *christianus alter Christus* and giving prominence to the *sacerdos alter Christus*, which has in fact been more to the fore in Catholic thought (to the limited extent that this terminology is actually used).

For the description of the Christian as another Christ to be understood and justified, there is need first for a serious study of the common priesthood as a true and proper priesthood, as a prelude to re-evaluating or recovering the theology of baptismal anointing as true priestly anointing—an anointing which is no way opposed to but which is different from the anointing by the sacrament of Orders (the difference has to do with the consecration and the role in which the recipient shares). The first step in this direction can be detected in the theology of Möhler, but it was not until the first half of the 20th century that it began to take hold, eventually emerging in the great doctrinal flowering of the Second Vatican Council.[38] It is interesting to note that this theology of baptismal priesthood is found in the teaching of Blessed Josemaría Escrivá, as can be seen, for example, from the fact that he applies the terms *alter*

---

37 P. Dabin, op. cit., p. 389. Some texts are given on pp. 384–5, 388–9.
38 Cf. A. Elberti, *Il sacerdozio regale dei fedeli nei prodromi del Concilio Ecumenico Vaticano II (1903–1962)* (Rome, 1989).

Christus, and *ipse Christus* to the individual member of the faithful.[39]

d. *'Sacerdos alter Christus' in 20th-century Magisterium*[40]

The expression *sacerdos alter Christus* has been used with some frequency by the contemporary Magisterium, and that use—that wording and its meaning—is a proximate source for the use that Blessed Josemaría makes of it on occasion. However, there are no traces in 20th-century Magisterium of the expression *christianus alter Christus*.

In fact we have not found the Christian literally described as 'another Christ' in any part of Catholic tradition, be it Patristic, dogmatic, spiritual or pastoral,[41] although similar expressions bearing the same meaning do occur. In contemporary writing it is sometimes mentioned as expressing a traditional teaching, but the actual words do not seem to be traditional.[42] It is impossible to say where the actual expression originates. Nor can we say exactly where Blessed Josemaría got it from; but that is beside the point here. (One suggestion might be that he got it mainly by transferring the phrase *sacerdos alter Christus* to the Christian as such, a transfer based on his profound priestly view of the person and being of the baptized.)

---

39 Cf. J.L. Illanes, 'El cristiano "alter Christus—ipse Christus". Sacerdocio común y sacerdocio ministerial en la enseñanza del Beato Josemaría Escrivá de Balaguer', in *Biblia, exégesis y cultura* (Pamplona, 1994).

40 Cf. R. Gerardi, ' "Alter Christus": la Chiesa, il cristiano, il sacerdote', in *Lateranum* 47 (1981), pp. 111–23; G. Rambaldi, ' "Alter Christus", "in persona Christi", "personam Christi gerere"'. 'Note sull'uso di tali e simile espressioni nel magistero da Pio XI al Vaticano II, e il loro riferimento al carattere', in *Teología del sacerdocio*, V (Burgos, 1973), pp. 211–64.

41 We know of only one exception: the expression occurs as a rubric in the Liturgy of the Hours: Week XII, fer. II, *ad off. lect.*

42 There were also no leads given in fn. 40. As Gerardi says (in his fn. 49), the passages mentioned by E. Mersch, *Le Corps mystique du Christ* (Paris and Brussels, 1936), p. 461, under the title 'chrétien, autre Christ', do not contain this expression literally (but obviously its meaning is there).

Nor do we know the immediate origin of the phrase *sacerdos alter Christus*. When the contemporary Magisterium uses it, it has a traditional ring to it. Truth to tell, it, like the other expression, is not found literally, but, as we have seen, its meaning is. We must conclude, with Gerardi, that despite the possible lines of research suggested by some, no hard and fast results have emerged.[43] In 1934 Cardinal Mercier described it as 'a sort of theological adage' used by Christian tradition to express its feeling about the priesthood.[44] What we do know for sure is that, at that time, it was used literally mainly by Popes Pius X, Benedict XV and Pius XII; prior to them, there do not seem to be any exact references to it. There very well may be no point in searching for a direct literal origin outside these sources.

Generally speaking, the texts of the Magisterium sometimes use *sacerdos alter Christus* in an exhortative sense, implying an invitation to imitate and be more like Christ, whom the priest represents. Thus it is, for example, for St. Pius X in his encyclicals *E supremi apostolatus* and *Haerent animo*;[45] and, similarly, for Benedict XV in the two texts where he uses the phrase.[46] And, confining ourselves to pontificates prior to or contemporaneous with Blessed Josemaría, it occurs in some documents of Pius XI,[47] Pius XII[48] and Paul VI.[49]

---

43 Cf. R. Gerardi, op. cit., p. 116.

44 Cf. D.J. Mercier, *La vie interieur* (Louvain, 1934), p. 143; quoted by Gerardi, op. cit., p. 115, fn. 20.

45 Cf., respectively, ASS 36 (1903–4), p. 135; ASS 41 (1908), p. 569.

46 Cf. Discorso ai parroci di Roma, AAS 11 (1919), p. 113; Ep. ad episcopos Czecoslovachiae, AAS 13 (1921), p. 555.

47 Cf. Letter, *Con singular complacencia* to the bishops of the Philippines, January 18, 1939.

48 Cf. Apos. Letter *Haud mediocrem*, to the Bolivian bishops: AAS 34 (1942), p. 234; Apos. Exhort. *Menti nostrae*, AAS 42 (1950), p. 659; Address to new priests in *Discorsi e Radiomessaggi* 18 (1957), p. 35; Address (not delivered, due to his death) to seminarians of Puglia: AAS 50 (1958), p. 966.

49 Cf. Address to the parish priests of Rome March 26, 1968 in Paul VI, *Siervos del pueblo. Reflexiones y discursos sobre el sacerdocio ministerial*

The theological context in which the popes use this wording is a traditional one, that is to say, it occurs in the context of a theology of priestly ministry centered on the notion of character and on the doctrine (connected with that) of *agere in persona Christi*.[50] With this same meaning of acting in the person of Christ, but applied to the Church as such, it occurs in a text of Pius XII.[51]

3. Roots in spiritual tradition

The last section of our inquiry into the theological basis of the expression *alter Christus* is the rich vein of spiritual tradition. Here, too, as in earlier sections, we notice that there are no instances of the *literal* use of the phrase, but there are clear references to its meaning. We spoke earlier of the boldness of the Christian assertion that every baptized person is called to eschatological identification with Christ, an identification which, even when the person is still on earth, is real though imperfect and in need of progress. Well, the route that progress takes, progress based on baptismal conformation and occurring in the sacramental, pastoral and prophetical bosom of the Church is the same for all Christians and has

---

(Salamanca, 1975), p. 120; Address to priests, in *Insegnamenti di Paolo VI* 6 (1969), 83; Homily preached in Manila, November 28, 1970, in *Siervos del pueblo...*, op. cit., p. 45; Address to priests in *Insegnamento* IX (1972), p. 862.

50 Cf., for example, Pius XI, Enc. *Ad catholici sacerdotii*, AAS 28 (1936), p. 10, where he writes: '...alter Christus est, cum eius gerat personam...'; Pius XI, Enc. *Menti nostrae*, where it says: '...alter Christus est, cum indelebile sit character insignitus, quo viva Salvatoris nostri quasi imago efficitur...'.

51 Cf. Enc. *Mystici Corporis*, AAS 35 (1943), p. 231: '(Ecclesia) quae hisce in terris veluti alter Christus eius personam gerit...'. Pius XI used it also in a text on St. Francis of Assisi, in which, speaking in the context of his imitation of and profound union with Jesus, he says: 'recte alter Christus nuncupatus est' (cf. Enc. *Rite expiatus*, AAS 18 [1926], p. 154). In the Second Vatican Council documents the formula is not used, although some requests were made for it (cf. Gerardi, op. cit., 114, nos. 18–19). John Paul II used it in his Letter to priests for Holy Thursday 1991 (cf. no. 2).

been given in Christian theological-spiritual language an exact name: *following and imitating Christ*.[52]

The source and conceptual content of these two terms is to be found in the New Testament: *following* Christ (*akolouthein*) is mentioned mainly in the Gospels, whereas *imitating* Christ (*mimeisthai*) is largely a Pauline idea.[53] The first, although it is used in a context which could also seem to mean a purely external following, a 'going after', is mainly meant in a moral sense: sharing in Christ's lot (Jn 12:26), following his example by carrying the cross (Mt 10:38; Mk 8:34-35; Lk 14:27),[54] and above all being his disciple, that is, keeping a special link with him which Jesus himself describes in the phrase, 'Follow me' (Mt 9:9; Mk 2:14; 10:21; Lk 9:59; 18:22; Jn 1:43).[55] The idea developed over the course of the New Testament, as understanding grew of the meaning of 'disciple', which came to be synonomous with 'Christian'. One could say that this was a development of the religious elements implicit in the Synoptics. Already in St. John, following Jesus has many dimensions to it—believing in him, leaving one's own world to share in his

---

52 This important subject is examined in depth in: E. Cothenet, P. Ledeur, P. Adnes, and A. Solignac, 'Imitation du Christ', in *Dictionnaire de Spiritualité*, v. VII, (Paris, 1971) col. 1536–1601; G. Turbessi, 'Imitación y seguimiento de Cristo' in E. Ancilli (ed), *Diccionario de Espiritualidad*, v. II (Barcelona, 1983), pp. 295–8; D. Mongillo, 'Seguimiento', in S. de Fiores and T. Goffi (eds), *Nuevo Diccionario de Espiritualidad* (Madrid, 1983), pp. 1254–63; B. Proietti, L. Perrone, G. Gouilleau, J. Leclercq and T. Matura, 'Sequela Christi e imitazione' in *Dizionario degli Istituti di Perfezione*, VIII (Rome, 1988), cols. 1287–1314.

53 An interesting recent study is F. Martin, 'Critique historique et enseignement du Nouveau Testament sur l'imitation du Christ', en *Revue thomiste* 93 (1993), pp. 234–62.

54 The expression 'to carry the cross' is one of the authentic *logia* of Jesus; cf. F. Martin, op. cit., p. 255; J.G. Griffiths, 'The Disciple's Cross' in *New Test. Stud.* 16 (1970), pp. 358–64; R. Pesch, Das Markus-evangelium' in *Herders theologischer Kommentar zum Neuen Testament*, II/2 (Freiburg, 1984), p. 60.

55 Cf. A. Schultz, *Nachfolgen und Nachahmen. Studien über das Verhältnis der neutestamentlichen Jüngerschaft zur christlichen Vorbildethik* (Munich, 1962), pp. 195–7.

destiny of death and resurrection; living in union with him through grace. In fact, the notion develops mainly through the step from a pre-paschal to a paschal meaning of 'following', with the result that the linking with the person of Jesus becomes also a linking with his message and putting into practice clearly defined moral attitudes.

Even the evolution of the notion in the Gospel passages seems to show that following and imitation converge in meaning, and that one implies the other.[56] 'Imitation' is a term that occurs often in Paul's writing as an exhortation by the Apostle to the faithful to align their behavior with the model of God (Eph 5:1), of Christ (1 Thess 1:6; 1 Cor 11:1), of Paul himself (1 Cor 4:16; Phil 3:17; 2 Thess 3:7) and of others. But the key meaning, even though sometimes other models are interposed, is *imitating Christ's example*—his love as manifested in his incarnation and on the cross (Phil 2:5ff), his generosity (2 Cor 8:9), his readiness to forgive (Phil 4:32; Col 3:13), his self-giving inspired by love of others (Eph 5:2).

This ethical sort of imitation has an ontological basis for St. Paul—the conformation of the baptized person to Christ in his death and resurrection. It is not mere external copying, but an active tailoring of one's life to the model of the incarnate Son, a model that the Holy Spirit impresses on the faithful: the Christian should strive to 'die with Christ' voluntarily, through his own daily actions, to the point that he acquires such feelings as Christ had in his heart (Phil 2:5). In St. Paul's teaching, 'conformity to the image of the Son of God [...] is the true meaning of the imitation of Christ. It is a process of transformation brought about by the Holy Spirit (2 Cor 3:18), whereby the Mystery, the revelation of the divine plan in the death and resurrection of Christ, is made present in time, generation after generation, in the in-

---

56 'Quid est enim sequi, nisi imitari?', writes St. Augustine: *De sancta virginitate*, 17: PL 40, 411.

ner life of the Church and through her, who is the Body of Christ.'[57]

This New Testament way of following the one and only Master and imitating the only model is the highway of Christian holiness, and it is one the Church has repeatedly reminded and encouraged Christians to take from the very beginning up to our own time.[58]

In the history of Christian spirituality, whose essential feature is the fact that it is Christocentric, there are important milestones for devotion to and imitation of the Humanity of Christ. All of them, reflecting as they do New Testament teaching, are naturally in tune with the content of the *christianus alter Christus*, even though that wording may not be used. In the writings of the great spiritual masters, whose personal life is also an admirable example of identification with Christ, many similar turns of phrase are used. There is no doubt but that, albeit implicitly, the notion of the Christian as *another Christ* is part of the common heritage of Christian spirituality.

---

57 F. Martin, op. cit., p. 258.

58 The Second Vatican Council documents, for example (to mention recent texts), often refer to following and imitating Christ as being expressions of the nature of baptismal vocation and the obligations it involves. All the faithful are exhorted to: follow Christ's example (LG, 37b), follow in his footsteps and conform to his image (LG, 40b), imitate his charity and humility and closely copy our Lord's self-emptying (LG, 42e), follow the path opened up by Christ (in so doing, life and death are sanctified and given a new meaning; GS, 22c), imitate the example of Christ's holy life and work (GS 43a), follow him in the spirit of the beatitudes (AA, 41) .... In addition to these passages addressed to all the faithful, there are others addressed to those who have particular roles. Thus, for instance, priests are encouraged to imitate our Lord's example when performing their ministry (PO, 14a); or religious: to follow Christ according to the Gospel is the norm of religious life (PC, 2a), and they are taught that in their case following or imitating Christ is done through practicing the evangelical counsels (PC, 1). For all, whoever they are, the only Christian way to holiness is that of following-imitating Christ. 'The forms and tasks of life are many, but holiness is one—that sanctity which is cultivated by all who act under God's spirit and, obeying the Father's voice and adoring God the Father in spirit and in truth, follow Christ, poor, humble and cross-bearing, that they may deserve to be partakers of his glory' (LG, 41a).

Among many examples we might cite that of St. Francis of Assisi. The imitation of Christ as 'following in his footsteps' (cf. 1 Pet 2:21), immersed in knowledge of him and in his love, becoming changed in form to the point of becoming *alter Christus* is, so to speak, his spiritual program. His great devotion to the Humanity of Christ and through that to his Divinity, expresses itself in various ways, especially in love of poverty and humility and in a desire to enter into the mystery of Jesus Christ's passion.[59] In the life of St. Francis written by Celano it says: *Christus vivebat in eo*,[60] and also *videbatur [...] quod Christi et beati Francisci una persona foret*.[61] In the context of Francis' life and the spirituality born of his example and teachings, one often finds significant doctrinal development concerned with following Christ and being spiritually identified with him.[62]

Another example of Christ-centered spirituality, which had a considerable influence on later writers and trends in spirituality, is that of St. Teresa of Avila. Her life and teachings resound with a call to seek familiarity with the sacred Humanity of Christ, which is implicitly a part of the *alter Christus* content; she and all the great spiritual writers give their own nuance to this idea. Her spirituality has been described as 'a wonderful experience of Christ',[63] the core of which is closely bound

---

59 Cf. N. Nguyen-Van-Khanh, *Gesú Cristo nel pensiero di S. Francesco secondo i suoi scritti* (Milan, 1984).

60 Cf. *2 Cel.*, 211 in *Analecta Franciscana*, X (Quaracchii, 1926–44), p. 252.

61 Ibid., no. 219; p. 257.

62 Cf. for example, A. Blasucci, 'L'anima della spiritualità francescana', in *Miscellanea francescana* 62 (1962), pp. 3–15; and his 'San Francisco de Asis', in E. Ancilli, *Diccionario de Espiritualidad*, II, 131–42: A. Rotzetter, V. Van Dijk and T. Matura, *Un camino de evangelio. El espíritu franciscano ayer y hoy* (Madrid, 1984).

63 S. Castro, *Christo, vida del hombre. El camino cristológico de Teresa confrontado con el de Juan de la Cruz* (Madrid, 1991), p. 129. See also a recent, important work on St. Teresa's anthropology containing ideas valuable for our subject, M. Isabel Alvira, *Vision de l'homme selon Thérèse d'Avila. Une philosophie de l'heroïsme* (Paris, 1992), pp. 125–38.

up with his glorified humanity. Christian following of Christ aims at a communion of feelings and life with Jesus, resolutely following his person, having a 'very great determination' to be one with him. This holy foundress' teaching on the spiritual life is, quite simply, Christ and following Christ.

Through the gifts she received, Teresa learned to practice and teach the presence of Christ in the soul and the transformation that that brings about in the Christian. Her spiritual way consists, in line with Pauline doctrine (Gal 2:20), in conformation to Him. Christ is, for her, the innermost center of man, something etched and stamped on him. That is why the process of spiritual transformation described throughout her writings necessarily passes through experience of the Cross and suffering. 'The life of our Lord becomes the goal to which everything tends—being, living, suffering with Him. This can be clearly deduced from countless passages in her writings.'[64]

Like these, many other examples could be given to show that Christ-centered spirituality has managed to describe very profoundly certain aspects of the ordinary way of identifying oneself with Christ. Each of these contains elements proper to it; those who led the way—most of them great saints and, in the examples given and in the case of Blessed Josemaría Escrivá, great founders—received special gifts and lights which enabled them to contemplate and proclaim fresh nuances on the mystery of the Christian's conformation to Christ. Doctrinally, the great masters of Christian spirituality are at one. They are distinguished only by different accents, different ways of looking at the only Model, different approaches depending on their particular focus on what it means to follow Christ.

---

64 S. Castro, op. cit., p. 105.

III. 'Alter Christus, Ipse Christus' in the thought of Josemaría Escrivá

The last part of our study brings us right into the core of Blessed Josemaría Escrivá's spiritual Christ-centeredness, and the important role played in it by the *alter Christus, ipse Christus* description. That description synthesizes, as it were, his spiritual thought and his way of looking at the mystery of Christ and the mystery of the Christian which is contained in and lit up by the former. It helps us to contemplate both these mysteries (by contemplation we mean here profound charismatic study of the revealed content of those mysteries). This description, whether taken as a whole, or taken in either part (as *alter Christus*, or *ipse Christus*), accompanied by appropriate verbs and in an appropriate context, as we shall go on to discuss, makes it possible to examine, and turn into a spiritual and pastoral proposal, the theological space that extends between the Humanity of God incarnate and the earthly life of Christians, called as they are to imitate that Humanity.

Blessed Josemaría's thought is normally to be found within that theological space, and there it tends to work as a matter of course in two ways—first, detailed analysis, rather phenomenological in style, of the mystery of the God-Man, and then going on to project the essential elements of that mystery onto the life of man. It could be described as an intense, tireless Christological hermeneutic (based on Catholic tradition and enlightened by his own charism) which becomes in turn an anthropological hermeneutical key, and then a spiritual and pastoral proposal. As I see it, his thought works in the way I have described: the idea of man that is reflected in his writings is the product of his prior Christological insight, and not the other way round. And this, with all the richness of his supernatural experience as a founder, is what he proclaims in a summarized form by the wording *alter Christus, ipse Christus*.

Having reached this point in our study, we can take one or the other of two possible approaches: a) an analysis of the wording used in the light provided by his prior Christological insight, and then deducing the basic elements in Blessed Josemaría's view of man; or else, b) starting with his view of man in order first to fix the meaning of the wording, and then to infer from the result what his underlying Christological view is. We are, logically, going to take the second approach, because our starting point is his spiritual teaching, which is the vehicle of his view of the Christian person and the life of that person. We have to work from below upwards—a route which takes us from the anthropological to the Christological keys via the bridge of the *alter Christus, ipse Christus*.

If we knew at the start the keys of Blessed Josemaría's christological hermeneutic, that would be the logical place from which to begin studying the *alter Christus, ipse Christus*. But as far as those keys are concerned, we know only 'part'—that constituted jointly by Catholic dogma on the mystery of Christ, and by traditional Christocentric spirituality, from which his theological reasoning and intellectual habits draw nourishment. However, there is another, quite essential 'part' not available to us—that dependent on the charismatic enlightenment which the Holy Spirit gave Blessed Josemaría, which, when projected on the first-mentioned part, will open up new perspectives in Christian spirituality. It is not possible for us to establish *a priori* the specific way of understanding the mystery of the Redeemer which comes with that charismatic enlightenment, but we may be able to approach it via the reflection it has left in his spiritual teaching.

So, we shall take as our starting-point that side of the *alter Christus, ipse Christus* bridge, and try to get to the other side in order to arrive at the Christological key referred to, and attempt a theological evaluation.

1. 'Alter Christus, ipse Christus': the texts

In the published works of Blessed Josemaría, the only ones on which we have worked, the expressions *alter Christus* and *ipse Christus* appear literally in thirty passages. Sometimes just one, sometimes both; in the original they come in Latin or Spanish. Of the thirty passages:

— Ten mention only *alter Christus*.[65] Twice (both in *The Way*), the expression is applied to the priest, who is *another Christ*.[66] The other passages refer to Christians in general (as we shall see later, the term 'Christian' has very precise nuances in Blessed Josemaría's thinking).

— In six of the passages only *ipse Christus* is used;[67] always with reference to the Christian.

— Finally, the other fourteen passages link both wordings, sometimes in both Latin and Spanish.[68] In three of these passages, they are applied to the priest;[69] in the rest, to Christians.

a. Verbal forms used

Independently of which of the two wordings occurs, the verb used to apply it to the subject is the verb 'to be'.[70] It is used in different moods and tenses, and usually combined with other verbal forms which make the meaning of the sentence exact. Here are some examples:

---

[65] Cf. *The Way*, 66, 67, 687; *The Forge*, 25, 450, 553; *Christ Is Passing By*, 21, 150; *Friends of God*, 13, 128.

[66] Cf. *The Way*, 66-7.

[67] Cf. *The Way of the Cross*, tenth station, 5; *The Forge*, 74; *Christ Is Passing By*, 109, 115, 120, 121.

[68] Cf. 'A priest forever' in *Love for the Church*, 38; *The Way of the Cross*, sixth station; *Furrow*, 45, 166, 200; *Conversations*, 58; *Christ Is Passing By*, 11, 79, 96, 104, 106, 183, 185; *Friends of God*, 6.

[69] Cf. 'A priest forever', op. cit.; *Furrow*, 45; *Christ Is Passing By*, 79.

[70] Only on two occasions are other terms used in an analogous context: 'knowing yourself to be another Christ' (cf. *The Forge*, 450) and 'becoming another Christ' (cf. *Friends of God*, 128).

Subject	Verb 'to be' + accompanying verbal form	Description
the priest [71]	is	another Christ
the priest [72]	is	alter Christus, ipse Christus
the Christian [73] or the Catholic [74]	is called to be	another Christ
each Christian [75]	is to be	ipse Christus
each Christian [76]	is to be	another Christ, Christ himself
all of us Christians [77]	have to be	ipse Christus
all of us Christians [78]	can and should be	other Christs, Christ himself
we Christians [79]	are	other Christs, Christ himself
the Christian [80]	is obliged to be	alter Christus, ipse Christus
all of us Christians [81]	are, want to be	ipse Christus

Many other similar examples could be given: 'feeling and knowing yourself to be another Christ';[82] 'have we made up our minds to be other Christs?';[83] 'urging each one of you on, to become another Christ';[84] 'we will be

---

71 Cf. *The Way*, 66–7.
72 Cf. 'A priest forever', op. cit.; *Furrow*, 45; *Christ Is Passing By*, 79.
73 Cf. *Furrow*, 166; *Christ Is Passing By*, 21.
74 Cf. *Friends of God*, 13.
75 Cf. *Christ Is Passing By*, 120.
76 Cf. *Furrow*, 200.
77 Cf. *The Forge*, 74; *Christ Is Passing By*, 183.
78 Cf. 'A priest forever', op. cit.; *Conversations*, 58.
79 Cf. *Christ Is Passing By*, 106.
80 Cf. ibid., 96.
81 Cf. ibid., 121.
82 Cf. *The Forge*, 450.
83 Cf. *Christ Is Passing By*, 121.
84 Cf. *Friends of God*, 6.

other Christs';[85] 'each Christian is not simply *alter Christus*, but *ipse Christus*';[86]. . . .

In addition to the different subjects of the sentences (as mentioned above) the first two interesting things to note are:

— The verb 'to be' is always being used to mean something in time—not an eschatological event. All the passages are referring to the Christian (or the priest) in this life, when one already is or should be spiritually Christ. So, he is looking at Christian life in this world, viewed from the perspective of the divine-human reality of Christ. Also, this historical reality (being another Christ or Christ himself) is described sometimes in the present tense: 'is Christ', 'we are Christ', or else in the future tense: 'we should be', 'is called to be', 'decide to be Christ'... . That is to say, sometimes identification with Christ is spoken of as already a fact, like a gift already given, and at other times (most times) as a goal to strive for, as something which is in the process of coming about.

Clearly the theological substratum on which Blessed Josemaría's thought and language is based is the biblical teaching on conformation to Christ, where we can see at one and the same time the sacramental gift that brings this conformation about and the supernatural process of gradual assimilation to the image of Christ, sometimes termed the process of 'christification'. The dynamic of the gift is such that it is something which still has to be obtained more perfectly in the future but is already possessed now. But the focus is always on time, not eschatology: in the eschatological situation there is no room for a process to operate.

---

85 Cf. *The Way of the Cross*, sixth station.
86 Cf. *Christ Is Passing By*, 104.

— It should also be noted that Blessed Josemaría uses indistinguishably the terms *alter Christus* and *ipse Christus*, either together or separately. This seems to indicate that he is giving the same meaning to each, for, although each has its own nuance, both have and express the same essential content—being spiritually Christ. Later we shall see more clearly that the two wordings show exactly what we have first said—the fact of already being that which one must come to be more perfectly. Both indicate something already possessed and the process towards more perfect possession, but whereas in the *alter Christus* the focus is more on the starting-point, in the *ipse Christus* it is more on the goal. In any event, this is something which needs to be gone into further.

b. *The subject of the description*

In the passages we are studying these descriptions are applied to the priest, to each Christian person, or to all Christians. On one occasion the subject is the Catholic, in another the 'apostolic man'. If these descriptions shed some light on Blessed Josemaría's view of the subject to which he applies them, the reverse can also be said to be true. So, it is useful to look more closely at the subjects concerned, in order to better understand the descriptions. We have here a case in which the sentence 'A is B' indicates an identity between subject and predicate which is not absolute, for not only A (for example, the priest) is B (for example, another Christ): we also find him saying that C (for example, the Christian) is the same B. So, whichever the subject is, light is thrown on the meaning (common to both) which should be given the predicate.

On the priest as *alter Christus, ipse Christus* there are five passages in these writings of Blessed Josemaría. Three of them clearly evidence Catholic tradition, because they refer to the *anointed* condition proper to the priest, which makes him *another Christ* or else *Christ himself*. The traditional source being used, explicitly or implicitly, in these passages is Psalm 104 (*nolite tangere christos meos*).[87] In one case it involves a reading of a passage from St. Catherine of Siena.[88] The passage in question contains a statement very relevant to our study: 'Some people keep searching for what they call the identity of the priest. How clearly St. Catherine expresses it! What is the identity of the priest? That of Christ. All of us Christians can and should be not just other Christians, *alter Christus*, but Christ himself: *ipse Christus*. But in the priest this happens in a direct way, by virtue of the sacrament.'

This gives us a lead to understanding the meaning Blessed Josemaría gives to these expressions used here that is, 'other Christs', 'Christ himself'. If the priest is said to be another Christ through the sacrament he has received, that is, 'by virtue of the sacrament', what is the content of the sacramental gift which can also be predicated of any Christian? Clearly, one cannot predicate of an ordinary member of the faithful the specificity of the priest's ministerial consecration-mission, that is, his power to act *in persona Christi Capitis*. Having ruled that out, what is left? What is left is the priestly condition taken in its most radical sense, as the capacity to mediate and to offer a sacrifice acceptable to God; what is left, then, is baptismal participation in the mystery of Christ, understood as an essentially priestly mystery. The priest is, in a singular and essentially different way, *qua* minister, what each member of Christ's faithful is and is called to be more perfectly by nature of his Baptism. In the passage mentioned the Christian is being viewed from the angle of his baptismal priesthood. This could mean, and we just mention it here to support it further on with more facts, that *alter Christus* and *ipse Christus* always have priestly content, irrespective of who their subject is.

---

87 Cf. 'A priest forever', op. cit.; *The Way*, 67; and implicitly, *The Way*, 66 and *Christ Is Passing By*, 69.

88 St. Catherine of Siena, *Dialogue*, ch. 116; quoted in 'A priest forever'.

So, as I see it, applying the description *alter Christus, ipse Christus* to the priest throws light on the central meaning of these expressions and also (indirectly) on the meaning of their application to the other subject, that is, the Christian as an ordinary member of the faithful. What do those texts have to say which specifically state this second application?

This extensive group of texts allows us to go somewhat further in the same direction, confirming our results so far and shedding some new light. To show this in an orderly way, we need first to analyze what the term 'Christian' means in this context. We read that 'each Christian', 'all Christians', or 'the Christian' as such, is or should be another Christ. But does the word 'Christian' refer just to someone who is baptized, or does it have some nuance which needs to be taken account of?

We need to bear in mind that Blessed Josemaría, in these texts we are studying, always has in his sights, as the forms of the verb 'to be' indicate, both the baptismal gift (which makes someone a *christ*, an anointed person) and the dynamism of that gift, which calls for a process of 'Christification' to be set in motion, for which the subject's free cooperation is essential. The Christian who is being spoken about here, the subject described as being *alter Christus, ipse Christus*, is the Christian who in addition to being baptized is cooperating in that process of Christification. He is the Christian who has consciously accepted his *Christian vocation* (an expression which also carries accents of its own in Blessed Josemaría's thought).[89]

The passages are quite explicit, such as this one, for example: 'You need interior life and doctrinal formation. Be demanding on yourself! As a Christian man or woman, you have to be the salt of the earth and the light of the world, for you have a duty to give good example with holy shamelessness.

---

89 Cf., for example, *Conversations*, 22, 58, 59; *Christ Is Passing By*, 58, 60, 71, 120.

'The charity of Christ should urge you on. Feeling and knowing yourself to be another Christ from the moment you told him that you would follow him, you must not separate yourself from your equals—your relatives, friends and colleagues—any more than you would separate salt from the food it is seasoning.

'Your interior life and your formation include the piety and the principles a child of God must have in order to give flavour to everything by his active presence.

'Ask the Lord to ensure that you are always that good seasoning in the lives of others.'[90]

One immediately notices, on reading these words, that the Christian person described as 'another Christ' is he or she who has taken that gift (and its demands) to heart 'from the moment you told him you would follow him', that is to say, ever since he came to see his baptismal vocation as a gift which he has received and a process that has to develop, one in which he has freely agreed to cooperate. Being and becoming *alter Christus, ipse Christos* means, therefore, being aware of one's baptismal consecration-mission and of the need to carry it forward. 'Embracing the Christian faith', Blessed Josemaría would write, 'means committing oneself to continuing Jesus' mission among men. We must, each of us, be *alter Christus, ipse Christus*, another Christ, Christ himself. Only in this way can we set about this great undertaking, this immense, unending task of sanctifying all temporal structures from within, bringing to them the leaven of redemption.'[91]

Thus, the *alter Christus* Christian is the Christian who strives to live his faith, giving it a vocational meaning. But, taking up the subject of the priest which we touched on earlier, it might be asked: does the subject of the *alter Christus, ipse Christus* also include the ordinary member of the faithful as seen by Blessed Josemaría Escrivá from the

---

90 *The Forge*, 450.
91 *Christ Is Passing By*, 183.

angle of priesthood? I think that this is indeed the case and that it comes across very clearly in the texts. For example, the following one in which he is speaking about the passion and death of Christ, the supreme act of his priestly ministry: 'The tragedy of the passion brings to fulfillment our own life and the whole of human history. We can't let Holy Week be just a kind of commemoration. It means contemplating the mystery of Jesus Christ as something which continues to work in our souls. The Christian is obliged to be *alter Christus, ipse Christus*, another Christ, Christ himself. Through baptism all of us have been made priests of our lives, "to offer spiritual sacrifices acceptable to God through Jesus Christ" (1 Pet 2:5). Everything we do can be an expression of our obedience to God's will and so perpetuate the mission of the God-man.'[92]

Here everything is being viewed, as we said, from the angle of priesthood— Christ's passion, his entire mission, his mystery, 'something which continues to work in our souls' (an expression of great theological depth), baptismal consecration... Clearly, then, the meaning of the *alter Christus*, when the subject of the sentence is the ordinary member of the faithful, is focused on in the same light as when the subject is the priest. It refers to priestly consecration and mission, mediation through sacrifice, redemption from sin, salvation, and the elevation of redeemed man and of all creation: 'Each of us is to be *ipse Christus*, Christ himself. He is the one mediator between God and man (cf. 1 Tim 2:5). And we make ourselves one with him in order to offer all things, with him, to the Father. Our calling to be children of God, in the midst of the world, requires us not only to seek our own personal holiness, but also to go out onto all the ways of the earth, to convert them into roads that will carry souls over all obstacles and lead them to the Lord. As we take part in all temporal activities, as ordinary citizens, we are to become leaven (cf. Mt 13:33) acting on the mass (cf. 1 Cor 5:6). [...] Look: The redemption was

---

92 *Christ Is Passing By*, 96.

consummated when Jesus died on the Cross, in shame and glory, "to the Jews a stumbling-block, and to the Gentiles foolishness" (1 Cor 1:23). But the redemption will, by the will of God, be carried out continually until our Lord's time comes. It is impossible to live according to the heart of Jesus Christ and not to know that we are sent, as he was, "to save all sinners" (1 Tim 1:15) with the clear realization that we ourselves need to trust in the mercy of God more and more every day. As a result, we will foster in ourselves a vehement desire to live as co-redeemers with Christ, to save all souls with him, because we are, we want to be, *ipse Christus*, Christ himself, and "He gave himself as a ransom for all".'[93]

And there are many more passages along similar lines, which confirm what we have been saying. I do not want to close this section without adding to the record a similar passage, which I think is especially relevant to our subject. It reads as follows: 'You cannot separate the fact that Christ is God from his role as redeemer. The Word became flesh and came into the world "to save all men" (cf. 1 Tim 2:4). With all our personal defects and limitations, we are other Christs, Christ himself, and we too are called to serve all men.'[94]

One notices here an essential presupposition in Blessed Josemaría's Christ-centered thinking—the absolute inseparability of being and role in Christ; this is a basic theological principle on which his spirituality is constantly drawing. Explicitly or implicitly, this principle, which could be called 'structural' to his thought, is being reflected all the time in all his writings. This light also illuminates his whole view of the Church and of Christian life. So, one can say that, in his thought, the indestructible connection between being and role indicates the theological identity of Christ, of his Body which is the Church, and of its members, Christians. The importance of this principle cannot be exaggerated.

---

93 *Christ Is Passing By*, 120–1.
94 Ibid., 106.

To a great extent our present study also draws on this light. Above all, because it helps us to see that the Christological content of the expressions *alter Christus* and *ipse Christus* is identical: both focus on the one and only *Christus*, the incarnate Son of God and Redeemer of man in his original and defining unity. The difference between one wording and the other (both referring to the Christian in the light of Christ) lies not in their being two different ways of looking at Him: rather, they refer to the Christian at two different stages in the spiritual process of 'Christification'.

The *alter Christus* is the baptized person, conformed by the Holy Spirit to Christ, whom he follows by freely taking on the duties of his consecration-mission; that is to say, the *alter Christus* is the Christian in his state of growing to be like the Redeemer Son, becoming progressively more identified with Him, both personally and in his active sharing in the mission of the Church. The *ipse Christus* is not some other Christian but the very same Christian, just as Christ is one and the same, but Blessed Josemaría is viewing him now not only as the subject of the process of identification with Christ but as someone who is already, at each stage in the process, sharing in the ultimate goal, even though the process is still ongoing. If he is 'another Christ' in the indestructible unity of consecration-mission in which he shares, he is already as 'Christ himself' in terms of salvific efficacy, in which he also shares. The *alter Christus,* given a capacity for and called to progressive identification with the Redeemer Son, is already, while still en route, making Christ present among men:[95] he is already a living image of Christ; he is already 'Christ himself' at every point where he is an effective instrument of co-redemption.

---

[95] The expression 'Christ's presence among men' or similar ones, sometimes including the expression *ipse Christus*, in Bl. Josemaría's writings, shows just what we have been saying. Cf. the very title of *Christ Is Passing By* and many passages in that book: for example, 112, 115. Similar passages occur, for example, in 138, 150, 183.

So, the *alter Christus* is, here and now, *ipse Christus*—Christ himself, who continues to be *present among men*, insofar as the efficacy of his shared-in redemptive role is present. When the *alter Christus* exercises his apostolic role, the redemptive efficacy of Christ is being actualized: the effective activity of the Redeemer is being made present in that of the co-redeemer. In this way Jesus continues to 'make his way' among men. Although Blessed Josemaría usually formulates this teaching by speaking of the *Christifidelis* as an individual person (and, in certain passages, by speaking of the priest), because he is the normal subject of the *alter Christus, ipse Christus* in his writings, it applies also to all Christians, that is, to his view of the whole Church. As regards the Church, the Body of Christ united to its Head, one could also say, following this line of thought, that the Church is *ipse Christus* in the exercise of its mission among men. Although Blessed Josemaría does not normally use this expression to describe the Church (it is an expression evocative of St. Augustine's 'total Christ'), he does expressly preach this doctrine when he says, for example, 'The Church is Christ present among us',[96] in which one can see the logical connection between his Christological, ecclesiological and anthropological thought.

2. 'Alter Christus, ipse Christus': the context

An analysis of the thirty passages chosen is important to our study, because it allows us to see more clearly the meaning of this expression by setting it within a wider framework. For this purpose, we are now going to examine two contextual elements: one of them, the immediate context, consisting of explanatory phrases used by Blessed Josemaría Escrivá in those passages; and another, broader one—the notions of *following, imitation of* and *identification with Christ* which he uses. We shall begin with the latter, to get a better overview, and then we shall focus more closely on the explanatory phrases applied to the *alter Christus, ipse Christus*.

---

96 *Christ Is Passing By*, 131.

a. Broader context: following, imitating and identifying with Christ

The ideas which we are now analyzing in Blessed Josemaría's writings—all of them (each in its own way, as is true of any spiritual teacher) an expression of the spiritual Christ-centeredness of the author—constitute material open to more detailed analysis, inappropriate here. Now, we want simply to study how they form a contextual framework for Josemaría Escrivá's thought on the *alter Christus*, as well as the supernatural anthropology that underlies it.

Both aspects (his thought and his view of men) are set, as we have seen, in the context of a biblical, dogmatic and spiritual tradition which goes back many centuries. Blessed Josemaría's teaching, as that of other trail-blazers of holiness in the Church, always draws on the tradition of received doctrine and, without ceasing to do that, it carries it forward by transposing into it (first by pastoral activity, and then spiritually and theologically) his own particular insights, confirmed by appropriate approval of the Church. From what we have seen so far by looking at the texts, this combination of tradition and development is patently present in the teaching of the formula of Opus Dei, but this is something we can appreciate even better if we study the nuances he gives in his writings to the Christocentric notions mentioned (following, imitation, identification). The first two of these are to be found in all Christian spiritual writing; the third, which is closely connected to them in Blessed Josemaría's thought (it is a later explication of them) is a function of his teaching on the *alter Christus, ipse Christus*, and contains some characteristics which are more specifically his own.

- *Following Christ*

In a total of 57 passages in his published writings Blessed Josemaría uses an idea of 'following Christ' which is very evocative of tradition and also of his own style, and which evidences a unity of thought and language. This 'following' is undoubtedly the same thing as taught in the entire tradition (as a Christian way of holiness); and also the Christ whom one is invited to follow is the only Christ, the model for all his disciples. But the action of following which Blessed Josemaría talks about always has reference to the great 'addressee' of his teaching—each Christian, all Christians: the *alter Christus ipse Christus*. And, especially relevant to our study, that protagonist, that follower, will always contribute his own theological individuality, thereby giving his own accents to the very notion of what it means to follow Christ. With Josemaría Escrivá a new spiritual and pastoral way is opened up to understanding and formulating this idea.

What is the traditional element and what are the 'Escrivá' nuances to be found in these passages? While it is true that this is something which needs to be gone into more closely and can only be touched on here, I shall try to give a brief outline.

— *Traditional elements* (some examples)
- following in Christ's footsteps[97], [98]
- followers of Christ[99]
- following Jesus closely (like our Lady, the Apostles)[100]

---

97 Cf. 'The supernatural aim of the Church' in *In Love with the Church*, p. 28; *Furrow*, 320; *The Forge*, 155; *Conversations*, 62; *Friends of God*, 127, 223, 252. In addition to the New Testament resonance of the phrase 'following in his (Christ's) steps' (cf. 1 Pet 2:21), one can readily see the personal resonance it must have had for Bl. Josemaría, whose vocation can be traced back to an episode in which he was impressed by the footprints of a friar in the snow.

98 Cf. *The Way of the Cross*, fourteenth station; *Christ Is Passing By*, 74; *Friends of God*, 238.

99 Cf. *The Forge*, 997; *Christ Is Passing By*, 9; *Friends of God*, 111, 198.

100 Cf. *The Way*, 797; *Furrow*, 978; *The Forge*, 6, 860; *Christ Is Passing By*, 2, 54, 107; *Friends of God*, 114, 140, 204, 299.

- following him, to be fishers of men[101]
- following him in his suffering (in his Passion, carrying the Cross, etc.)[102]

— *Special nuances* (some examples)
- following him by 'fulfillling the mission God has given you, in the place and in the environment indicated by his Providence'[103]
- following him, to be an 'apostle of apostles'[104]
- following him, 'so you can journey through this earthly life, sowing peace and joy'[105]
- following him, by becoming 'contemplative souls, in the street', in the midst of one's work[106]
- following him, in marriage, which is 'a real supernatural calling'[107]

The novelty in these special nuances lies in the fact that the people that Blessed Josemaría is exhorting and teaching *to follow Christ* are Christian men and women who, aware of their vocation to holiness, have to strive to attain holiness wherever they are, staying in their place in society, in the state-in-life proper to them. It is a notion of Christ-following by the ordinary Christian (or by the secular priest) that is intensely nuanced, as we have said, by the person's theological individuality—a notion which retains all the features normally found in Catholic tradition, but which now acquires a special tonality: it is strongly

---

101 Cf. *Christ Is Passing By*, 45; *Friends of God*, 259.
102 Cf. *Furrow*, 249, 700; *Christ Is Passing By*, 9; *Friends of God*, 111.
103 Cf. *Conversations*, 60.
104 Cf. *Christ Is Passing By*, 1. The expression 'apostle of apostles' is very much Bl. Josemaría's.
105 Cf. *Friends of God*, 141. The expression 'sowers of peace and joy' is typical of Bl. Josemaría.
106 Cf. *Friends of God*, 238. The expression 'contemplatives in the midst of the world' is characteristic of Bl. Josemaría and a summary of his teaching.
107 *Christ Is Passing By*, 23.

accentuated by secularity, by the apostolic mission of the Christian lay person (co-redemption) and by the evangelizing activity of Christians in and from within society.

These accents, however, although they give an air of novelty to the idea of being a 'follower' and to what that means in practice, do not in any way change its theological essence, which continues to be rooted (in Blessed Josemaría's teaching, as in that of all tradition) in biblical doctrine on the exemplarity of the earthly life of the God-Man, as also of his death and resurrection. The passages of the New Testament that were frequently quoted by him—such as, for example, Philippians 2:5–8,[108] Matthew 11:28–30,[109] or John 14:6,[110]—eloquently prove what we say.

Within this framework, the description *alter Christus, ipse Christus* is easier to understand. The Christian person is described (as understood by Blessed Josemaría) as the person who follows Christ closely, committed like Him to doing the Father's will, the mission of Redemption, without any need to change his place in the world in order to follow in the Redeemer's footsteps; to be on such close terms with Him that he can be a contemplative in the street, fully committed to performing his ordinary duties and his role in the Body of Christ ... The figure of the *alter Christus, ipse Christus* takes on a sharper outline in this context.

---

108 'Have this mind among yourselves, which was in Christ Jesus, who, though he was in the form of God, [...] humbled himself and became obedient unto death, even death on a cross'. This Pauline passage is the New Testament text most quoted in *Christ Is Passing By* and *Friends of God* (eleven times).

109 'Come to me, all who labor and are burdened [...]. And learn from me; for I am gentle and lowly in heart [...].' This is the second most quoted New Testament passage in those two books (nine times).

110 'I am the way, and the truth, and the life; no one comes to the Father, but by me.' He quotes it on seven occasions.

- *Imitation of Christ*

As we have already noted, following and imitating Christ are not seen in spiritual tradition as two different things. Their meaning are not so much different as complementary, for Christ can only be imitated by following him, and he can only be followed by imitating him. However, in line with biblical terminology,[111] it is customary to speak of both actions and to use both expressions.

The action of imitating Christ is explicitly mentioned on occasions in the passages we are studying—and implicitly, of course, in many more. I shall give a short outline of these, too, distinguishing traditional elements from special nuances.

— *Traditional elements* (some examples)
- imitating Christ, the Master [112]
- imitating his virtues (his detachment,[113] his humility,[114] his obedience,[115] his charity towards all[116])
- learning from his life[117]
- learning froma the way he lived[118]

— *Special nuances* (some examples)
- imitating particularly his thirty years of work at Nazareth[119]

---

111 Cf. What we said above in the section on 'Roots in spiritual tradition' (pp. 151ff).
112 Cf. *Furrow*, 806; *Friends of God*, 252.
113 Cf. *The Forge*, 523; *Friends of God*, 114.
114 Cf. *The Forge*, 590; *Christ Is Passing By*, 18.
115 Cf. *Christ Is Passing By*, 21.
116 Cf. *The Forge*, 859; *Friends of God*, 225.
117 Cf. *Friends of God*, 154.
118 Cf. ibid., 136.
119 Cf. *Conversations*, 70; *Christ Is Passing By*, 20; *Friends of God*, 56.

- imitating Christ, *perfectus Deus, perfectus homo*, by being very human and very supernatural, fulfillling one's obligations perfectly[120]
- imitating him, so as to make him known through the way one lives one's ordinary life[121]

So, in Josemaría Escrivá's thinking, imitation extends to every point in Christ's life and to all aspects of his sacred Humanity. What these passages offer us is a contemplation of the mystery of Jesus' life in which the accent is put on that life as a paradigm for the life of the sons and daughters of God, that is, of the *alter Christus, ipse Christus*. The Christian is seen in his Model, and the Model is viewed from the angle of his filial mystery of self-giving, whether in the fullness of the paschal event, or in his public life or in his years of ordinary working, family and social life in Nazareth.

On this last-mentioned aspect, in which so many everyday attitudes are taken up and sanctified by Christ, Blessed Josemaría seems to focus particularly closely. His teaching, addressing the *christifidelis* who strives to imitate his Maker in his ordinary life, goes much further than the contributions of other great teachers. Although we cannot go into this here, we should notice that the words we shall go on to quote contribute something quite new to the notion and to the actual practice of following Christ:

'Since 1928 I have understood clearly that God wants our Lord's whole life to be an example for Christians. I saw this with special reference to his hidden life, the years he spent working side by side with ordinary men. Our Lord wants many people to ratify their vocation during years of quiet, unspectacular living. [. . .] I dream—and the dream has come true—of multitudes of God's children, sanctifying themselves as

---

120 Cf. *Friends of God*, 50, 74, 75, 104, 121.
121 Cf. *The Forge*, 452; *Friends of God*, 299.

ordinary citizens, sharing the ambitions and endeavors of their colleagues and friends. I want to shout to them about this divine truth: If you are there in the middle of ordinary life, it doesn't mean Christ has forgotten about you or hasn't called you. He has invited you to stay among the activities and concerns of the world. He wants you to know that your human vocation, your profession, your talents, are not excluded from his divine plans. He has sanctified them and made them a most acceptable offering to his Father.'[122]

These words show very clearly Blessed Josemaría Escrivá's thinking about the essence of the imitation of Christ by the *alter Christus, ipse Christus*. They carry special spiritual and pastoral nuances which arise from the condition of the person concerned. All the richness of the traditional notion is retained, but interesting new values attach to it. Also essential to this way of looking at the imitation of Christ is the strong accent placed on its apostolic dimension: 'This is the love of Christ which each of us should try to practice in his own life. But to be Christ himself, we must *see ourselves in him*. It's not enough to have a general idea of the spirit of Jesus' life; we have to learn the details of his life and, through them, his attitudes. And, especially, we must contemplate his life, to derive from it strength, light, serenity, peace. [...] If we want to bring other men and women to our Lord, we must first go to the Gospel and contemplate Christ's love. We could take the central events of his passion, for, as he himself said: "Greater love has no man than this, that a man lay down his life for his friends" (Jn 15:13). But we can also look at the rest of his life, his everyday dealings with the people he met. In order to bring men his message of salvation and show them God's love, Christ, who was perfect God and perfect man, acted in a human and a divine

---

122 *Christ Is Passing By*, 20.

way. [...] It makes me very happy to realize that Christ wanted to be fully a man, with flesh like our own. I am moved when I contemplate how wonderful it is for God to love with a human's heart.'[123]

Blessed Josemaría does not focus first on the traditional notion of imitation and then on the *christifidelis* who should apply it to his life: first he looks at Christ and then at the *alter Christus* called to a holy and co-redeeming life in his place in the world—which accounts for the pastoral and spiritual accents he gives the notion.[124]

- *Identification with Christ*

The nuances and stresses the *alter Christus, ipse Christus* gives to the notions of following and imitating Christ lead Blessed Josemaría's thinking towards another notion central to his texts—that of identification with Christ. This is very close to the *ipse Christus*, which immediately suggests that this idea too must have a specific weight in the way he sees things. To my mind, it, along with the description we are studying, is the most typical feature of his spiritual Christ-centeredness. It would make a fine subject for a monograph.

Given the light it throws on our present subject, we shall now point out some aspects of its theological background, as revealed by the 32 passages in which it occurs literally in his published work.[125]

— *Identification with Christ* is, above all, the goal of the *alter Christus, ipse Christus* process of following and imitating Christ.[126] This explains why all three

---

123 *Christ Is Passing By*, 107.
124 See also *Conversations*, 70; *Christ Is Passing By*, 150.
125 Cf. 'A priest forever', op. cit., *The Way*, 947; *Furrow*, 273, 655, 728, 889; *The Forge*, 155, 288, 397, 468, 818, 1022; *Conversations*, 70, 72, 91; *Christ Is Passing By*, 19, 31, 32, 56, 58, 96, 106, 110, 120, 138; *Friends of God*, 111, 128, 212, 236, 256, 281, 300.
126 Cf. *The Forge*, 155, 486, 1022; *Conversations*, 70; *Christ Is Passing By*, 19, 32, 56; *Friends of God*, 111, 128, 136.

ideas commonly occur in the same passage together with their subject.[127] Two of the texts throw helpful light on the subject of this identification by linking the Christian's personality with spiritual identification with Christ, thereby showing how deeply the Christian is conformed to his Model: '[...] You need to have your own personality, agreed. But you should try to make it conform exactly to Christ's.'[128] Insofar as it is the goal of following and imitating Christ, identification is itself conceived as the goal of the *Christian vocation* as such ('Our Christian vocation, this calling which our Lord makes to each of us personally, leads us to become identified with him').[129]

— *Identification with Christ* is synonymous with the holiness to which all Christians are called by Baptism: 'We cannot stay still. We must keep going ahead toward the goal St. Paul marks out: "It is not I who live, it is Christ that lives in me" (Gal 2:20). This is a high and very noble ambition, this identification with Christ, this holiness. But there is no other way if we are to be consistent with the divine life God has sown in our souls in baptism. To advance we must progress in holiness. Shying away from holiness implies refusing our Christian life its natural growth.'[130] As is only logical in a spirituality of the ordinary member of the faithful as *alter Christus*, this also applies within marriage: 'The purpose of marriage is to help married people sanctify themselves and others. For this reason they receive a special grace in the sacrament which Jesus Christ instituted. Those who are called to the

---

127 Cf. *Friends of God*, 128, 299.
128 *The Forge*, 468; cf. *Christ Is Passing By*, 31: 'make the foundation of my personality my identification with you'.
129 *Friends of God*, 256; cf. *Furrow*, 728; *Christ Is Passing By*, 120.
130 *Christ Is Passing By*, 58; cf. *The Way*, 947; *Furrow*, 655; *The Forge*, 397.

married state will, with the grace of God, find within their state everything they need to be holy, to identify themselves each day more with Jesus Christ, and to lead to God those with whom they live.'[131]

— *Identification with Christ* always means sharing in his redemptive mission: 'All the ways of the earth can be an opportunity to meet Christ, who calls us to identify ourselves with him and carry out his divine mission—right where he finds us.'[132] Carrying out his mission, or being a co-redeemer with him, means, as we said earlier, making Christ present among men, 'identifying ourselves with Christ's desire to redeem'.[133] 'The Christian is obliged to be *alter Christus, ipse Christus*, another christ, Christ himself. Through Baptism all of us have been made priests of our lives, "to offer spiritual sacrifices acceptable to God through Jesus Christ" (1 Pet 2:5). Everything we do can be an expression of our obedience to God's will and so perpetuate the mission of the God-man. [...] It is a good time to examine how much we really want to live as Christians, to be holy. [...] The experience of sin should lead us to sorrow; we should make a more mature and deeper decision to be faithful and truly identify ourselves with Christ, persevering, no matter what it costs, in the priestly mission that he has given to every single one of his disciples.'[134] The priestly essence of this shared mission, and consequently of being identified with Christ, is confirmed in an especially clear way in its intrinsic reference to the cross, as shown, for example, in the rather auto-

---

131 *Conversations*, 91.
132 *Christ Is Passing By*, 110.
133 Ibid., 138.
134 Ibid., 96.

biographical awards of Blessed Josemaría Escrivá which we quoted at the start of this essay: 'You did this, Lord, to make me see that having the Cross means happiness, joy. And the reason—I see it more clearly than ever—is this: having the Cross is being identified with Christ, it means being Christ, and, therefore, being a son of God.'[135]

— Finally, in a passage which is a summary of Blessed Josemaría's ascetical teaching, he himself provides what he calls 'stages' in identification with Christ (we can see here, also, the essential Marian dimension of his notion of identification, something which warrants further study): 'I have distinguished, as it were, four stages in our effort to identify ourselves with Christ: seeking him, finding him, getting to know him, loving him. It may seem clear to you that you are only at the first stage. Seek him then, hungrily; seek him within yourselves with all your strength. If you act with determination, I am ready to guarantee that you have already found him, and have begun to get to know him and to love him, and to hold your conversation in heaven (cf. Phil 3:20). I beg our Lord to help us make up our minds to nourish in our souls the one noble ambition that matters, the only one that is really worthwhile: to get close to Jesus, like his Blessed Mother and the Holy Patriarch St. Joseph did, with longing hearts and self-denial, not neglecting anything. We will share in the joy of being God's friends - in a spirit of interior recollection, which is quite compatible with our professional and social duties—and we will thank him for teaching us so clearly and tenderly to fulfill the Will of our Father who dwells in heaven.'[136]

---

135 Cf. fn. 3 above.
136 *Friends of God*, 300.

b. The immediate context: phrases accompanying the description

Having looked at the broader context of the spiritual Christ-centeredness in which the description we are studying is set, we shall now look at the matter through the actions he predicates of the subject. How should someone act who is by virtue of his Christian vocation another Christ, Christ himself? How is he to make progress until he arrives at complete identification, holiness? We can find answers to these questions by examining the verbal forms or explanatory phrases which accompany the *alter Christus, ipse Christus*; these replies, which I can give only in outline, will bring us closer to the goal of our research.

Subject	Description	Explanatory phrase
an apostle[137]	is another Christ	if he follows Jesus, by carrying out his duty
the Christian[138]	is called to be another Christ	has to do things as a child of God would; and to encourage people to share in the Redemption
Christians[139]	are asked by God to be other Christs	by sanctifying their everyday work and the responsibilities of their particular state in life
Christians[140]	have to be *ipse Christus*	by putting on the Lord Jesus Christ and dialoguing with him

---

137 Cf. *The Way*, 687.
138 Cf. *Christ Is Passing By*, 21.
139 Cf. ibid., 150.
140 Cf. *The Forge*, 74.

Subject	Description	Explanatory phrase
every Christian[141]	to be *ipse Christus*	needs to learn the details of his life and his attitudes, and to meditate on his life and get involved in it, as if one were a protagonist, following him as closely as Mary and the Apostles did
the Christian[142]	by being *ipse Christus*	has to make Christ present among men, making the Love of God known through his human love
each Christian[143]	has to be *ipse Christus*	by being made one with Christ, the only Mediator, so as to offer with Him all things to God
we Christians[144]	are, want to be *ipse Christus*	eager to be co-redeemers with Christ, to join him in saving all souls
all of us Christians[145]	will be other Christs, Christ himself	by faithfully imitating the features of his life
each Christian[146]	should be *alter Christus, ipse Christus*	because God's call, baptismal character and grace enable him to make the Faith his own, as he ought

---

141 Cf. *Christ Is Passing By*, 107.
142 Cf. ibid., 115.
143 Cf. ibid., 120.
144 Cf. ibid., 121.
145 Cf. *The Way of the Cross*, sixth station.
146 Cf. *Conversations*, 58.

The Christian, alter Christus, ipse Christus, ...

Subject	Description	Explanatory phrase
the Christian[147]	is obliged to be *alter Christus, ipse Christus*	because he is made a priest of his own life through Baptism, perpetuating the mission of the God-Man
each Christian[148]	is not just *alter Christus*, but *ipse Christus*	uniting oneself to Him through faith, and letting his life be seen in us
we Christians[149]	are other Christs, Christ himself	called to serve all men, because the Word became flesh to save all men, and it is not possible to separate the fact that Christ is God-Man from his mission as Redeemer
each Christian[150]	has to be *alter Christus, ipse Christus*	committing himself to continue the mission of Jesus, sanctifying all temporal structures from within, thereby bringing to them the leaven of Redemption
each Christian[151]	if he makes up mind to be *alter Christus*	is told by God, `You are my his son'
each Christian[152]	should feel the urgency to be another Christ, *ipse Christus*	that is to say, he is conscious that his daily conduct has to be consistent with the norms of faith

---

147 Cf. *Christ Is Passing By*, 96.
148 Cf. ibid., 104.
149 Cf. ibid., 106.
150 Cf. ibid., 183.
151 Cf. ibid., 185.
152 Cf. *Friends of God*, 6.

If we read down the third column, ignoring repetitions and condensing the ideas, it will give us a panoramic view of the traits of the *alter Christus, ipse Christus* who makes Christ present among men. Here are some of the things he is saying:

The *alter Christus, ipse Christus*:

— contemplates the life of Christ
— imitates his actions
— does things like a son of God
— follows Jesus by doing his duties
— united to Christ, allows the Master's life to express itself through him
— moves others to share in the Redemption
— is a priest of his own life
— realizes that he is called to serve all men as Christ did
— offers all things to the Father with Christ the Mediator
— is committed to continuing Christ's mission and to do so by sanctifying earthly structures from within, bringing to them the leaven of Redemption
— sanctifies his everyday work and the duties of his state-in-life
— thereby perpetuates Christ's mission among men.

That is how Josemaría Escrivá sees the Christian. Here we can see the traits of the Christian's supernatural identity as a son of God and co-redeemer, as well as the priestly essence of his vocation in Christ—the content of his sacrifice, which is always linked to that of the Redeemer (the central place of the Eucharist is, in this regard, a key point in Blessed Josemaría's thinking), the effectiveness of his activity as a mediator sharing in Christ's mediation. If our study were designed to be more reflective than descriptive, we would have a fine field of work exploring all these aspects. But all we are aiming here is to prepare the ground, setting down markers for later study.

IV. Conclusion: his underlying image of Christ

By examining Blessed Josemaría's spiritual thought, from which his view of Christian life emerges, we have come closer to his underlying view of man and to showing it to be condensed in the figure of the *alter Christus, ipse Christus*, and in the whole gamut of actions in which he is the protagonist. We have worked up to this point gradually, trying to find in this description the hermeneutical key to Blessed Josemaría's view of man. In analyzing that description, our declared intention was to use it as a bridge to discovering its Christological root.

Josemaría's image of this *alter Christus, ipse Christus* has special features which give his own nuances and accents to the great traditional notions of spiritual Christ-centeredness. But it is an image which only partly derives from that manifold Catholic tradition. In fact, its main specific source is his theological experience of the mysteries of the Faith, particularly the mystery of Christ, experience that always took shape with the help of the charismatic gifts he received as someone called to be a founder.

In other words, we should not forget that we are studying the thought of a master of the spiritual life who was also a founder, which is the same as saying he was a charismatic person 'sifted' by the Holy Spirit. All his teaching, even that which derives from earlier tradition, has a tonality that comes from the lights given him to enable him to carry out his mission, and some elements of his message derive exclusively from his fundamental charism. For example, his sense of the apostolic activity of the *alter Christus, ipse Christus*, which he would describe as 'putting Christ at the peak of all human activities'. We can see this, for example, in the following passage:

'Our Lord has treated me like a child: if, when I was given my mission, I had realized what it was going to involve, I would have died. I had no interest in being a founder of anything. As far as myself and my work go, I have been hostile to new foundations. As I see it, all the old foundations, as well as those of recent centuries, are very much in being. True, our Work—the Work of God—arose to bring back to life a new and old spirituality of contemplative souls, in the midst of all sorts of everyday affairs, sanctifying the ordinary tasks of this earth: putting Jesus Christ at the peak of all noble realities that men are involved in, and loving this world, which fled from its Creator.'[153]

A person who has been given the gift and foundational mission to implant that new way of holiness (a spirituality of 'contemplative souls in the midst of the world'), to sanctify the world from within and thereby to establish in the world, cooperating in the mission of the Church, the kingdom of Jesus Christ, necessarily has to live and to teach others to live a deeply Christ-centered life. 'Putting Christ at the peak of human endeavor' means one has to see human work, and the men and women who do it (the Christian who is and is called to be *alter Christus, ipse Christus*) from the angle of the lordship of Christ, though the glorification of his holy Humanity; that is, one needs to have a deeply Christological outlook.

---

[153] Letter, September 4, 1951, 3, 'It is the task of Christians, in his name, to reconcile all things with God, placing Christ, by means of their work in the middle of the world, at the peak of all human activities', *Conversations*, 59; 'Work always and in everything with sacrifice, in order to put Christ at the peak of all human activities' (*The Forge*, 685); 'We will make it easier for others to recognize Christ; we will help to put Christ at the center of all human activities' (*Christ Is Passing By*, 156); 'Jesus reminds all of us: "et si exaltatus fuero a terra, omnia traham ad meipsum", "And I, if I be lifted up from the earth, will draw all things to myself". If you put me at the center of all earthly activitites, he is saying, by fulfillling the duty of each moment, in what appears important and what appears unimportant, I will draw everything to myself. My kingdom among you will be a reality!' (*Christ Is Passing By*, 183); 'This is the secret of the holiness which I have now been preaching for so many years: God has called on us all to imitate him. He has called you and me so that, living as we do in the midst of the world—and continuing to be ordinary everyday people—we may put Christ at the peak of all noble human activities' (*Friends of God*, 58).

It also has to be said that that charismatic foundational sureness, full of Christological meaning, was also from the very start bolstered by considerable supernatural support. We need only recall, for example, the extraordinary event of which Blessed Josemaría was the protagonist, in Madrid on August 7, 1931, when he was saying Mass: 'The time of the Consecration came', he writes in an autobiographical account: 'at the point of raising the Sacred Host, without losing the proper recollection—I had just mentally made the offering to merciful Love—there came to my mind, with exceptional force and clarity, those words of Scripture *et si exaltatus fuero a terra, omnia traham ad meipsum* (Jn 12:32). Normally, in the presence of something supernatural, I feel afraid. Then comes the *ne timeas!*, it is I. And I realized that it will be the men and women of God who will raise up the Cross by means of Christ's teachings on the pinnacle of every human activity ... And I saw the Lord victorious, attracting all things to Himself.'[154]

Is it possible, we ask, by reasoning it out, to establish the Christological image on which his thought is built? Can we move from his theological-spiritual statements and his view of man on which they are based, towards the deeper, Christological basis, via the bridge of the *alter Christus, ipse Christus*? It is a matter of looking away from the formula, the wording, we have been studying and focusing on its theological core, that is, the *Christus* contained (and, more than that, contemplated) in them.

Blessed Josemaría's contemplation of the mystery of Christ is, so to speak, global: it takes in each and every aspect of the revelation of the Word made man, from his incarnation to his resurrection and ascension. Even though in one or another passage in his writings he may be directly referring to some particular point in Christ's life, there is no doubt that Josemaría is always contemplating it within the context of the mystery as a whole

---

154 Quoted by A. del Portillo, *Una vida para Dios* (Madrid, 1992), pp. 163–4.

and, in that sense, from the angle of his glorious Humanity. One could say that the primary (not necessarily the principal) key to his Christological hermeneutic lies in the very fact that he is contemplating everything to do with Christ from the angle of his present place in glory *ad dexteram Patris*. The source of the meaning of all the various 'mysteries of the life of Christ' lies in the fact that they are part of a whole and reflect, each in its own way, the ultimate light—the exaltation of his Humanity in glory.

If the mystery of Christ is taken as a whole, and all illuminated by his glory in heaven, which gives full meaning to his ordinary life and his self-surrender to death, then that final light in glory is a fusion of two elements—Jesus' divine filiation and his totally faithful performance of his redemptive mission. It is plain to see how strongly these two elements are etched on the figure of the *alter Christus, ipse Christus* drawn by Josemaría Escrivá—a sure sign that these two same elements previously marked his contemplation of Christ. Divine filiation and complete self-giving to the mission of Redemption are jointly the translation into practice of the inseparability of being and role in Christ, a central point in Blessed Josemaría's conception of things.

But this unity between divine filiation and redemptive self-giving in the God-man are manifested in fact (that is to say, in the reality of his earthly life and of his life in glory) in the priestly mystery of his holy Humanity. If one studies Blessed Josemaría's thought carefully, looking at other aspects in addition to those dealt with here, one will be able to understand even better what we have been saying—that his spiritual and pastoral teaching is conceived and expounded within a priestly framework. His conception of the baptismal vocation, of Christian activity in the world, of the mission of the *alter Christus*, is decidedly priestly: it hinges constantly on the notions of mediation, sacrifice, salvation, glory of God ... Surely the priesthood of the Son of God is shining its light here. Can one not see here, then, the profound grasp of that priestly mystery Blessed Josemaría charismatically managed to attain?

To end with: I think (and I leave the matter open, to study it more) that the question we were looking at earlier (the foundational Christological image on which the founder of Opus Dei's thinking is based) is precisely the one just mentioned—the priestly condition of Christ's sacred Humanity and of his mission. Here Blessed Josemaría acquires a profound ecclesiological outlook based on the unity, difference and complementarity that exists between the common priesthood and the ministerial priesthood, an outlook that stamps all his work as a founder and his considerable literary output.

Christians, the life of the world

Giuseppe Dalla Torre,
Rector of the Libera Università Maria SS. Assunta, Rome.

I. Introduction

For the student of the history of canon law and ecclesiastical institutions, one area of special interest is the long process, from the Middle Ages onwards, whereby the papacy gradually reserved for itself matters to do with beatification and canonization.

I refer to the way in which the law eventually managed to bring into proper balance two powers, each having constitutional status. On the one hand, the power of the Christian people, which in the last analysis has the right to pronounce judgment on the personal holiness of individuals occurring within it and the right therefore to exercise a public function (which might be described as juridical-constitutional) in so doing. On the other, the power and might of the ecclesiastical institution to control, check and confirm the people's judgment, the so-called 'reputation for holiness'. The reform of Benedict XIV (in which this historical process eventually jelled) meant that public cult could not be given to non-canonized saints, nor could saints be canonized without the people first making its mind known.[1]

This dynamic relationship throws light on many aspects of the complex system of constitutional checks and balances in the canonical legal system, which has its own peculiar qualities. One can see the specifically juridical characteristics of declaring an individual a canonized saint (as distinct from the sanctity which must be at-

---

1 On all these aspects I refer the reader to G. Dalla Torre, 'Santità ed economia processuale. L'esperienza giuridica da Urbano VIII a Benedetto XIV', in *Archivo giuridico*, 221 (1991/1), pp. 9–48.

tained by all those who are saved). Indeed this dynamic relationship is of more interest than the actual procedures which are used to arrive at the truth. These procedures have been simplified and made less rigorous in recent times because of the help given by modern science, and particularly in the historical method.

Due precisely to the dynamic which underlies this 'demography of heaven', to use Gabriel Le Bras' telling expression,[2] and due also to the active part canon law plays in decision-making in this field, causes of beatification and canonization constitute both a great effort by the Church to know itself, and a considerable degree of cultural productivity in the widest sense.

In other words, investigating the complexities of each experience of holiness (which is what causes of beatification and canonization are all about) helps the Church, as the people of God, to know itself and its history through the history of its members and therefore through the history of holiness that has occurred in it over the course of time. And, even in the case of saints who, according to our poor ways of categorizing them, might be thought 'lesser' (because we don't know enough about them or because they were not founders of orders or builders of great ecclesial or social undertakings), we are still helped to acquire a deeper knowledge of the Church, as a divine institution—to understand its purpose and message better, and to see how that message can be applied in each historical context.

All this makes for a rich cultural heritage, growing all the time, keeping pace with the growth of the 'demography of heaven', a treasure of inestimable value which should not be allowed to become tarnished but should be generously passed on so that all may enjoy it. This is necessary for many reasons, including this: the experience of the holiness of others shows the 'expansive force' of holiness—the way it can act as leaven in

---

2 Cf. G. Le Bras, *La Chiesa del diritto. Introduzione allo studio delle instituzioni ecclesiastiche* (Bologna, 1976), p. 125.

human relationships, far beyond what might be deduced from the ups and downs of history, provided that that holiness is not mediated via the holy pictures typical of a certain kind of hagiography. It needs to be seen in all the robustness of the genuine, original article.

Looking at things from this angle, reflecting once again on the teachings of Blessed Josemaría Escrivá de Balaguer, as one would look at any other experience of holiness, also involves making contact with the 'expansive force' of holiness, to become leaven, and to prepare suitable human ground for the seed to grow.

Specifically, to reflect on how Christians are to give life to the world is equivalent to looking at the essential and solid core of Blessed Josemaría's teachings—his clear awareness of ordinary life as the place and means of sanctification, the universal call to holiness.

This awareness, which had begun in a supernatural experience, on August 7, 1931, during the celebration of the Eucharist, led Josemaría Escrivá to understand with unexpected depth the full significance of the words of verse 32 of chapter 12 of the Gospel of St. John: 'Et ego, si exaltatus fuero a terra, omnia traham ad meipsum'. This divine irruption in his soul—as it has been termed so well[3]—caused him to see, beyond the literal sense of John's words, that it is up to the Christian to put Christ at the peak of all upright human activities, in such a way that, by the force of attraction which that elevation causes, the world may be reconciled to God, his Kingdom may begin to be established, and the transformation of earthly realities may become a means of sanctification for oneself and others.

This intuition he had of the deeper meaning of the passage had a strong influence on his concept of Christian life in the world—which in turn considerably influenced the renewal of the Church in the second half of this century.

---

3 Cf. P. Rodriguez, in his fine essay, ' "Omnia traham ad meipsum". Il significato di Giovanni 12, 32 nell'esperienza di Mons. Escrivá de Balaguer', in *Annales theologici* 6 (1992/1), pp. 5–34.

We shall come back to that later. Now we shall return to what we were discussing when we began. It is worth pointing out perhaps that it is no accident that there has been a great growth in the number of causes of beatification and canonization during the present age of the Church; this is a phenomenon which only superficial observers criticize. The growth in the number seems to be an authoritative and unambiguous response by the Magisterium to the doctrine of the universal call to holiness; holiness is for the man in the street; it is something available to everyone and not just a chosen few. 'Do you really want to be a saint?', Escrivá asks in *The Way*. 'Carry out the little duty of each moment: do what you ought and concentrate on what you are doing.'[4]

II. Christianity and the world

History shows us that there has always existed a dialectical tension between Christianity and the world; quite often it has not been clear how Christianity should deal with the world; sometimes it is even argued that Christianity and the world are enemies.

Christian experience over the centuries has had to cope with two opposed temptations—that of fleeing from the world (the world being seen as something intrinsically bad, something incorrigible, irredeemably lost ever since the fall of man); and the other, deriving from the certain conviction that the structures of the temporal order can be fully rescued and entirely rechannelled in line with God's original plan. The first temptation, one charged with a heavy pessimism, argues that flight from the world is the only hope of salvation: it is just not possible for one to ensure one's spiritual integrity if the *magna latrocinia*[5] (fallen world) get in the way—and they do in the earthly city; the second temptation says that the dirt in which the earthly city is immersed can-

---

4 *The Way*, 815.

not stain angels, and it can be cleared away, allowing all creation to shine out, in its original and intrinsic beauty.

The first temptation induces an exaggerated and disembodied spiritualism; a manicheeism alien to the correct notion of man; a theology which loses sight of the essential reasons for and the inevitable consequences of the Incarnation; a detachment from things temporal so pronounced that it runs the risk of not listening to the lesson our Lord taught, as Acts bears witness—*pertransivit benefaciendo* (he went about doing good).[6]

The second temptation, on the other hand, leads inevitably to a secularization of our outlook and experience; increasing worldliness, forgetful of heaven; blind confidence in man's ability to shape a perfect world; and it gives rise to aberrant forms of social reform through revolutionary action, because it is inspired by the conviction (good in itself) that man is able to change social structures, ridding them of evil. One could say that, to a large extent, the revolutionary movements of the last two centuries have been secularized and aberrant forms of Christian moral imperatives.

To round off the analysis, one might point out that in the two thousand years of Christianity the world has suffered from two symmetrical and antithetical temptations—that of sacralizing earthly realities, especially earthly power, which reduces everything to the level of politics and makes politics lord of all; and that of secularization (especially effective in its laicist form), which banishes religion and the sacred from social life.

Clearly, these two temptations, operating in the two ways indicated, are the result of false premises and lead to conclusions which could be disastrous. As regards the Church, one need only recall the instances of flight from the world which occurred even in the early years of

---

5 St. Augustine, *De civitate Dei* IV, 4.
6 Acts 10:38.

Christianity, and which St. Paul wrote against;[7] or the aberrations of certain medieval heresies, especially if you view them in the light of the balanced teaching of St. Francis;[8] or the way some people, even good people, became timid and closed in on themselves in the face of growing secularism and events which clearly showed the devil to be at work in the world.[9] From the opposite point of view, there is the personal and social degeneration that has taken place which in some cases (in the area of ecclesial commitment as well as in political affairs) has given rise to the so-called theology of liberation; or in general the idiotic error of kneeling down before the world (a phrase Maritain coined)[10] committed by those Christians who believed (and believe) that there is no Kingdom of God other than the world, and that the world absorbs that kingdom into itself.

It is also clear that the mystery of the Incarnation sends us in a completely different direction, that of the Christian's relationship with the world; that relationship has *already* been established and yet it has *still* to come;

---

7 In this connection cf. the views of W.A. Meeks, *I cristiani dei primi secoli. Il mondo sociale dell'apostolo Paolo* (Bologna, 1992).

8 Speaking about Francis and his movement, Manselli observes how 'whereas the Cathars reject any pleasure which derives from the things of the world, his attitude is one of joy, but free from sins or fault [...]. The Cathars' view of the cosmos, sun, stars, water as being evil, Francis counters by his enthusiastic hymn of love to the universe as a splendid creation of divine Providence, in his *Hymn to Brother Sun*; and it is no accident that all this should lead up to a trusting praise of death, not as a gateway that is foreboding or as the start of a new incarnation, as the Cathars believed, but as the beginning of life eternal': R. Manselli, *Studi sulle eresie del secolo XII*, 2nd ed. (Rome, 1975), pp. 291f. Cf. F. Cardini, *Francesco d'Assisi* (Milan, 1989), pp. 117ff for an interesting reconstruction of the connections between early Franciscanism and Cathar teaching.

9 Typical of this is the disorientation that affected very many Christians in the face of the revolutionary upheaval at the end of the 18th century and subsequent events; these Christians were quick to interpret these events as basically anti-Christian. For a survey of such attitudes and a comparison of them with writings of those who tried to see Christian traces in these events, cf. V.E. Giuntella, *La religione amica della democrazia. I cattolici democratici del triennio rivoluzionario (1796–1799)*, (Rome, 1990).

10 J. Maritain, *The Peasant of the Garonne; an old layman questions himself about the present time* (New York, 1968), pp. 53ff.

the Christian confidently puts his hope on a Kingdom of God that is to come, but he also has the certainty that, with the coming of our Lord into this world, that Kingdom is already in the process of being implanted.

This is not the place to elaborate on this point. What we have said about the dialectical tension which has always been, in various ways, typical of Christians' attitude to the world, can teach us another interesting lesson from history which more directly serves our present purpose.

I refer to this: because of this dialectical tension the Church, almost in every generation, has had to re-learn what the true Christian way is, with reference not to a theoretical world but to actual historical circumstances, which can be very diverse. The entire history of the Church could be read in terms of a recurring need to recover its primitive purity (*Ecclesia semper reformanda*), returning to the way the first Christians lived, because the example they set is the closest to the example set by our Lord when he was on earth.)

But the history of the Church also shows that, from time to time, partly due to the social and cultural context of the time, there has also been a need to delve deeper into the Christian message; to become more aware (not only through *sapientia rationis*, but also through *sapientia cordis*) what the essential, most genuine, content of that message is, and to discover the lessons that content teaches. In the last analysis, the entire history of the Church evidences this tendency; and the history of holiness also, in a different way, shows us how to relearn the Christian message, insofar as the saint is someone who, in a particular human, cultural, social and historical context, has managed to do the will of God in an exemplary way.[11]

---

11 Cf. in this connection P. Molinari, 'La santità canonizzata', in *La santità cristiana* (Rome, 1980), pp. 349ff. There are interesting ideas on this subject in A.C. Jemolo, 'Chi è il santo?', in Pio IX. *Studi e ricerche sulla vita della Chiesa dal Settecento ad oggi*, I (1972), pp. 15ff.

Seen from this point of view, the figure of Monsignor Escrivá and the work he did are very eloquent.

This is a century marked by a feeling that everything is progressing to its final solution; it sees a need to discover in the world, and even in the cosmos (one cannot avoid thinking of the anguished adventure of a Teilhard de Chardin!)[12], the sign of God's great salvific plan and man's role in it. In this context Monsignor Escrivá's life clearly shows his great desire to get back to what being a Christian in the world really means, and it also shows the original contribution he made to the Church's constant search to make people more aware of their Christian calling. His basic teachings on the ways of holiness in the midst of ordinary life contain two key features.

From one point of view we have here a teaching and a personal experience which, although they have a personality of their own, can be set in the framework of the great lay movement which has been taking shape over the past century and a half, a movement involving various kinds of commitments and initiatives, and which has its own share of failures and remarkable undertakings. They all have one thing in common: they all derive from an attempt to help Christians today, in the context of the society in which they live, to discover what their specific mission is, in other words, the mission of sanctifying themselves. The people of God, guided by the Holy Spirit, has managed to become aware once more of what it means to be a *christifidelis*, and the laity have become more aware of what their role is in relation to earthly realities. And the Magisterium—from the great social encyclicals to the teachings of Vatican II— has authoritatively confirmed the achievements of the laity.

But, in addition to that, Monsignor Escrivá's teachings also constitute an original contribution to our understanding of the *sensus plenior*, the fuller meaning, of what is involved in being a Christian in the world.

---

12 J. Maritain spoke of a 'new gnosis' which 'is, like all gnoses–a poor gnosis', with regard to the thought of Teilhard, in *The Peasant of the Garonne*, pp. 116 ff.; pp. 264 ff. (the cited expression is on p. 122).

III. Christians, the life of the world

Christian 'animation' of the world, that is, changing the structures of the temporal order to bring them into line with the salvific mission of the Church, sums up the Magisterium of Vatican II on this subject, though the term *'animatio'* does not occur in the Council documents.[13]

Those documents frequently speak about *instauratio mundi* or they use similar words such as *aedificatio, extructio, institutio mundi* (clearly language deriving from St. Paul)[14], to show that the Church is committed to building the temporal order on the solid foundation established by Jesus Christ.

Also of Pauline origin, and widely used in ecclesiastical tradition, are other expressions used by Vatican II to indicate why the Church is entitled to strive to give earthly realities their true structure, that is, to share with Jesus in his dominion over all creation—or to indicate that the Christian, who has been recreated in Christ, is authorized to renew the world.

Always in this same connection, the Council uses other expressions such as *consecratio mundi* or *santificatio mundi*: the former expression came into general use as a result of theological reflection on the great lay movements of the 19th and 20th centuries (it refers to a role *proper* to lay people); the second expression is more closely linked to the Council itself and associated with the idea of lay people being leaven in the world (a point that Vatican II laid a lot of stress on).

It has often been pointed out that these and other expressions used in the Council documents to indicate the mission of *christifideles* (and, especially, lay people) have

---

13 One should see, on this theme, the wonderful and timely essay of M. Bleda Plans, 'Animazione cristiana del mondo', in *Dizionario enciclopedico di spiritualitá*, ed. E. Ancilli. New ed., v. 1, pp. 146–152 (Cittá Nuova, Rome, 1990).

14 Cf. 1 Cor 3:11; Eph 2:20.

fallen into disuse in postconciliar theological writing because of the possible danger of their being interpreted as meaning a more or less pronounced 'sacralization' of earthly realities. And, as we have pointed out, this is not only incompatible with a sound theological outlook grounded on the principle of the autonomy of the temporal order; it is also incompatible with Vatican II teachings, which are the most reliable point of reference on this subject.

For this reason we come back to the expression 'Christian animation of the world' or 'Christian animation of the temporal order': although not used in the Council texts these expressions have a long and authorized tradition, one closely linked to the relationship between Christians and the world. Thus, we can read in the *Epistle to Diognetus*: 'the relation of Christians to the world is that of a soul to its body. As the soul is diffused through every part of the body, so are Christians through all the cities of the world. The soul, too, inhabits the body, while at the same time forming no part of it; and Christians inhabit the world, but they are not part of the world.'[15]

First and foremost, the idea of Christians being the life of the world implies in no way a negative or pessimistic view of temporal realities. The world, a divine creation, is beautiful and good in itself: the Creator in his wisdom has inscribed an order on all its dimensions (from physical, chemical, biological, economic and other laws, which regulate material things, to the natural law, designed to regulate interpersonal relationships). It is no accident that Vatican II should speak of the 'autonomy' of earthly realities.[16]

---

15 *Epistle to Diognetus*, VI, 1–3.

16 Cf., for example, *Gaudium et spes*, 76. On the notion of autonomy in this passage see G. Dalla Torre. 'Stato laico e autonomia temporale', in *Il primato della coscienza. Laicità e libertà nell'esperienza giuridica contemporanea* (Rome, 1992), pp. 73–97.

It is man, with the concupiscence which derives from original sin, who disrupts the order of things and puts it out of joint with God's original plan which made man lord of all creation. He does this in two ways. Either by breaking the laws established by divine wisdom he fails to respect nature, (as we can see in the ecological problem) and even breaks moral laws (with resultant disorder, injustice and violence in personal and social relationships), or he is tempted to regard created things as his ultimate end, thereby closing himself off from others and from God.

In light of all this, the idea that Christians are the light of the world means this: that the *christifidelis*, thanks to the lessons learned from history, and his awareness that after the original fall man is not good deep down (contrary to the utopian thought of old and new forms of enlightenment), and also his realization that earthly things have a definite part in God's plan— thanks to this the Christian can and should act in such a way as to ensure that God's plan for the world is respected and fostered. Man knows that sin renders him incapable of putting God's plan into effect,[17] but that, by virtue of Christ's work of redemption, his own nature can be restored and healed.

Recognizing the autonomy of the temporal order does not mean, then, bringing more or less wide expanses of freedom under the control of 'ecclesiastical authority' or, to put it another way, 'sacralizing' them. On the contrary, it means accepting that earthly things are governed by principles and rules which should be respected, if they are to develop in a harmonious way in keeping with their own proper structure.

---

17 Cf. in this connection Gn 3:6–7, 16–19; 11:1–9, and also the text on Genesis by U. Neri with an introduction by G. Dossetti in *Biblia. I libri della Bibbia interpretati dalla grande Tradizione* (Turin, 1986) pp. 50ff.

It is worth noting that the Constitution *Gaudium et spes* speaks of 'autonomy', not of 'independence': for the principles and rules which govern the natural order are different but not separable from those that rule the spiritual order.

Also, the *christifidelis*, as the book of Genesis teaches, is also clearly aware that he is not only something *created*: in some way he shares in God's creation of the world. This is very evident in the area of work, through which, in a practical way, man carries on and 'completes', day after day, the work of the Creator. Scripture shows us that work precedes the fall of man; therefore, before it became a form of punishment, it was man's natural condition.

Christian 'animation' of the world means, therefore, not just shaping temporal affairs in keeping with God's plan but also sharing in the divine creation of the world (which is also part of that plan). John Paul II has outlined this idea very clearly in his Encyclical *Laborem exercens*.[18]

And there is still more to Christians' being the life of the world.

We know, for one thing, that from the history of the sin of Adam and the countless sins that have happened in its wake, evil comes from man, as we read in the Gospel of St. Mark (7:18–23): 'Do you not see that whatever goes into a man from outside cannot defile him, since it enters, not his heart but his stomach, and so passes on?[...] What comes out of a man is what defiles a man. For from within, out of the heart of man, come evil thoughts, fornication, theft, murder, adultery, greed, wickedness, deceit, licentiousness, envy, slander, pride, foolishness. All these evil things come from within, and they defile a man.' We also know that sin impacts negatively on earthly realities. Consequently, the irruption of

---

18 Cf. John Paul II, Enc. *Laborem exercens*, September 14, 1981, esp. no. 25. F. Viola, *Il lavoro umano e la dottrina sociale della Chiesa* (Palermo, 1991) goes into these points further.

God into human history through the Incarnation, must also leave its mark on earthly realities. The world has become a place of amendment and ransom; and, following the example of our Lord, who worked and suffered, man's work in the world has become a means of redemption.

Furthermore, by engaging in temporal affairs, the Christian can sanctify these things. In particular, the proper dimension of man (work) can be sanctified and, once sanctified, it sanctifies the worker and the worker can sanctify others by virtue of the apostolic dimension intrinsic to sanctified work. 'If we work with this spirit,' we read in a passage from Blessed Josemaría, 'our life, despite its human limitations, will be a foretaste of the glory of heaven, of that communion with God and his saints where self-giving, faithfulness, friendship and joy reign supreme. Your ordinary work will provide the true, solid, noble material out of which you will build a truly Christian life. You will use your work to make fruitful the grace which comes to us from Christ.'[19]

In this way, the Christian cooperates with the Lord Jesus in the task of drawing the universe towards the Father, in the eschatological perspective of the fulfillment of God's great salvific design, by virtue of which, St. Paul wrote, 'the whole creation has been groaning in travail

---

19 Bl. Josemaría Escrivá, Homily 'In Joseph's workshop', in *Christ Is Passing By*, 49. 'Your human vocation is a part—and an important part—of your divine vocation. That is the reason why you must strive for holiness, giving a particular character to your human personality, a style to your life; contributing at the same time to the sanctification of others, your fellow men; sanctifying your work and your environment—the profession or job that fills your day, that gives your personality its special features; your home and family; and the country where you were born and which you love' (ibid., 46). On the originality of Monsignor Escrivá's teachings on the sanctification of work, which certainly constitute a new chapter in the history of Christian spirituality, see the well-documented pages of the *Positio super vita et virtutibus*, prepared for the process of beatification (Romana et Matriten. Beatificationis et Canonizationis Servi Dei Iosephmariae Escrivá de Balaguer, Sacerdotis, Fundatoris Societatis Sacerdotalis S. Crucis et Operi Dei, *Positio super Vita et Virtutibus. Studium criticum super virtutum heroicitate* (Rome, 1988), pp. 895–925.

together'.[20] As Vatican II so incisively put it, 'all human activities, which are daily endangered by pride and inordinate selfishness, must be purified and perfected by the cross and resurrection of Christ'.[21]

IV. The Church and Christians, the life of the world

It is part of the job of the Church to bring about the Christian 'animation' of the world.

Vatican II is very clear on this point: 'The mission of the Church is not only to bring men the message and grace of Christ but also to recreate and improve the whole range of the temporal by means of the Gospel spirit.'[22] Therefore, 'it is the duty of the whole Church to equip men to establish the proper scale of values on the temporal order and to direct it towards God through Christ'.[23]

And the Pastoral Constitution on the Church in the World spells this out further: 'Christ did not bequeath to the Church a mission in the political, economic or social order: the purpose he assigned to it was a religious one. But this religious mission can be the source of commitment, direction and vigor to establish and consolidate the community of men according to the law of God.'[24]

Therefore, it is the Church as a whole that is entrusted with this mission and with the Christian 'animation' of the world. And, therefore, all the *cristifideles*, on account of their common Baptism, are called to carry out this task. But it is worth saying, too, that the Christian 'animation' of the world is a specifically lay activity.[25]

---

20 Rom 8:22.
21 Second Vatican Council, Const. *Gaudium et spes*, 37.
22 Second Vatican Council, Decr. *Apostolicam actuositatem*, 5.
23 Ibid., 7.
24 Second Vatican Council, Const. *Gaudium et spes*, 42.
25 A theological reflection on this subject is to be found in various authors, *Chi sono i laici. Una teologia della secolarità* (Milan, 1987).

The whole question has been much debated, as we all know. Undoubtedly, Vatican II rejected certain traditional ideas which regarded the lay person as a kind of tool that the Church, or, better yet, the hierarchy, could use for acting in the world; but it also rejected certain trends in ecclesiology which tried to establish the difference between lay people and clergy by arguing that the mission of the clergy lay *in the Church*, whereas the mission of the laity was *in the world*. So, the conciliar teachings stressed the oneness of the people of God, and their unitary participation in the *one* mission of the Church, while leaving it quite clear that there is a diversity of roles and ministries which differentiates the various kinds of people who make up the people of God.[26]

To identify the mission of the lay person, there is a passage in the Decree *Apostolicam actuositatem* which is very revealing. It says that lay people, carrying out the Church's mission to permeate and improve the whole range of the temporal with the Gospel spirit, 'exercise their own apostolate therefore in the world as well as in the Church, in the temporal order as well as in the spiritual. These orders are distinct; they are nevertheless so closely linked that God's plan is, in Christ, to take the whole world up again and make of it a new creation, in an initial way here on earth, in full realization at the end of time.'[27]

If, going beyond the difference in *status* between lay person and cleric, one looks at their diversity of functions *within* the ecclesial community, one can get much closer to the definition of what a lay person is. Whereas, by looking at their different roles, clerics can be defined

---

26 To understand conciliar teaching on this, including the legal problems it raises and what they imply at the level of actual Christian experience, A. del Portillo's thoughts in *Fieles y laicos en la Iglesia*, op. cit., are essential reading; they have particularly inspired subsequent canon law studies in this regard.

27 Second Vatican Council, Decr. *Apostolicam actuositatem*, 5. For further reading on some of these points I might suggest my own *Considerazioni preliminari sui laici in diritto canonico* (Modena, 1983).

as those members of the faithful given sacred ministries, and religious are those who are called to give public witness, in the name of the Church, to the spirit of the beatitudes and the 'new heaven' and the 'new earth' through *separatio a saeculo*. Lay people should be seen as those members of the faithful 'to whom it belongs by their special vocation to seek the Kingdom of God by engaging in temporal affairs and directing them according to God's will.'[28] That is to say, to quote the famous conciliar statement, 'their secular character is proper and peculiar to the laity'.[29]

Recapitulating, one can sum up as follows the responsibility proper to lay people by virtue of their vocation and condition (which gives rise to a true ecclesial *munus* proper to them): to engage in temporal affairs, imbuing the activities and structures of the *civitas terrena* with Christian spirit, by becoming the soul of society in the world of work, professional life, culture, and all other dimensions of civil life. In this connection, *Lumen gentium* goes on to say that lay people 'are called by God that, being led by the spirit of the Gospel, they may contribute to the sanctification of the world, as from within like leaven'.[30] And the postsynodal Exhortation on the Vocation and Mission of Lay People in the Church and in the World says that 'The vocation of the lay faithful to holiness implies that life according to the Spirit expresses itself in a particular way in their *involvement in temporal affairs* and in their *participation* in earthly activities.'[31]

---

28 Second Vatican Council, Const. *Lumen gentium*, 31.

29 Ibid. As G. Lo Castro observes, in his *Il soggetto e i suoi diritti nell'ordinamento canonico* (Milan, 1985), p. 83: 'lay character is not merely descriptive of a social and ecclesial commitment (sanctification of temporal realities) but is also a constituent element of a juridical condition in the Church—that of the lay person.'

30 Second Vatican Council, Const. *Lumen gentium*, 31.

31 John Paul II, Apos. Exhort. *Christifideles laici*, December 30, 1988, 17.

As theological teaching has shown, to bring all this about lay people need to have certain prerequisites, such as an ability to carry out the activity proper to them with all due natural perfection. And, therefore, they need to have the necessary work skills; they need a strong 'civic sense' (allow me to use that non-theological expression), rooted in a sense of justice and solidarity, along with which should go a deep awareness of their responsibilities both as citizens and as Christians;[32] they need a deep knowledge of the Christian Faith, which is the light that will illuminate their minds and sustain them in their doings; and they should have a deep interior life, nourished by the Word of God, the sacraments and prayer.[33]

It is important to stress, especially as regards the way contemporary man can be 'conditioned' by the 'spirit of the age',[34] that the work a Christian does to give life to the world is something that is linked to objective values, and it is up to the Magisterium of the Church to identify these and ground them properly: it is its mission to enunciate and explain the doctrinal principles which should show people the way, here and now, to set in motion the Christian 'animation' of the world.[35]

---

32 On the joint responsibility for the common good as a moral duty, cf. Mt 22:21. See also The Catechism of the Catholic Church, nos. 2238 ff.

33 On this point, I again refer the reader to M. Belda Plans, *Animazione cristiana del mondo*, op. cit., pp. 151ff.

34 Suffice it to think of that extolling of liberty which goes so far as to make it an absolute and the source of ethical values, thereby leading to full-blown subjectivism on moral questions; this is something which John Paul II rightly stigmatizes in his enclyclical *Veritatis splendor*, August 6, 1993, esp. in nos. 31–4. Insights into the so-called 'spirit of the age' are to be found in J. Ratzinger, *A turning point for Europe? The Church in the modern world: assessment and forecast* (San Francisco, 1994).

35 Cf. in this connection the views of a canon lawyer: C.J. Errázuriz, *Il 'munus docendi Ecclesiae': diritti e doveri dei fedeli* (Milan, 1991), esp. pp. 77ff.

V. Between tradition and renewal

We have already referred to the fact that the teaching and spiritual experience of Blessed Josemaría Escrivá de Balaguer has simultaneously deepened the furrow of a tradition which in the past two centuries has put forward a more balanced and consistent concept of the Church, and is a most original contribution to our deeper grasp of what Christian life means.

We should say something here about Christian experience. For Monsignor Escrivá's contribution to the great heritage of spirituality and culture which sanctity builds up over time and which constitutes an invaluable treasure for the Church, is not (or is not primarily) a new theological doctrine, no matter how original such a doctrine might prove to be and no matter how much it might help towards a better understanding of the Christian mystery. No, what it is, rather, is a spiritual and supernatural experience which, like a light flooding in from outside, helps bring about a deeper appreciation of that mystery and opens up for Christians new ways in the *sequela Christi*, the following of Christ. So, while there was much theological writing that prepared the cultural ground for Vatican II,[36] the work of Monsignor Escrivá formed part of a series of Christian experiences which in some way anticipated *Lumen gentium* and *Apostolicam actuositatem*, and which yielded their spiritual fruit many years prior to the holding of the Council.

If one wants to discover one of the core elements in his contribution, one must surely start from that deep stimulus which pushed him to seek out new ways within the Church. I refer to the emphasis running through all his writings on that great temptation forever threatening the Christian living in the world—that of leading 'a

---

36 For example, as regards the question of lay people in the Church, there is Y.M. Congar's essential work, *Lay people in the Church; a study for a theology of laity* (Westminster, 1965).

double life: on the one side, an interior life, a life relating to God; and on the other, a separate and distinct professional, social and family life, full of small earthly realities'. On the contrary, Monsignor Escrivá almost shouted, 'We cannot lead a double life. We cannot be like schizophrenics, if we want to be Christians. There is just one life, made of flesh and spirit. And it is this life which has to become, in both soul and body, holy and filled with God. We discover the invisible God in the most visible and material things.'[37]

One consequence of that spur, that stimulus, was that supernatural experience we referred to at the beginning. As Monsignor Escrivá himself recalled, 'For many years now, ever since the foundation of Opus Dei, I have meditated and asked others to meditate on those words of Christ which we find in St. John: 'And when I am lifted up from the earth I shall draw all things unto myself' (Jn 12:32). By his death on the Cross, Christ has drawn all creation to himself. Now it is the task of Christians, in his name, to reconcile all things to God, placing Christ, by means of their work in the middle of the world, at the peak of all human activities.'[38]

This intuition would involve going beyond (but not excluding) a series of inherited notions about Christianity which had been gaining acceptance over recent decades. For example (in the area of apostolate), the idea of 'Christian witness'; or (in connection with Christians' civil responsibilities), the ideal of commitment in the sphere of politics and economics which (in the wake of Leo XIII's great encyclical) was such a feature of the first fifty years of the social teaching of the church.[39]

---

37 Bl. Josemaría Escrivá, 'Passionately loving the world', in *Conversations*, 114.

38 Ibid., 59.

39 For an overview, cf. A. Acerbi, *La Chiesa nel tempo. Sguardi sui progetti di relazioni tra chiesa e società civile negli ultimi cento anni* (Milan, 1979). 'His (Christ's) hidden years are not without significance, nor were they simply a preparation for the years which were to come after—those of his public life': *Christ Is Passing By*, 20.

Monsignor Escrivá's experience goes much further than that. It throws light on a key fact: the way that Jesus Christ lived his human life (including long years of hidden and 'ordinary' life, to which Monsignor Escrivá used to so insistently call attention)[40] is the best possible life, the most just, the happiest, the most human.[41] That is why he stands as an example, legitimating and encouraging the Christian's commitment to give life to the world.

But, to the degree that Christians follow the Lord's example, become one with him and make him manifest, raising him up for all to see, the salvific mission of drawing all things to himself is being continued on this earth.

'Stay with us, for it is toward evening and the day is now far spent.' That beautiful passage in St. Luke's Gospel,[42] the literary attractiveness of which helps to make its meaning clear, marvellously reveals our Lord's very human way of acting, which could not but draw people to him. 'Did not our hearts burn within us while he talked to us on the road, while he opened to us the scriptures?',[43] the disciples asked each other in surprise, once Jesus had disappeared from sight. And truly, their invitation for him to stay still conveys to us, despite the intervening centuries, the tensions of souls who, without realizing it, had been enjoying the Lord's company and now were afraid he would leave them, no matter how much they needed him.

The experience of Blessed Josemaría Escrivá de Balaguer helps us to get past the literal meaning and understand better the profound significance of the message which this passage contains.

---

40 Cf., for example, *Christ Is Passing By*, 20.
41 On holiness as the perfection of man, cf. P. Palazzini, 'La santità coronamento della dignità dell'uomo', in *Miscellanea in occasione del IV Centenario della Congregazione per le cause dei Santi* (Vatican City, 1988), pp. 221ff.
42 Lk 24:29.
43 Lk 24:32.

Work, justice, charity

José-Luis Illanes, University of Navarre

Someone who studies the person and teachings of Blessed Josemaría Escrivá de Balaguer cannot but notice the force, and even the clarity, of the charism which was the underlying inspiration behind his activity from that crucial day, October 2, 1928, when he realized that God wanted him to devote his life and all his energies to the foundation and furthering of Opus Dei.

After that date, of course, there was a broadening and a development and a whole process of deepening whereby his actual experience and his personal reflection and prayer enabled him to spell things out more exactly and in a more elaborate way. But the documentary sources and the recollections of those who were with Josemaría Escrivá during the first stages of the history of Opus Dei all testify to the fact that, from the very beginning, not only did he have a very strong grasp of the basic 'blueprint' but he also had a way of putting things, a language, which enabled him to communicate very clearly the message he felt impelled to pass on.

This is true also in connection with the subject we are going to look at— work. Among other possible examples, we will propose a paragraph from his 'Apuntes íntimos' (private notes) which dates from June 1930 and in which, in a very few words, he describes precisely— sculpts, so to speak— the characteristics of the spiritual and apostolic reality he knew he was called to spread and which, around that very time, he had begun to call Opus Dei, Work of God: 'Ordinary Christians. A fermenting mass. Ours is the ordinary, with naturalness. Medium: professional work. All saints!'[1]

---

1 'Apuntes íntimos' (private notes), 35.

I. Work, the core element in Blessed Josemaría Escrivá's spiritual teaching

The density of these few words suggests that we should analyze them and comment on them in some detail to work out what they mean and set his message on the subject of work into that context.

As I see it, these words can be seen to contain three great assertions:

— First and foremost, the proclamation of the universal call to holiness: 'All saints!' Christ died for every human being. Everyone needs to know that he is loved by God, and loved in a special, immediate way; even more than that—he is called by name, to share in God's friendship. No Christian—in fact, more radically still, no human being—is just an individual, just one among many, part of a mass. If mankind sometimes seems to be a shapeless mass, that is because God's call has been forgotten, or people don't know about it; in which case it needs to be stirred up, to be leavened, until each and every person recognizes his true identity as a son or daughter of God, as beings with an infinite capacity, beings open to eternity.

— Secondly, these words show Opus Dei to be an institution made up of Christians who, having become aware of the divine call that Baptism implies, aspire to spread that awareness among those around them, and to do so not 'somehow' but through their very lives as 'ordinary Christians', committed to the tasks and involvements that they share with people in general. In this way they show, not in a theoretical but in a practical way, with the simplicity and eloquence of life—'ours is the ordinary, with naturalness'—that nothing is alien to God, that daily life, with all the little events that go to make it up, is meant to be the place, the occasion, for an encounter with Christ and, in Christ, with God.

— Lastly, there is the idea of work—'medium: professional work'—being a key element in human and Christian life and, consequently, being *the* place to bear witness to the nearness of God, and the place to draw close to him, that is, to respond lovingly to the love that God himself has shown us.

These three assertions stand on different levels—first, the theological-dogmatic level; second, the ecclesicenteral and institutional; third, the anthropological. However, in the message of Blessed Josemaría Escrivá de Balaguer (and in the life of Opus Dei) they go to make up a single, profound unit. From the point of view of logic and ontology, the primary dimension is, undoubtedly, the assertion of the universal call to holiness and apostolate: this sheds its light on both the sanctifiable and sanctifying value of human work, and on Opus Dei as an institution designed to foster, in the midst of the world, an effective search for holiness. In one sense, from a historical-biographical point of view, the order is different: what Monsignor Escrivá de Balaguer perceived on October 2, 1928 was the divine call to organize a pastoral initiative of Christian life in the world, and, in connection with that, and at its center, to promote Opus Dei as an institution. So, the universal call to holiness is as it were the backdrop, the basic presupposition, and at the same time the goal, of the mission God invited him to undertake and to which, from that first moment (that is, October 2, 1928), he in fact devoted all his energies.

This is not the right place to discuss the universal call to holiness or the institutional aspects of Opus Dei; rather, we must focus our attention on what this 1930 quotation has to say about the value of ordinary life, and, in that context, about work.[2] What do these statements imply; where do they come from and where are they leading?

---

2 Other papers read at the symposium have already dealt with the first of these themes; I would also refer the reader to what I have said in this connection in my *Mundo y santidad* (Madrid, 1984), pp. 65ff. As regards the second theme, and more specifically on the light which those reflections throw on theological appreciation of Opus Dei as an institution, see P. Rodríguez, F. Ocáriz and J.L. Illanes, *Opus Dei in the Church* (Dublin, 1994), esp. pp. 4–9 and 122–4.

In his preaching, and especially in his earliest preaching, Blessed Josemaría (except occasionally) did not go into formal argument: his style was assertive. He did not speak like a thinker or a theologian who, having come to a conclusion, wanted to get it across to others by giving arguments and reasons: he spoke in a spiritual way, like a man who had experienced the nearness of God and was bearing witness to that experience to those around him with a forcefulness which derived from his personal encounter with God, and also from increasingly profound reflection on the Gospel to which that encounter led him. In other words, the constant reference to ordinary life and work which one finds in the writings of Blessed Josemaría is not the outcome of his reflection on man and the history of man: it is a result of his spiritual experience of October 2, 1928—of his awareness of the task which that experience laid on him and which was intimately linked to the call to sanctification in the middle of the world and the reference to work.

This does not mean, of course, that that reference to ordinary life and the pride of place given to work did not imply anthropological presuppositions, or that his preaching was devoid of argumentation and reasons; it simply means that those arguments and reasons, that spelling out of the presuppositions, were not the point from which he started, but something, so to speak, which came later, a further stage, as a sort of intellectual probing of his original spiritual experience. The foundational impulse which Monsignor Escrivá de Balaguer received on October 2, 1928 led him to address men and women of all walks of life, in order to make them aware of what being a Christian meant, and to encourage each person to sanctify his or her position in the world and his or her work. So, in the context of that real life, of his personal experience, he was gradually explaining and spelling out the implications of his original charism (and this meant, very particularly, explaining the full implications of human work). So, before we try to answer the questions posed above (and to give a fuller answer to them), it will be useful to look a bit closer at Monsignor Escrivá's life.

If there was one distortion of Christianity which Blessed Josemaría Escrivá fought against his whole life long, it was undoubtedly what the French call *surnaturel plaqué*, supernatural veneering (quite close to the terminology Josemaría Escrivá used), a cleavage between the man and the Christian—a way of thinking and, in some instances, a lifestyle in which faith has no real influence on one's thoughts and actions, with the result that Christian truth, even though one accepts and professes it, is confined to shadows, and one's real life goes on regardless.

His work as a priest in Saragossa and Madrid in the thirties brought him into contact with many Christians who lived consistently with their faith, but also gave him contact with environments sometimes steeped in a laicism which excluded the Christian element from social structures and, even more so, from culture, and other environments marked by a pietistic devotion which locked the Faith inside the prison of an ethereal and historically irrelevant interiority. From the very depth of his being, Blessed Josemaría strove to heal those breaches and, especially, to provoke, in sincere but run-of-the-mill or superficial Christians, a spiritual crisis, a conversion, which would bring them to see the all-embracing power of faith. Being a Christian is not something 'adjectival', something that affects the person only externally or tangentially: it is a vigor, a life, which lies at the very depths, the very core of one's being, shedding light on all aspects of one's life, showing one that life can and should be lived as a calling from God and lived in communion and dialogue with him.

In a homily he gave in 1967 on the campus of the University of Navarre, Monsignor Escrivá referred to those yearnings of his in the early years. The truth of Christianity—the intimate connection it establishes between the divine and the human, between the physical and the spiritual, as can be seen from the dogma of the

Incarnation and from the Eucharist—is misunderstood, he began, 'whenever people have tried to present the Christian way of life as something exclusively "spiritual", proper to "pure", extraordinary people, who remain aloof from the contemptible things of this world or, at most, tolerate them as something necessarily attached to the spirit while we live on this earth. When things are seen in this way,' he went on, 'churches become the setting *par excellence* of the Christian life. And being a Christian means going to church, taking part in sacred ceremonies, being taken up with ecclesiastical matters, in a kind of segregated "world", which is considered to be the antechamber of heaven, while the ordinary world follows its own separate path. The doctrine of Christianity and the life of grace would, in this case, brush past the turbulent march of human history, without ever really meeting it.'[3]

Against that attitude, against that disembodied spirituality, 'I often said,' he went on, 'to the university students and workers who were with me in the thirties, that they had to know how to "materialise" their spiritual life. I wanted to keep them from the temptation, so common then and now, of living a kind of double life. On one side, an interior life, a life of relation with God; and on the other, a separate and distinct professional, social and family life, full of small earthly realities. No! We cannot lead a double life. We cannot be like schizophrenics, if we want to be Christians. There is just one life, made of flesh and spirit. And it is this life which has to become, in both soul and body, holy and filled with God. We discover the invisible God in the most visible and material things.'[4]

I have given a rather long quotation, but I think it is useful. Let us say something about it. First, there is one thing we need to remember: the root of what it means

---

[3] *Conversations*, 113. This homily can also be found in the book *Josemaría Escrivá de Balaguer y la Universidad* (Pamplona, 1993), pp. 113–130.

[4] *Conversations*, 114.

to be and live as a Christian lies not in the person himself or in the world, but in Christ: it is none other than the grace given the Christian in Baptism and reaffirmed in the subsequent calls and gifts he receives from God.[5] But grace takes shape in and through history, in man's free response, in the actions, great and small, which go to make up each and every day that passes. And, in the case of the ordinary Christian called by God to sanctify himself in the midst of the world and through the world, that 'world' is the world in which he lives and where God wants him to be. So, for the ordinary Christian, his situation in the world, the obligations, interests and aspirations which that implies, is the 'material' (as Josemaría Escrivá puts it)[6] which, imbued with grace, is to produce a holy life, to shape and develop man as a Christian as that life in the world unfolds.[7]

That situation in the world (as we have just said, but it is worth stressing) involves a whole gamut of things and tasks—work, family life, friendship, social or political activities, entertainment, rest, contemplation of nature, thought, art etc... All these things, each in its appropriate way, have to be imbued with grace. The totality of ordinary life is, for the average Christian, 'material' he has to use to build holiness: in other words, this Christian is called, as Blessed Josemaría puts it, 'to sanctify ordinary life, sanctify oneself in ordinary life and sanctify others through ordinary life', to make ordinary life, all of it, an opportunity to meet God and to fill out all the dimensions of Christian living.[8]

---

5 This baptismal grounding of Christian experience, as found in the preaching of Bl. Josemaría Escrivá, is identified in P. Rodríguez, *Vocación, trabajo, contemplación*, 2nd ed. (Pamplona, 1986), pp. 105ff.

6 Cf., for example, *Conversations*, 70.

7 On the meaning and scope of the phrase 'ordinary Christian' which we have already used twice here (and will use further) as found in the writings of Bl. Josemaría, see what we have said in *Opus Dei in the Church*, op. cit., pp. 131–420.

8 Perhaps the most relevant text is the homily 'The greatness of ordinary life', in *Friends of God*, 1ff.

The synthetic and programatic phrase we have just quoted ('sanctifying ordinary life, sanctifying oneself in ordinary life and sanctifying others through ordinary life') occurs frequently in Monsignor Escrivá de Balaguer's writings and preaching, but there is one he uses even more often, almost an identical one: 'sanctifying one's work, sanctifying oneself in work, and sanctifying others through work'.[9] Do these two expressions really mean exactly the same thing? In other words, why, out of the whole range of things which make up life in the world, in the ordinary circumstances in which people live, why does the founder of Opus Dei single out work in this way?

To get the answer it is helpful—necessary, in fact—to go back to the 1930 text in order to underline one key thing: what Blessed Josemaría is talking about is not work in a generic, imprecise sense but, rather, 'professional' work concretely and specifically. Something he was always conscious of, a constant reference-point in his writing and preaching, was not work in the sense of just an intellectual or manual activity, but work in all its anthropological and social dimensions, work as a stable occupation which both authenticates the person and involves him in building human society and shaping its future.[10]

'Professional' work presupposes knowledge and skills, it shapes one's attitudes and ways of thinking, it leads to friendship and companionship, it helps one to support oneself and one's family, it provides resources for the society of which the worker forms a part, it puts him in contact with the ideas, aspirations, needs and problems that affect that society and explain its history . . .

---

9 Cf., for example, *Christ Is Passing By*, 46ff.

10 We had occasion to explore these aspects of the founder of Opus Dei's teaching in an essay published in various editions: cf. *La santificación del trabajo*, 6th ed. (Madrid, 1981), esp. pp. 37-44; the first edition came out in 1966 and was published in English as *On the theology of work* (Dublin and New York, 1982).

in other words, 'professional' work (and, more specifically, the actual, efficient doing of that work) not only takes up a good proportion of a person's time (usually much more than other activities): by its very nature it implies and sets up a dynamic which affects some of the deepest aspects of the human being. 'Professional' work means, really, ordinary life in its totality; life as a whole as seen from the angle of one of the factors or elements which, impacting strongly on the person (man grows and matures through work), in turn helps to shape and develop societies.

Sanctifying ordinary life and sanctifying work ('professional' work) are things which go hand in hand: each has reference to the other. One cannot speak of sanctification of work except in the context of a decision to orient one's entire life so that one lives it with one's sights set on God. And one cannot conceive of a sanctification of ordinary life unless there is real, effective sanctification of work. A theological life which fails to influence how one does one's work would inevitably be a life lived on the margin of real life and therefore on the periphery of one's personality: it would produce that cleavage between the man and the Christian we spoke about earlier. However, a theological life which develops to the point of influencing one's profession (that is the totality of the dimensions that the exercise of 'professional' work implies) affects or is going to affect one's entire existence, and through that personal existence it will impact on the fabric of society.

II. Professional work and Christian living

'Work, all work, bears witness to the dignity of man, to his dominion over creation. It is an opportunity to develop one's personality. It is a bond of union with others, the way to support one's family, a means of helping to improve the society in which we live and the progress of all humanity.

For a Christian these horizons extend and grow wider. For work is a participation in the creative work of God. When he created man and blessed him, he said: "Be fruitful, multiply, fill the earth, and conquer it. Be masters of the fish of the sea, the birds of heaven and all animals living on the earth" (Gen 1:28). And, moreover, since Christ took it into his hands, work has become for us a redeemed and redemptive reality. Not only is it the background of man's life, it is a means and path to holiness. It is something to be sanctified and something which sanctifies.'[11]

These words, taken from a 1963 homily, are a good example of how far Monsignor Escrivá's thought matured as a result of his constant meditation over the years since 1928; and they also splendidly sum up what we have been trying to say in the previous paragraphs. Here we see work being depicted as something in which the human and the Christian intersect to the point of becoming fused together: work is a task thanks to which man and history develop, and an activity which at its very roots is illuminated by the light shed by Christian faith. This work is 'professional' work, work in the sense of a permanent, socially accepted occupation, work as such and as it is shaped in each historical moment in line with the different forms of profession that develop. It is what the Christian who lives in the world is called to sanctify, recognizing and proclaiming its full Christian value. It is not just the 'setting' in which a life takes place but which is in the last analysis alien to it, it is 'something to be sanctified and something which sanctifies' and therefore it is a constituent, integral part of one's development as a Christian. Furthermore, given the central position professional work holds in all ordinary Christian life (as a structural element which shapes it) one can go so far as to say that Christian existence, which is born of Christ and grace, has professional work as its

---

11 *Christ Is Passing By*, 47.

'axis' or 'hinge'.[12] In fact, it is around work, in and through the doing of work, that, for the ordinary Christian whom God wants to be in the midst of the world, the life of grace is supposed to develop and grow.

It is not surprising that, working from these premises, Blessed Josemaría should devote so much of his time and interest to showing in a practical way (as befits someone who, more than anything else, was a great educator of souls) how the key elements of the Christian ideal can be channelled into professional work. Living in the world, working hard at his profession, the Christian, can, no longer despise the world, but being fully committed to his work, and actually availing himself of the world and work, can really put the Gospel ideal into practice and reach the heights of holiness.

'An hour of study, for a modern apostle, is an hour of prayer,' he says in *The Way*.[13] Many years later, in 1960, he is still talking along the same lines: 'We would be on the wrong path if we were to disregard temporal affairs, for our Lord awaits us there as well. You can be sure that it is through the circumstances of ordinary life, ordained or permitted by the infinite wisdom of divine Providence, that we have to draw close to God.'[14] And, in another passage, already quoted, which comes from 1963: 'We see the hand of God, not only in the wonders of nature, but also in an experience of work and effort. Work thus becomes prayer and thanksgiving, because we know we are placed on earth by God, that we are loved by him and made heirs to his promises. We have just been rightly told, "in eating, in drinking, in all that you do, do everything for God's glory" (1 Cor 10:31).' He concludes: 'Faith, hope and charity will come into place in your professional work done for God. The inci-

---

12 The words in quotes are Monsignor Escrivá's own: cf., for example, *Christ Is Passing By*, 45.

13 *The Way*, 335; this point is found, in another wording, in the book that preceded *Camino* (*The Way*), that is, *Consideraciones espirituales* (Cuenca, 1934), p. 34.

14 *Friends of God*, 63.

dents, the problems, the friendships which your work brings with it, will give you food for prayer. The effort to improve your own daily occupation will give you the chance to experience the cross, which is essential for a Christian. When you feel your weakness, the failures which arise even in human undertakings, you will gain in objectivity, in humility and in understanding for others. Successes and joys will prompt you to thanksgiving and to realize that you do not live for yourself but for the service of others and of God.'[15]

To these passages, which summarize his thinking, we could add others, fuller and more complex texts in which he puts before us the full gamut of aspects and dimensions of living out Christianity—the rich, broad world of the virtues, prayer, contemplative dialogue, sharing in Christ's cross, service of others, fraternity and apostolate . . . Work, the everyday exercise of one's profession, with all the obligations it implies and all the little events that make it up—that work, if faced up to with faith, aware of how near God is, leads to dialogue with God, identification with his will, and solid growth in virtue. This same work also constantly provides opportunities to contribute to the welfare of others, to do one's bit for the common good, to open, for one's friends and colleagues, horizons of theological and Christian life by means of a testimony and a word which arise in the context of work and everyday events.[16]

All this (and this is the key point) happens not only apropos of work, but in and through work, sanctifying it, doing it competently, down to the last detail. Becoming holy through work and sanctifying others through work are, in fact, the same thing as sanctifying work: they are not just things that happen at the same time, or side by side: they are all aspects of a single process, one and the same spiritual dynamic. For, let us not forget, the work being spoken about here is not just keep-

---

15 *Christ Is Passing By*, 48 and 49.
16 For more on this cf. *La sanctificación del trabajo*, op. cit., pp. 71ff.

ing one's hands and mind occupied, but 'professional' work, with all the demands, chores, interests, relationships and duties that it involves. So it is a fully human enterprise in which the whole man sees himself committed and which therefore involves not only all his faculties, but affects his deep-rooted attitude to life. Here man engages his entire being: everything he does helps towards his self-expression and his growth as a man and a Christian.

Work, in the sense of 'professional' work, is not just using some one or many of one's human faculties (that would only tangentially touch the person); it is an activity which, deep down inside him, commits the worker to what he is doing; it is an activity, all of whose aspects (objective and subjective, 'productive' and person-building) are mutually interdependent and interactive. The ideal of the sanctification of work, as Blessed Josemaría proclaimed it and made it known, implies two basic convictions or presuppositions to which we have been referring from the start but which now, having reached this point, we might summarize somewhat better:

— On the one hand, he sees professional work as a constitutive part of the human condition and a key factor in shaping both the person *qua* person and society as a whole. Working—more specifically working with the seriousness, stability and competence that professional dedication implies—is at one and the same time an expression and a source of human maturity: a person who faces up to his work shows that he is really serious about his life and the obligations it involves, and he has set in motion a process in which his personality is forged and developed. Work is, at one and the same time, something that man does and a task through which he matures; it is an act which presupposes the spiritual condition of the person who carries it out, and his ability to take responsibility for his own life; and a task through which that life is in fact engaged and which makes him grow in his own humanity.

— On the other hand, he is very keenly conscious of the truth and depth of the redemption wrought by Christ, and therefore of the vivifying power of grace, which, rooted as it is in the very core of the human being, redounds (aspires to redound) to the benefit of his entire being. Nothing in the Christian should remain foreign to faith, to man's condition as someone redeemed by Christ, made part of Christ's body and, in Christ and through the Holy Spirit, led to live in communion with God the Father. The Christian should feel called to imbue all aspects of life with faith—allowing all the energy which comes from Christ to spread out and to impel him to always love with the love of Christ himself.

These two presuppositions combine to create the ideal of the sanctification of work; and whether or not the energies produced by these presuppositions actually do combine depends on the sanctification of work. In other words, the sanctification of work presupposes that the man and the Christian are involved there together: 'if, for there to be work (human work) well done, the *man* needs first to be present, so that sanctification of work can result (that is, the elevation of work to the order of grace), this task (work) needs to be undertaken by someone who is (also prior to the action) *a Christian.*'[17] This means that in the process of work, in the effort to sanctify work in fact, the man and the Christian grow inseparably and jointly.

All this is equivalent to saying that the ideal of the sanctification of work is not achieved in an impersonal or automatic way: like every ideal, it becomes real through the exercise of man's freedom, and in real time, in a dynamic and progressive way. For someone to ap-

---

17 P. Rodríguez, *Vocación, trabajo, contemplación*, op. cit., p. 191; see pp. 188–93.

preciate this ideal properly, he must first be aware (to a minimum degree at least) of what it means to be a man and a Christian: he needs to have some degree of both human and Christian maturity. And the effort to put that ideal into practice calls for and helps towards a genuine human and Christian lifestyle and needs to be increasingly rooted in that dual maturity.

III. At the summit of all human activities

More than once, in the course of what we have said above, when quoting from Blessed Josemaría Escrivá or commenting on the text, we have referred to the many facets of professional work, and more specifically to the fact that that work concerns not only the individual but society in general; up to this point, however, we have focused our attention on spiritual growth or development. However, it is worth looking also at the other ('horizontal') aspect of the question, in order to get a more complete notion of what 'professional' work is and of what Blessed Josemaría Escrivá's message is in this regard.

The end of the 19th century and the beginning of the 20th saw a considerable flowering of lay associations and institutions. Many of them were designed to foster social and civic action, or, to use the terminology widespread at that time, to 'rechristianize' society. In a historical and cultural context marked by profound change and, not uncommonly, by laicist or secularizing political attitudes, it was to be expected that initiatives should arise which aimed at encouraging Catholics (and therefore the Christian spirit) to make their presence felt in social life and institutions. During those same years Blessed Josemaría was given the light which gave rise to Opus Dei and it was then that he began his work, which eventually grew and developed. Those who witnessed this process, on hearing his preaching and noticing how vigorously he asserted the divine calling of the ordinary Christian, might have had the impression that Opus Dei was one more expression, one more instance, of the sort of initiatives in the field of Christian social action to which we have referred. In fact that was not the case, for the inspiration which gave rise to Opus Dei had special accents of its own, which distinguish it from those other movements etc., as Josemaría Escrivá himself stressed, unambiguously, from the very start.[18]

Of course, even when he was beginning his pastoral work, Blessed Josemaría's apostolic horizon did include the radiation of the Christian message in society and in social structures: that was only to be expected, for the goal of his priestly work was the spread of holiness and apostolate in the midst of the world. From early youth and from the time he was training to be a priest, he was deeply affected by the ideal of harmony between faith and reason, between Christianity and human culture. And, from 2 October 1928 onwards, he was aware that the Work he was called to develop could and should make a big contribution to the lives of Christians who, motivated by a strong faith, aspired to imbue their actions and therefore human institutions generally with the Spirit of Christ.

That goes without saying. And yet there is this fact we mentioned—that Opus Dei is not part of the movement of ideas or the institutions to which we have previously referred. In his early years and throughout his life Blessed Josemaría Escrivá's work as a priest did not have as its direct aim the transformation of social structures and of cultures, or, in more general terms, Christian 'animation' of the world: what he was looking for was the sanctification of concrete, individual persons; he wanted men and women to meet Christ; by his word and his message he wanted people to realize that they were called to a personal relationship with God, and to be personally committed to God. In other words, Christian transformation of the world was not, according to

---

18 On this point we have written at length in A. de Fuenmajor, V. Gómez Iglesias and J.L. Illanes, *The Canonical Path of Opus Dei. The History and Defense of a Charism* (Princeton and Chicago, 1994), pp. 45ff, whose conclusions we summarize here.

Blessed Josemaría's own way of seeing things (or as Opus Dei continues to see things), a goal: it was rather a result, a foreseen effect or consequence, even something to be expected, but not because it was sought directly: it would come about as a logical and necessary consequence of what he was directly trying to do and bring about, that is, holiness sought and found in the midst of the world.

Having said this (and it is something not to be lost sight of), it must be said again that that result or effect is something confidently foreseen and sincerely expected, as a well-known point of *The Way* makes clear: 'A secret, an open secret: these world crises are crises of saints. God wants a handful of men "of his own" in every human activity. And then . . . *"pax Christi in regno Christi*—the peace of Christ in the kingdom of Christ.'[19] Nor is this point of *The Way* an isolated passage or a stray remark in Blessed Josemaría Escrivá's writings and preaching; on the contrary, it echoes one of his most intensely felt spiritual and mystical experiences.

That experience took place on August 7, 1931, on a day on which (in Madrid, at that time) the feast of the Transfiguration of Christ was being celebrated; he was saying Mass and, immediately after lifting up the sacred Host, as he himself wrote, that very day, in his 'Apuntes íntimos' (private notes): 'The time of the Consecration came,' he writes in an autobiographical account: 'at the point of raising the Sacred Host, without losing the proper recollection—I had just mentally made the offering to merciful Love—there came to my mind, with exceptional force and clarity, those words of scripture: *et si exaltatus fuero a terra, omnia traham ad meipsum* (Jn 12:32). Normally in the presence of something supernatural, I feel afraid. Then comes the *ne timeas!*, it is I. And I realized that it will be the men and women of God who will raise up the Cross by means of Christ's teachings on the pinnacle of every human activity... And I

---

19 *The Way,* 301.

saw the Lord victorious, attracting all things to Himself!'[20]

Over the course of his life Monsignor Escrivá de Balaguer often went back to that event and the light he received then, to comment on what it meant.[21] Christ, lifted up on the Cross, attracts the entire universe to himself. And he does this through the Christian, through making all mankind part of his own body and his own life. It is real, actual, men and women who come in being and shape history: it is these men and women who, becoming part of Christ's body, identifying themselves with him, make Christ present in the world, thereby helping to make the divinizing force that resides in Christ spread into all the real world.

To explain this, we might be tempted to use terminology consecrated by use —by speaking, for example, in terms of a task or a mission—but words like that don't go far enough, because what Blessed Josemaría is saying refers not so much to the sphere of action as to the sphere of being and, only by way of consequence or effect, to action insofar as it is an expression of being. By the very fact of being a Christian and to the degree that he really is one, a Christian makes Christ present, 'places' him, through his life, inside, at the center or top of those human activities which he happens to be involved in. The spreading of the Faith, the increase in the numbers of Christians (and of Christians who, whatever their human limitations, are conscious of their calling)— this extends the presence of Christ through the length and breadth of history, making that presence real in all the many *environments* and involvements in which Christians (just like any other men or women) happen to live. And, as a result of all that (that is, as a result of the presence of Christ, to whom Christians bear witness and

---

20 'Apuntes íntimos', 217.

21 This 1931 episode and Bl. Josemaría Escrivá's later references to it are commented on in P. Rodríguez, ' "Omnia traham ad meipsum". El sentido de Juan 12, 32 in la experiencia espiritual de Mons. Escrivá de Balaguer' in *Annales theologici* 6 (1992), pp. 5–34.

whom they make known) one conclusion, or better yet, one hope, applies—that there will reverberate throughout the entire universe (even now; and later on, in the *eschaton* fully) the fullness of reconciliation which Christ brought about by being raised up on the Cross.

This gives one a vision or understanding of history as a process through which the full effects of the Redemption unfold. Blessed Josemaría spoke about this on various occasions; sometimes with direct reference to the text of John 12:32, interpreting it via his 1931 experience; sometimes in creationist terms or, more specifically, in terms of the dialectic between sin, which broke up the unity and goodness that were features of the Origin, and grace, seen as the re-establishment of union with God and of the harmony of creation. We shall quote a passage in which we can see these two viewpoints coming together.

It comes from a homily given on the feast of Christ the King, in which, after saying that the Kingdom of Christ is a kingdom of justice, love and peace, he exclaimed very vibrantly and as if taking issue with those who might think that these convictions based on faith are utopian and an illusion: 'This can be done; it is not an empty dream. If only we men,' he goes on, 'would decide to receive the love of God into our hearts! Christ our Lord was crucified; from the height of the cross he redeemed the world, thereby restoring peace between God and men. Jesus reminds all of us: "And I, if I be lifted up from the earth, I will draw all things to myself (Jn 12:32). If you put me at the center of all earthly activities, he is saying, by fulfillling the duty of each moment, in what appears important and what appears unimportant, I will draw everything to myself. My kingdom among you will be a reality!'

'Christ our Lord,' he immediately goes on to say, coming to that view of history we referred to earlier, 'still wants to save men and the whole of creation— this world of ours which is good, for so it came from God's hands. It was Adam's offence, the sin of human pride, which broke the divine harmony of creation. But God the Father, in the fullness of time, sent his only-begotten Son to take flesh in Mary ever Virgin, through the Holy Spirit, and re-establish peace. In this way, by redeeming man from sin, "we receive adoption as sons" (Gal 4:5). We become capable of sharing the intimacy of God. In this way, the new man, the new line of the children of God (cf. Rom 6:4-5) is enabled to free the whole universe from disorder, restoring all things in Christ (cf. Eph 1:9-10), as they have been reconciled with God (cf. Col 1:20).'[22]

Hope in work producing a good result, not purely transcendental and eschatological but also here and now, undoubtedly played a big part in Blessed Josemaría's interior life—and in his preaching. If one were to forget all about this good result, or downplay its importance, that would mean deforming entirely the scope of his message and the spiritual impact it produced and continues to be called on to produce. But we need to make two points in order to identify exactly what the view of history contained in these recently quoted passages is, so as to see how that view impacted on his spirit and on his teachings.

— What need to be stressed particularly are the radical differences between his pastoral and apostolic approach and the attitudes of 'confessional institutionalism' or a 'restorationism' with their yearnings after Christendom. Putting Christ on the pinnacle or peak of human activities is not, in the writings and preaching of Blessed Josemaría, meant to be either a kind of 'decorative-confessional' operation or any sort of politico-cultural program. It is clearly, decidedly and exclusively something evangelical and spiritual: it is all about a deepening of Christian faith which leads a genuine believer to identify himself with Christ to the point of being totally one with him. It is people (the

---

22 *Christ Is Passing By*, 183.

'men and women of God', whom the 1931 text talks about) who are to bring Christ into human activities and tasks, and they are to do this not so much by means of external gestures but, much more profoundly, by their own lives. What really and truly makes Christ present are not signs, symbols or declarations, but the Christian himself (and that includes the ordinary Christian, whose time is spent in secular occupations and all the various forms professional work takes), when his actions are imbued, sincerely, deeply, by the spirit of the Gospel.[23]

— The second point rounds off and extends the first one. To put it succinctly: his approval combines very profoundly two apparently opposite attitudes—an awareness that history is meaningful, and an awareness also that its meaning is opaque. In other words, on the one hand, the affirmation that life is worthwhile and on the other, accepting that that worthwhile life has to be lived without being seen: it has to be taken on faith; that is, we are not always allowed to see its full value and meaning. Monsignor Escrivá de Balaguer had a deep sense of freedom as being an essential and defining attribute of the human person, and, being a man of deep faith and refined dealings with God, he also proclaimed equally vigorously that our destiny is radically a transcendental one. Whichever way you look at it you must draw this conclusion, which Blessed Josemaría spelled out unambiguously on more than one occasion: every-

---

23 'I respect', we read in one of his Letters, in a paragraph not devoid of irony, 'those who think that, to be a good Christian, one needs to hang a collection of scapulars or medals round one's neck. I have a lot of devotion to scapulars and medals, but I have more to possessing sound doctrine, whereby people acquire a profound knowledge of religion.' 'So,' he goes on, 'to show that one is a Christian, there is no need to deck onself out with a fistful of distinguishing marks, because Christianity will show itself. In all simplicity in the life of those who know their faith and who strive to put it into practice' (Letter, March, 24 1930).

thing that happens in this world, in the context of history or time, is provisional, or transitory. It is quite impossible to consider history finished, or to identify the kingdom of God with any human achievement.

In one of his writings he says that 'in creating us, God took on the risk and adventure of our freedom. He wanted true history to be made, one formed from our genuine decisions and not something fictitious or a game. Each person should experience his personal autonomy in facing chance, trial and error and, at times, the unknown.' Further stressing the unknown factors in the course of history he adds: 'Let us not forget that God, in giving us the security of our faith, does not reveal the meaning of all human events.'[24]

The situation of man in history can be compared (the comparison is Josemaría Escrivá's own) to someone looking at the back of a tapestry when it is in the making: he sees unconnected patches of color, threads which seem to go nowhere, knots apparently tied at random . . . ; in other words something that makes no sense at all. And yet all these knots, threads and colors do have a purpose, which you discover when, after the tapestry is finished, you look at it from the front: now you see the whole design in all its beauty; all the work was leading up to this. The tapestry of history is something hidden to us who are here, in history: it is God who is arranging all the threads, and only from God's angle (only from beyond history) can all its beauty and meaning be perceived.[25] If we forget this, if we

---

24 'The riches of the Faith', an article published originally in *ABC* (Madrid), November 2, 1969 and much later in *Position Papers* (Dublin).

25 Bl. Josemaría left a testimony of the moment in which, for the first time, this metaphor unfolded in his thoughts in a remark to Mons. Alvaro del Portillo: 'Once I visited a tapestry workshop in which they were making a copy of a tapestry from the royal palace. A good portion of the work had already been completed and the designs were executed with precision and vivacity: men, armor and a sky in a very beautiful shade of blue. Afterwards, I saw the back of it, and it was all knots and threads in no apparent order. Our life is much the same: everyday we slip up again and again and have to tie off a knot and press on, continuing to work without realizing the beauty of our task. But if we could ever see the tapestry

try to give absolute value to something that is only provisional and relative, the inevitable result is crisis, drama and anxiety.

If one approaches things in this profound way, then one's awareness of the eschatological orientation of human existence, one's consciousness of the provisional nature of things and one's appreciation of pluralism are to the fore. But that in no sense implies apathy or scepticism: on the contrary, it rules them out. For the very same sense of the spiritual and eternal dimension which leads one to affirm the relativity or finitude of what happens within history, shows the deep meaning of history: time is shot through with eternity, and the finite with infinity. Man needs to confront his life (and its complex and rich task, which work is), conscious that, through that work, he not only contributes to the temporal development of history but (what is more important) the shape of eternity itself.

---

from the front, we would see how magnificent the combination of all those threads really is, thanks to God and our own small, daily effort.' (from a comment of Msgr. Alvaro del Portillo in *Instrucción*, May 1935/November 14, 1950, 52).

IV. On developments in the theology of work

As I had occasion to point out some years ago, theological thinking on the subject of work has increased over the past century and has evolved quite a lot.[26] In the early stages, when the theology of work was coming into its own (that is, from the mid-1940s and '50s) one question attracted a lot of attention—the connections between time and eschatology and, more specifically, the continuity between them; that is, the preparation or anticipation in time of the image of a world destined to endure, or, to put it in biblical terms, the connection between human activity and the new heaven and the new earth which Scripture speaks about.[27] This debate went on up to the Second Vatican Council, where it had an influence on the studies and debates which eventually led to the pastoral Constitution *Gaudium et spes*, specifically its third chapter, on 'man's activity in the universe', which ends with a section which focuses on the subject from the angle of the new heaven amid the new earth.[28]

The doctrinal and theological ground covered during those years of reflection and study was certainly considerable, because it sank its roots in a basic Christian truth—the continuity between history and eschatology. But even during the conciliar debates it became evident that that line of thought was, so to speak, played out: it had done its work. In other words, nothing more was to be gained by ploughing that furrow; so, in order to give an impetus to philosophical-theological thinking on the subject of work, a new point of departure had to be found. From then on reflection focused, sometimes, on a possible theol-

---

26 Cf. 'Trabajo, historia y persona. Elementos para una teología del trabajo en la "Laborem exercens"', in *Scripta theologica* 15 (1983), pp. 223–5.

27 The key works in this line are undoubtedly: G. Thils, *Théologie des realités terrestres* (Paris, 1947) and M.D. Chenu, *Pour une théologie du travail* (Paris, 1955).

28 Const. *Gaudium et spes*, 39.

ogy of revolution or (in other terms and with a deeper focus) a theology of political liberation; and, at other points, attempts were made to analyze work *qua* act of the person—in other words, going in the direction of anthropology. One of those who set out in that direction was the young professor and later bishop Karol Wojtyla, whose academic research and reflections clearly prepared the way for the teachings which, as John Paul II, he expounded in *Laborem exercens*, an encyclical very much in keeping with his personality and style.

Monsignor Escrivá de Balaguer always took interest in matters more or less directly to do with the universal call to holiness and the vocation and mission of lay people, which exercised the Church in his time; but, conscious of his responsibility as a founder, he always kept his distance. So, to the debate we have been just discussing we find no reference in his writings, or at least only very tenuous, indirect references. It would be a mistake, then, to try to ascribe a particular line of thought to him, because his teaching was on another level. However, there is no doubt that his teaching helped place the accent on the theological dimension and therefore to focus reflection on the subject of work by looking at it from the angle of the relationship between man and God. The texts quoted show this, and we could add another very significant one, taken from another of his 'Foundational Letters': 'We will sanctify work, if we are saints, if we truly strive to be saints.[...] You have to have a fire which comes from within, which stays alight, which sets fire to everything it touches ... That is why I have gone as far as to say that I don't want any work, any activity, if my children don't improve in the course of doing it.' And he goes on immediately to add, even more clearly: 'I measure the effectiveness and the value of activities by the degree of holiness which those who carry it out acquire.[...] Without the ascetical struggle, our life would be of no value, we would be ineffective, sheep without a shepherd, the blind leading the blind'.[29]

---

29 Letter, 15 October 1948, 20–1.

If that is the way he speaks, putting the accent, radically, on the theological dimension, does it not mean, despite any claims to the contrary, that he is falling into a kind of spiritualism? Not at all; he is adopting an attitude which makes for a well-rounded view of things and therefore of work, even work in the sense of a historical force, a source of social development and change. One of the very factors which we referred to only just now was the realization, which resulted from the conciliar debates and subsequent theological debate, that it just was not possible to develop a 'general theory' of work by looking at it from the eschatological-collective point of view or, more specifically, the contribution that the sum total of work made to the shaping of the End. If one focuses on the product, the change that work effects on the material world, it is not possible to get back to the worker himself: he tends to disappear, submerged in a process to which he contributes but which contributes nothing to his personal development. One needs to approach the matter from the other direction. When one focuses attention on the worker, one quickly sees how much more useful it is. By going from the man-who-works, taking account of his value and destiny, it is possible to access work and evaluate it as such, setting it into an anthropology and an eschatology which gives sense both to the totality of history and to each and every one of those who walk its stage.

The Encyclical *Laborem exercens* has been very influential in this regard. The enormous historical potential of work, glimpsed by ancient writers, but perceived clearly only in the modern period (from Adam Smith to Marx, all subsequent thinkers taking their cue from them) is fully recognized by John Paul II, who here (as usual) is totally modern. But the fact that he recognizes this does not lead him to explain man in terms of work, but rather, work in terms of man. Man is the subject of work and as such he is not a mere producer, a mere maker of things and producer of results: he is the subject of work as a person, as someone who has a value which is reflected in his actions. And that is the reason (there is no other) why work is endowed with such incalculable historical potential.[30]

The distinction between 'work in the objective sense' and 'work in the subjective sense', crucial to the structure of *Laborem exercens*, is basic to this whole approach and is responsible for the intellectual quality of the document.[31] Work is an activity involving control, an act whereby man changes the world around him and makes it serve goals which he devises and pursues. It is an act, which, because it comes from a subject who has an unlimited recall and learning capacity, sets in motion a cumulative process, as a result of which man's dominion over nature grows and develops. The fact that work is objectivized, in things produced, in knowledge, in technique, is undoubtedly why it has such special historical force and why it can bring about change. But it must not be forgotten that at the start and at the base of that process stands man, and he is there by virtue of his spiritual nature. This is what sets the historical process of work going, and this is what keeps it going. 'Objective' work never ceases to be dependent on man. And therefore it must be ordered and organized, with him in mind; otherwise it will destroy and annihilate itself as a process. Man who stands at the start of work stands also at the end: 'objective' work is ordained to 'subjective' work, that is, to the perfecting of man, the subject of work.

This ordering is not something automatic; like everything in history it is the outcome of intelligence and freedom; it depends on how well man understands himself and on how he in fact acts. This means that there can be tension or even rupture between 'objective' and 'sub-

---

30 For this analysis of *Laborem exercens* I have drawn on my 'Trabajo, historia y persona', op. cit., pp. 205–31; see also my 'Trabajo, productividad y primacía de la persona', in various authors, *Doctrina social de la Iglesia y realidad socio-económica* (Pamplona, 1991), pp. 911ff.

31 On this distinction, which is made repeatedly in *Laborem exercens*, see esp. 5 and 6 of the encyclical.

jective' work, between the development of the forces of production and the proper perfecting of man. But there is nothing *necessary* about such a rupture: it depends on the way man himself thinks and acts, the way he sees work, and therefore the way he actually works and the goals he pursues in work.

So, we can see that technique and ethics are two different things (better, two dimensions of the one thing), but they are not opposed to one another or heterogeneous: on the contrary each should influence the other. And that influence should be in line with a well-defined order or hierarchy: it is ethics, the science of values and ends, that should evaluate technique; it is the branch of knowledge which judges the means we use; and therefore it is ethics that should have the final say. Social problems are always, in the last analysis, problems about man, about the attitude man adopts to society and history; and they can be solved only in the light of the truth about man. Furthermore (and it is on this note that John Paul II ends his encyclical), it is not enough for that truth to be formulated and proclaimed: it needs to be taken to heart and put into practice; that is, man has to really act as a spiritual and transcendent being. Only someone who enters into himself and existentially grasps the fact that he is a spirit, is in a position to insert work really and effectively into a history imbued with the truth about man.[32]

Using as his starting-point not his view of the connection between ethics and technique, but, instead, the light radiated by his experience on 2 October 1928 and his experience too as a director of souls (which hinged on the former). Blessed Josemaría Escrivá arrived at a similar approach, a clear and intensely theological one. At the center of his message stands (as we have said) man, a being set before God, in fact, someone loved and called by God. And man is called all the time, every-

---

[32] This is the subject dealt with in the last chapter of *Laborem exercens*, on 'elements for a spirituality of work' (24–7).

where, even in his ordinary life and in the doing of his 'professional' work—work which can and should be done with a theological outlook, in communion and dialogue with God. It is this, this very thing, that gives rise to Blessed Josemaría's very forceful invitation to people to be serious (in a human as well as a supernatural sense) about their work and everything work involves.

So, we should not forget that what Monsignor Escrivá de Balaguer's writings (and also his preaching) invite us to do is not only to cultivate God, to be contemplative while living in the world (much less, be contemplative in spite of the world), but something much more profound and audacious—to be contemplative by 'availing oneself' of the world, nourishing one's contemplation (that is, dialogue and a loving response to God) with what it means to be and to live in the world and all the events and tasks that implies; for it is there, in that world, that God has to be found and it is that world that has to lead us to him. The divine and the human intersect, and this has a clear and (what concerns us here) decisive consequence—recognizing the value that work, and work well done, has as an integral part of man's relationship with God.[33]

Faith does not draw man away from the world around him, to lead him into a different world; it takes him into the deepest reality of this world (the only world there is) to discover its rich meaning. A theological sense of human existence, a contemplative attitude, does not draw a person away from the concrete reality of daily life; it does not alienate the Christian whom God has called to sanctify himself in the world, from human ideals and social problems, from concern about the efficiency or effectiveness of work, from taking things and events seriously. On the contrary, it helps him to accept all the incidents and situations of his life with the sense

---

33 For a later theological analysis of this point, see 'El trabajo en la relación Dios-hombre', in various authors, *Dios y el hombre* (Pamplona, 1985), pp. 717-24.

of responsibility of someone who realizes that it is through these very things that God is speaking to him, and in these very events that God awaits him.[34]

Monsignor Escrivá de Balaguer spoke about all this very often, in many different ways and giving all kinds of examples. Perhaps he had one favourite way of putting it: Christian perfection, living with one's sights on God, the sanctification of work, calls for human perfection; one has to do one's work well, perfectly, finished down to the last detail. 'You pray, you deny yourself, you work in a thousand apostolic activities, but you don't study. You are useless then, unless you change. Study—professional training of whatever type it be—is a grave obligation for us,' he says in *The Way*.[35] And in the *Letter* already quoted, in which he declared, in strong words, that he valued activities for the holiness reached by those engaged in them, he went on a few paragraphs later to say, equally forcefully: 'Work can never be a game for us, something we don't take seriously; nor is it something for *dilettanti* or 'enthusiasts'. What use is it to me, to be told that one of my sons is, for example, a bad teacher but a good son of mine? What good does that do me? For he is not, in fact, a good son of mine, if he has not used the means available to him to improve at his job. We have to work as well as the best of our colleagues. And if possible, better than the best. A man who doesn't take his job seriously is of no use to me.'[36] 'If we want to live this way, sanctifying our profession or job', as he sums it up in one of his homilies, 'we really must work well, with human and supernatural intensity.'[37]

The need to work well, doing one's job with professional competence and human perfection, can be illus-

---

34 On the style of prayer which all this implies, cf., for example, Bl. Josemaría Escrivá's homilies 'The Blessed Virgin, cause of our joy' and 'A life of prayer', in *Christ Is Passing By*, 171ff and *Friends of God*, 238ff, respectively.

35 *The Way*, 334.

36 Letter, October 15, 1948, 15.

37 *Christ Is Passing By*, 50.

trated by bringing in a whole range of arguments and motivations—such as, respecting the nature of things; the human maturity which every man and woman is called to attain; the responsibility which rests on someone who takes on a job of special importance; indeed, the responsibility which everyone has as a citizen. . . . Echoes of all these kinds of arguments can be found in Blessed Josemaría's writings; but wrapped around every such argument, and giving it full force, we always find (expressed in one way or another) an ultimate, definitive reason—the reference of work to God, a theological understanding of existence, the fact (witnessed to by Christian faith) that one's entire life, work included, is something that God sees, and therefore it should be done in a way worthy of God.

'An essential part of that enterprise [the sanctification of ordinary work] which God has entrusted to us,' we read in one of his Letters, is doing the work itself well, perfection (on the human level too), carrying out our professional and social obligations well.'[38] And in one of his homilies: 'It is no good offering to God something that is less perfect than our poor human limitations permit. The work that we offer must be without blemish, and it must be done as carefully as possible, even in its smallest details, for God will not accept shoddy workmanship. "Thou shalt not offer anything that is faulty," Holy Scripture warns us, "because it would not be worthy of him" (Lev 17:20). For that reason, the work each one of us does, the activities that take up our time and energy, must be an offering worthy of our Creator. It must be *operatio Dei*, a work of God that is done *for* God: in short, a task that is complete and faultless.'[39]

---

38 Letter, May 31, 1954, p. 18.
39 *Friends of God*, 55.

The passages I have quoted (to which many more could be added)[40] say all that needs to be said. We would first make the point that the passage from Leviticus quoted in the second passage occurs originally in a priestly context (describing sacrifices and especially holocausts). Theological life, awareness of being in God's presence, is thus linked, in this passage from Blessed Josemaría, to an understanding of Christian life as a priestly form of existence.[41] The Christian, equipped by Baptism to make his life an offering acceptable to God, exercises this priesthood also (and very especially) through work: the work of man's hands is, by virtue of man being a member of Christ's body, a sacrifice worthy of God. And this means not only that the worker must have the proper intention, presence of God, and an attitude of prayer, but also and inseparable from that, his work has to be humanly perfect. The same perfection as the Old Law required in victims to be offered in sacrifice must also exist in the content of the sacrifice of the New Law—the Christian's life united to the life of Christ; and this means that work, an essential component of that life, has to be perfect too.

V. Social responsibility, charity, justice

'Man's great privilege is to be able to love and to transcend what is fleeting and ephemeral. He can love other creatures, pronounce an "I" and a "You" which are full of meaning. And he can love God, who opens heaven's gates to us, makes us members of his family and allows us also to talk to him in friendship, face to face.' This privilege, which defines and characterizes the human

---

40 Ibid., 58 and 62, *Christ Is Passing By*, 50, etc.; and a later selection of passages in my *La santificación del trabajo*, op. cit., pp. 94–105, where I comment at length on this point.

41 On the common priesthood of the faithful in the teachings of Bl. Josemaría Escrivá see the essay *supra* by A. Aranda and my 'El cristiano "alter Christus—ipse Christus". Sacerdocio común y sacerdocio ministerial en la enseñanza del beato Josemaría Escrivá de Balaguer', in various authors, *Biblia, exégesis y cultura* (Pamplona, 1994), pp. 605–22.

being, affects his work, endowing it with dignity; the passage we are quoting concludes, 'This is why man ought not to limit himself to material production. Work is born of love; it is a manifestation of love and is directed toward love.'[42]

These words, taken from a homily which we quoted before, reaffirm that theological background ever-present in Blessed Josemaría's teaching about work; and they also take us one step further. As we said earlier, work cannot happen unless man is present, the mature man, because only someone who truly exercises his human nature can face up to what work, 'professional' work, involves; and the sanctification of work, raising it up to the supernatural, transcendental level, cannot happen unless the Christian is there, a Christian who is alert and aware of the implications of faith. We want at this point to look at our theme in the light of what we have just said, for in the last analysis the core, basis or touchstone of human and Christian maturity lies in love.

To speak of love—and more specifically of Love with a capital letter, as Monsignor Escrivá de Balaguer liked to say and write, a love, which by sharing in divine love, takes us across frontiers and limitations and opens up to fullness and to the eternal—is to speak of a force which, arising from the deepest depth of the human being, aspires to affect everything he does; the capacity to relate to others, which is consubstantial with human existence, reaches its full potential through love. To speak of love with reference to work means setting work right inside that active capacity to relate to others; it means appreciating how decisive a place work has in structuring the relationship between man and God.[43]

---

42 *Christ Is Passing By*, 48.

43 I refer the reader again to the article mentioned to in fn. 33; however, we do not yet have a good study of Monsignor Escrivá de Balaguer's teaching on love. The connection between work and love, and more specifically on the need to ground the dignity of work on love, is stressed by T. Melendo, *La dignidad del trabajo* (Madrid, 1992), a book which draws on the teachings of Bl. Josemaría.

Let us put it another way, and begin with the subject, the person who works. A man who realizes he is called to love God and, in God and from God—and, therefore, totally—every other human being and mankind as a whole, should express that love through the work he does, imbuing the whole work-process with love. From this it follows—as we have just said—that one's underlying view of life has repercussions on work, including the more technical, practical aspects of work. Work badly done, carelessly done, shows that the person doing it is acting in a superficial way, he is not putting all of himself into that work: love is missing. And the other way around, to put it positively, work well done, an activity done carefully, with attention to detail, shows that the worker feels fully committed to it and therefore is expressing himself in it and giving himself to it. In other words, he loves the work he is doing and, at a deeper level, in and through that work he is loving him or those (God and all mankind, from a Christian theological perspective) towards whom, in one way or another, that activity of his is oriented. 'Everything that is done out of Love acquires greatness and beauty.' 'Do everything for Love. Thus there will be no little things: everything will be big. Perseverance in little things for Love is heroism.' 'A little act, done for Love, is worth so much!' 'Lord, may I have due measure in everything ... except in Love.'[44]

To those points from *The Way* which I have just quoted, I could easily add many other things Blessed Josemaría said along the same lines; but I don't think I need to. What does need to be stressed is that we would be reducing the scope of his message, if, on reading or hearing words like these, we were to think it was a matter of vague feelings or that one just had to take care of the technical aspects of work or material details. Professional competence and attention to detail (care of 'little things', to use an expression of Blessed Josemaría's)

---

44 *The Way*, 427, 429, 813, 814.

undoubtedly play an important part in the ideal of the sanctification of work, because love expresses itself in practical things: great plans or declarations of intent are not enough; intentions need to be carried through until the job is finished, and every little detail is in place. But it is also true that that attention to detail, and more specifically to material details and technical perfection in work, does not express the full meaning of work: a theological love needs to apply to work.

Let us remember something which we have mentioned a number of times because it is one of the main lines running through this entire essay, and now its full relevance emerges: when we speak about work in connection with Josemaría Escrivá de Balaguer's teaching, we must remember that in his preaching and writings the word 'work' always means work in its full sense, that is 'professional' work; and 'professional' work is not just a material job one does; it is also, equally, a whole series of relationships which broaden the perspective, from the concrete material action one performs to all those other people engaged in the same work activity and, in the last analysis, to society and all mankind.

Sanctifying work, doing it with a theological outlook, means realizing that God is near, and that consciousness leads us to do our work very well and, while so doing, being aware of the social responsibility that is ours as men committed to a particular job and as members of human society. Both aspects have to be taken into account. One may make a big deal about one's regard for mankind, but that is of no use unless one actually does one's work well; it would be a form of deceit, and a sign that one is alienated from one's work. But equally indicative of alienation would be a job 'well done', but done without real social sensitivity. 'A man or a society that does not react to suffering and injustice and makes no effort to alleviate them is still distant from the love of Christ's heart.' Christians can have diverse views on temporal matters, but 'they should be united in having one and the same desire to serve mankind. Otherwise their Christianity will not be the word and life of Jesus;

it will be a fraud, a deception of God and man.'[45] Social responsibility is, then, an intrinsic dimension of human endeavor, and therefore, and more radically, of Christian endeavor.[46]

Monsignor Escrivá de Balaguer developed this point of his teaching, and, as regards the interior attitude one should have, he stressed the interconnection between two virtues—charity and justice. By justice (in line with classical and Christian tradition) he meant not only readiness to respect rights and give everyone his due but also a disposition of mind which leads one to be conscious of the demands of the common good, and therefore a strong desire to foster social harmony and development. And, in line with biblical teaching, charity is that attitude of mind and heart which leads one to see in each person an individual worthy of being loved, and therefore to love him in a unique, concrete, and personal manner. Understood in this way, we can see that these two virtues are different but complementary, in such a way that when they are properly integrated they contribute effectively and necessarily to give a person the kind of outlook that enables him to be a good member of society.

This is the way Blessed Josemaría expresses in his writings this connection between justice and charity:

— In the first place, he does this by a reflection which, with justice as his starting-point, he moves on towards charity, to show that one must not only respect people's rights but even needs to have a much more personal attitude. 'Justice' he says in one of his homilies, 'does not consist exclusively in an exact respect for rights and duties, as in the case of arithmetical problems that are solved sim-

---

45 *Christ Is Passing By*, 167.

46 On this point and its implications in connection with the notion of 'unity of life', a key element in Bl. Josemaría's spirituality, see my 'La responsibilidad social del cristiano en la enseñanza de Mons. Josemaría Escrivá de Balaguer', in various authors, *Educar en la solidaridad para la paz y la justicia* (Bilbao, 1993), pp. 61–3.

ply by addition and subtraction.' The Christian virtue of justice is 'more ambitious': it stirs us to be grateful and generous, to work hard, 'to uphold the right of all men to [. . .] own what is necessary to lead a dignified existence'. But, he goes on, even if one has that notion of justice and puts it into practice, justice is not enough; it is inadequate for building a society worthy of man. 'Justice does not go far enough', because it does not reach the center of the human heart. 'Be convinced', and here this passage of the homily ends, 'that justice alone is never enough to solve the great problems of mankind. When justice alone is done, don't be surprised if people get hurt. The dignity of man, who is a son of God, requires much more.'[47] Man does not just ask for his rights to be respected. He wants to be valued on his own account, to be recognized as a person, and therefore to be treated with appreciation and, really, with love.

— But if justice needs to be rounded off by charity, it should not be forgotten that charity calls for and presupposes justice. Only someone who keeps the law, who truly respects his fellow human being and strives to give that person the things he needs and has a right to, can truly say that he loves. To speak of charity and not meet the demands of justice is hypocrisy. Charity, love for another, implies, above all, being aware of the position in which the other person finds himself; it means being aware of his rights, and of the things he stands in need of. . . . One needs to go even further: to those rights must be added love—but all that comes before, all those rights in justice, have to be presupposed. 'Charity, which is like a generous overflowing of

---

47 *Friends of God*, 168–72. 'Your apostolic zeal,' he sums it up in one of his letters, 'has to push you not only to practice justice in a most refined way, but to go further still, in charity' (Letter, October 15, 1948, 27).

justice, demands first of all the fulfillment of duty.'[48] Therefore, he will say in another homily, Christians are asked for an 'overflow of charity, which brings with it also an overflow of justice'.[49]

These two approaches are two aspects of the same thing; the impulse to justice and charity is a single impulse. The relationship between charity and justice is not a relationship between two qualities or attributes which simply co-exist: it is a relationship between two points in one single vital dynamic governed by recognition of the value of the other person, recognition of his dignity and richness. For that very reason charity holds the primacy and it is the full flower of the deep sense of social responsibility the Christian should feel. Charity, love of the other person whom one recognizes to be a son or daughter of God, is the impetus which leads the Christian to identify with that person; it is the energy which impels him to confront and to do all one can to solve social problems.[50]

But the analysis should go further. Even though justice and charity (from the angle of the dispositions of the human heart) form the attitude which the social dynamic (and therefore work, as part of that dynamic) calls for, we should not forget that justice and charity (or injustice and lack of charity) lie not just in the spirit but also in physical things. Man, placed in the world, acts in line with the dispositions of his will and his spirit, but, at the same time and inseparably, he acts in line with his knowledge of the world around him, the world in which his action is meant to impinge upon. It should not be surprising, then, that in the writings of Blessed Josemaría references to the sanctification of work

---

48 *Friends of God*, 173.

49 Ibid., 233, in a context in which he is speaking about mercy and stressing that compassion must not be a mere feeling but should express itself in practical action.

50 On this subject, in addition to what is said in 'La responsibilidad ... ', op. cit., pp. 67–9, see also my 'Sentido de la justicia', in various athors, *Homenaje a Mons. Josemaría, Escrivá de Balaguer* (Pamplona, 1986), pp. 51ff.

and to the interconnection between charity and justice should be tied to a constant call, on the one hand, to study and to professional competence, and, on the other, to formation of conscience. For Christians this implies trying to know as much as possible concerning the truth about man and the world as revealed to us in the Gospel. Therefore, it means trying to have an adequate knowledge of the deposit of faith, moral theology and the social doctrine of the Church, which, by casting its light from above on man and his behavior, 'makes known the conditions indispensable for bringing about solutions that are worthy of man'.[51]

Divine perfection and human perfection, intelligence and will, charity and justice, professional competence and a Christian-formed conscience—all intersect and complement one another in the ideal of the sanctification of work; and this is true, too (assuming that grace is at work) in regard to the actual performance of work. All this lies on the horizon of a history in which man, building this world, opens his heart to God and communes with the eternal. Even if sketchy, these are the basic lines of a theological reflection on work as far as we have been able to derive it from Blessed Josemaría's teachings and writings.

---

51 A. del Portillo, 'Dottrina sociale e nuovo evangelizzazione', in *Studi cattolici*, 367 (1991), p. 582, later published in *Romana* 13 (1991), p. 267.

Responsibility to the world, and freedom

Jean-Luc Chabot, University of Grenoble (France)

I. Introduction

The writings of Blessed Josemaría Escrivá, founder of Opus Dei, are a sort of extension of his life and personality: accessible to all, they are pleasant and attractive to the reader; they grow out of real life; and they deal with difficult matters concerning faith and Christian morality and yet manage to do so without the dryness of a learned discourse. And, above all, everything he writes has a wonderful vitality about it; it is a call to arms addressed to Christians and men of good will. What gives this revolutionary spirit to his words, which rings so true and which has a telling effect, is his complete faith in Christ and in the Church. It is no accident that Pope John Paul II should have made this very point in his apostolic Letter of beatification (May 17, 1992): he 'has highlighted all the redemptive power of the Faith, and its capacity to transform both individuals and the social structures in which men and women work out their ideals and their ambitions.'[1]

These structures derive from the social dimension of man's activity, and they are the focus of that part of moral theology known as the 'social teaching of the Church'. Love for the world (without being worldly),[2]

---

[1] John Paul II, *Apostolic Letter for the beatification of Josemaría Escrivá de Balaguer, Priest, Founder of Opus Dei, May 17, 1992*: AAS 84 (1992), p. 1059.

[2] *The Way*, 939; *The Forge*, 569.

sanctification through work in ordinary life, which is what the role of lay people in the Church and in society is all about, and love for personal freedom—these are some of the elements in the teaching of the founder of Opus Dei which make an original contribution to the social doctrine of the Church. It is not so much that he outlines possible lines of development in this or that sector; what he does is go back constantly to the wellspring of social ethics, the human and Christian ethic which flows from the Man-God, the Redeemer. Thus, the ascetical and mystical dimension of Blessed Josemaría's writings extend out (by virtue of his profound secularity) to give very clear, practical and concise teachings about the social activity of man, based on the two inseparable notions of freedom and responsibility.

Boldly stating that the fullness of individual and collective human development can only be attained if one has a genuine Christian life, he maintains that the Christian's responsibility towards the world lies mainly in this—in being fully Christian. The social effects of that attitude will be characterized by the fact that one practices all the human virtues fully and that this will impact on social structures themselves so that the deepest yearnings of mankind will thereby be fulfillled. In this context importance must be given to freedom, which is one of the most precious gifts God has given man. So, one always needs to start out from the heart of man, if one is to achieve peace, justice, solidarity, and draw one's strength from the 'divinization' of mankind in Christ. This is the thrilling panorama set by the man who founded Opus Dei on October 2, 1928, who often proclaimed that 'the divine paths of the earth have been opened.'[3]

---

3 *Christ Is Passing By*, 8 and 150.

II. Christianity brings mankind to fulfillment

1. Christ-centered human and social advancement

Blessed Josemaría Escrivá, in his writings as also in his life, showed himself to have uncommon faith, a full, living faith, in Christ's person, actions, words and promises. Christ who is alive and who is always with us, 'the same yesterday and today and for ever' (Heb 13:8),[4] to such a point that he is at the center and summit of creation and, therefore, logically, of that part of creation which is the moral action of man. This area, commonly called the 'social teaching of the Church', is not an isolated section, for it centers on, is vivified and brought together in the central figure and key to the history of mankind—Christ, *perfectus Deus, perfectus homo*.

a. Christ, the perfection of human nature

This expression—'perfectus Deus, perfectus homo'—taken from the Athanasian Creed is used remarkably often in the published writings of Blessed Josemaría: it is, as it were, the fulcrum, the initial axiom, of his way of explaining things and in everything he does. it occurs no less than fourteen times, twelve of them in nine different homilies.[5] This perfect Man is always found at the summit of a creation which he has himself come to ennoble: 'we cannot say that there are things—good, noble or indifferent—which are exclusively worldly. This cannot be the case after the Word of God has lived among the children of men, felt hunger and thirst, worked with his hands, experienced friendship and obedience and suffering and death. "For in him (Christ) all the fullness of God was pleased to dwell, and through him to rec-

---

4 *Conversations*, 72 and 102.

5 Cf. *Christ Is Passing By*, homilies ' The Eucharist, mystery of faith and love', 83 and 89; 'Christ's presence among Christians', 107; 'The Ascension of our Lord', 117. And *Friends of God*, homilies, 'Time is a treasure', 50; 'Working for God', 56; 'Human virtues', 73, 75, 93; 'For they shall see God', 176; 'Living by faith', 201; 'A life of prayer', 241. *The Forge*, 290. *The Way of the Cross*, sixth station, point for meditation 1.

oncile to himself all things, whether on earth or in heaven, making peace by the blood of his cross" (Col 1:19–20).'[6] This Pauline reference to Christological fullness, used in three different homilies in *Christ is passing by*, occurs twice elsewhere in the same work in the passage after the one quoted, with the stress on the concept of fullness: 'We must love the world and work and all human things. For the world is good. Adam's sin destroyed the divine harmony of creation; but God the Father sent his only Son to re-establish peace, so that we, his children by adoption, might free creation from disorder and reconcile all things to God.'[7]

b. *'No one can surpass the Christian in human nature.'*

Insofar as the world is something good, one should 'love it passionately';[8] insofar as Christ is the perfection of human nature, 'It is inconceivable that, in order to be a Christian you need to turn your back on the world and become a defeatist with regard to human nature. Everything, even the smallest occurrence, has a human and divine meaning. Christ, who is perfect man, did not come to destroy what is human, but to raise it up. He came to share all man's concerns, except for the sad experience of sin.'[9] There is no room, therefore, for a Christian to have even a hint of a 'complex' about the modern world; there is no question of having to adapt an outdated Christianity to a contemporary world, which is replete with positive, attractive values. This world is something basically good; we men 'make it evil and ugly

---

6 *Christ Is Passing By*, 112.

7 Ibid. In similar words: '...The world is not evil, for it has come from God's hands; for it is his creation; for Yahweh looked upon it and saw that it was good (cf. Gn 1:7ff). We ourselves, mankind, make it evil and ugly with our sins and infidelities' (*Conversations*, 114).

8 'Passionately loving the world', the title of a homily preached on the campus of the University of Navarre, October 8, 1967; it forms the last section of *Conversations* (113–23); in it we find this profession of faith by the author: 'I am a secular priest, a priest of Jesus Christ, who is passionately in love with the world' (*Conversations*, 118).

9 *Christ Is Passing By*, 125.

with our sins and infidelities.'[10] The world needs to be opened up to Christianity, to the grace of Christ and to the interior spiritual strivings of Christians, so as to enable it to attain its excellence, its fullness of being: 'Let us be optimists. Moved by the power of hope, [. . .] we get a new joyful perspective on the world, seeing that it has sprung forth beautiful and fair from the hands of God. We will give it back to him with that same beauty, if we learn how to repent.'[11] Seen from this angle, the *aggiornamento*, the bringing up to date, which the Church has to undergo in relation to the modern world, 'should take place, primarily, in one's personal life so as to bring it into line with the "old novelty" of the Gospel. "Being up to date" means identifying oneself with Christ, who is not a figure of the past: Christ is living and will live for all ages: "yesterday and today and forever" (Heb 13:8).'[12]

This attitude, full of faith and logic, demolishes the religious and metaphysical relativism, and the over-cautious attitudes and complexes many Christians had fallen victim to as a result of the secularist climate of the times: 'It is within Christianity that we find the good light that will enable us to solve all problems: all you have to do is to strive sincerely to be good Catholics, *non verbo neque lingua, sed opere et veritate* (1 Jn 4:16), not with words or with the tongue, but with works and in truth. Speak up fearlessly, when the need arises (and if necessary look for opportunities), without being in any way shy.'[13] This is precisely the view the Magisterium of the Church has always maintained in its social teaching, asserting that 'there can be no genuine solution of the "social question" apart from the Gospel,'[14] because 'to know man, authentic man, man in his fullness, one

---

10 *Conversations*, 114.
11 *Friends of God*, 219.
12 *Conversations*, 72.
13 *Friends of God*, 171.
14 John Paul II, Enc. *Centesimus annus*, May 1, 1991, 5.

must know God'[15] Blessed Josemaría echoes this when he writes: 'Christians should be second to none as human beings'.[16]

2. The Christian revolution and rejection of ideologies

a. 'The greatest revolution of all time'

Religion itself is a revolution, 'the greatest rebellion of the man who refuses to live like an animal, dissatisfied and restless until he knows his Creator and is on intimate terms with him'.[17] This revolt on the level of nature becomes a revolution when Christian revelation comes on the scene: 'If we Christians really lived in accordance with our faith, the greatest revolution of all time would take place. The effectiveness of our co-redemption depends on each one of us. Think about that.'[18] 'Today it is not enough for men and women to be good. Besides, anyone who is content to be "almost good" is not good enough. You need to be "revolutionary". Faced by hedonism, faced by the pagan and materialistic wares that we are being offered, Christ wants objectors—rebels of Love!'[19] 'Take note of the words of that working man who commented so enthusiastically after attending a gathering you had organized: "I had never heard people speak as they do here, about being noble, honest, kind and generous." And he concluded in amazement: "Compared to the materialism of the Left or the Right, this is the true revolution".'[20]

---

15 A quotation from Paul VI in John Paul II's Enc. *Centesimus annus*, 55. Also, Leo XIII, Enc. *Rerum novarum*, May 15, 1891: 'The things of the earth cannot be understood or valued properly without taking into account the life to come. Exclude the idea of futurity, and forthwith the very notion of what is good and right would perish; indeed, the whole scheme of the universe would become a dark and unfathomable mystery.'

16 *Friends of God*, 93.

17 Ibid., 38; an identical wording is found in *Conversations*, 73, which leads to the conclusion that 'the study of religion is a fundamental need; a person who lacks religious training is a person whose education is incomplete.'

18 *Furrow*, 945.

19 Ibid., 128.

20 Ibid., 754.

What is needed to make this revolution succeed, to bring about the individual and collective 'fullness' of mankind in Christ? Beginning with Christians themselves, people have to reject materialistic attitudes and the like—all the reductionism which deprives mankind of its integrity, and alienates man from God by tempting him to idolatries old and new, devised by people who either do not know God or have set themselves against him. This Christian revolution rejects violence of any sort, because that it is not a 'suitable way either to persuade or to win over';[21] on the contrary, it is a revolution based on the exercise of a personal freedom which accepts the idea that 'life on earth is armed combat', a struggle, the nature of which Christ has taught us: it is 'a war each of us makes on himself. It is a constantly renewed effort to love God better, to reject our selfishness, to serve all men.'[22]

b. *The reductive anti-humanism of ideology*

Whatever form it takes, materialism is that 'reddish-blue wave of filth and corruption that has set out to conquer the world, throwing its vile spittle over the Cross of the Redeemer. Now he wants another wave to issue forth from our souls—a wave that's white and powerful, like the Lord's right hand—to overcome with its purity all the rottenness of materialism and to undo the corruption that has flooded the world. It is for this, and more, that the children of God have come'.[23] This applies both to Marxism, irrespective of its historical successes or failures, and to hedonism. As regards the former, Blessed Josemaría Escrivá had this to say in a homily preached in 1963: 'Can there be anything more opposed to the Faith than a system which is based on eliminating the loving presence of God from the soul?

---

21 *Conversations*, 44.
22 *Christ Is Passing By*, 74.
23 *The Forge*, 23.

Shout it aloud, so that your voice is clearly heard, that in order to practice justice we have no need whatsoever of Marxism.'[24] As regards hedonism, he denounced it as the origin of 'theories that make birth control an ideal, or a universal or general duty' and which he does not hesitate to describe as 'criminal, anti-Christian and humanly degrading'. 'And so,' he went on, 'paradoxically the countries where most birth control propaganda is found, and which impose birth control on other countries, are the very ones that have attained a higher standard of living.'[25] This 'demographic neo-colonialism'[26] is instigated by rich but dechristianized cultures, where the idolatry of 'having' inhibits the unfolding of 'being'.[27] It produces a harvest of sadness and loss of a sense of direction: 'What really makes a person—or a whole society—unhappy, is the anxiety-ridden, selfish search for well-being, that desire to get rid of anything upsetting.'[28]

These are the main forms of materialism, but there are also ideologies which are enemies of the 'fullness' of man

---

24 *Friends of God*, 171.

25 *Conversations*, 94.

26 Ibid. It is worth pointing out that these moral stances are in line with or even precede the Magisterium of the Church; the interview from which these quotations come took place shortly after the publication of Paul VI's *Populorum progressio* (cf. March 26, 1967) but anticipate the later development of ideas in John Paul II's writings, such as *Familiaris consortio*, November 22, 1981, no. 30 or *Sollicitudo rei socialis*, December 30, 1987, no. 25: 'On the other hand, it is very alarming to see governments in many countries launching *systematic campaigns* against birth, contrary not only to the cultural and religious identity of the countries themselves but also contrary to the nature of true development. It often happens that these campaigns are the result of pressure and financing coming from abroad, and in some cases they are made a condition for the granting of financial and economic aid and assistance. In any event, there is an *absolute lack of respect* for the freedom of choice of the parties involved, men and women often subjected to intolerable pressures, including economic ones, in order to force them to submit to this new form of oppression. It is the poorest populations which suffer such mistreatment, and this sometimes leads to a tendency towards a form of racism, or the promotion of certain equally racist forms of eugenics.'

27 Paul VI, Enc. *Populorum progressio*, 18 and 19; John Paul II, Enc. *Sollicitudo rei socialis*, 28.

28 *The Forge*, 767 and *Conversations*, 97.

and the cause of the worst kinds of sectarian intolerance: 'the fanaticism of the sectarians, since it bears no relation to the truth, keeps changing its dress. It raises against the Holy Church a bogey of mere words lacking in any factual content. Their "freedom" enchains men; their "progress" leads mankind back to the jungle; their "science" conceals ignorance. All their stall contains are only old damaged goods.'[29] This is an outspoken assertion of the superiority of Christian humanism over outdated or retrograde theories which falsify freedom: 'It's incredible that some people still want to regard the stagecoach as a good means of transport. This is how I feel about those who persist in unearthing musty and periwigged "Voltairianisms" or discredited liberalisms of the nineteenth century.'[30] The same is true of 'progressivism': 'We must not allow ourselves to be deceived by the myth of constant and irreversible progress. Progress, in an orderly manner, is good, and desired by God. But people seem to have more regard for another kind of progress, which is false and blinds many persons, who often fail to realize that, sometimes the human race moves backwards and loses some of the ground it had conquered.'[31] And of nationalism he says: 'If patriotism becomes nationalism, which leads you to look at other people, at other countries, with indifference, with scorn, without Christian charity and justice, then it is a sin. It is not patriotism to justify crimes or to deny the rights of other peoples.'[32]

Lastly, there is perhaps the oldest and most widespread form of revolt—indifferentism. 'Nonsectarianism. Neutrality. Old myths that always try to seem new. Have you ever stopped to think how absurd it is to leave one's Catholicism aside on entering a university, a professional association, a cultural society, or Parliament, like a man

---

29 *Furrow*, 933.
30 *The Way*, 849.
31 *Christ Is Passing By*, 123.
32 *Furrow*, 315 and 316.

leaving his hat at the door?'[33] Or this: 'The enemies of Jesus—and even some who call themselves his friends—come decked out in the armour of human knowledge and wielding the sword of power. They laugh at us Christians, just as the Philistine laughed at David and despised him. In our own days too, the Goliath of hatred, the Goliath of falsehood, of dominating power, of secularism and indifferentism, will also come crashing to the ground. And then, once the giant of those false ideologies has been struck down by the apparently feeble weapons of the Christian spirit—prayer, expiation and action—we shall strip him of his armour of erroneous doctrines, equipping our fellow men instead with true knowledge, with Christian culture and the Christian way of life.'[34]

III. The social impact of a genuine Christian life

1. The 'unity of life' principle and its social effect

Taking issue with the words of one of the fathers of ideological liberalism, who pronounced: 'private vices, public benefits',[35] Blessed Josemaría Escrivá proclaims that private virtues promote the welfare of society, and that the quality of social structures and of society is a function of personal effort to put the Christian ethic fully into practice: 'What eagerness many show for reform! Would it not be better for us all to reform ourselves, so as to fulfill faithfully what is laid down?'[36] This presupposes that there is a principle of 'unity of life', of continuity between the life of individual persons and that of society, in the sense that the second derives from the

---

33 *The Way*, 353.
34 *The Forge*, 974.
35 Bernard de Mandeville (1670–1733), a precursor of the thought of Adam Smith, *The Fable of the Bees: private vices, public benefits*, 1st part (1714), 2nd part (1729).
36 *Furrow*, 131.

first. What we have here is an application of the constant principle of the social teaching of the Church which upholds the excellence and primacy of the human person, not only as the beneficiary of social order but also and simultaneously as the protagonist responsible for social structures and social behavior.

a. 'These world crises are crises of saints'

'By the very fact of being a man, a Christian has a full right to live in the world. If he lets Christ live and reign in his heart, he will feel—noticeably—the saving effectiveness of our Lord in everything he does.'[37] If in the past century the world has been shaken by terrible wars, genocide, devastation, and all kinds of oppression, if it lurches from one severe social problem to the next, the reason for all this must be sought in man's heart; it will not be found by tinkering with social structures: 'It is useless to call for exterior calm if there is no calm in men's consciences, in the center of their souls, for "from the heart come evil intentions: murder, adultery, fornication, theft, perjury, slander" (Mt 15:19).'[38] 'Men are forever "making peace" and forever getting entangled in wars. This is because they have forgotten that they were advised to struggle within themselves and to go to God for help. Then He will conquer, and we will obtain peace for ourselves and for our own homes, for society and the world.'[39] There is a name for this struggle against oneself—holiness—and it leads Blessed Josemaría to introduce a sort of 'social mathematics of holiness': bit by bit sanctification of all mankind will be won by a few scattered people, acting like leaven in the mass, in

---

37 *Christ Is Passing By*, 183.

38 Ibid., 73.

39 *The Forge*, 102. See also *Christ Is Passing By*, 182: 'Some people try to build peace in the world without putting love of God into their own hearts, without serving others for the love of God. How could they possibly achieve peace in that way?'

all sectors of human activity: 'A secret, an open secret: these world crises are crises of saints. God wants a handful of men "of his own" in every human activity. And then...*pax Christi in regno Christi*—the peace of Christ in the kingdom of Christ.'[40] For, 'the foundation of all we do as citizens—as Catholic citizens—lies in an intense interior life. It lies in being really and truly men and women who turn their day into an uninterrupted conversation with God'.[41]

b *'We cannot lead a double life'*

Dualistic and reductionist views of man and the Christian are poles apart from this principle of permeability, this idea that personal holiness has an effect on the state of the world: 'There is a certain type of secularist outlook that one comes across, and also another approach which one might call "pietistic", both of which share the view that Christians somehow are not fully and entirely human. According to the former, the demands of the Gospel are such as to stifle our human qualities; whereas, for the latter, human nature is so fallen that it threatens and endangers the purity of the Faith. The result, either way, is the same. They both fail to grasp the full significance of Christ's Incarnation; they do not see that "the Word was made flesh", became man, "and dwelt amongst us".'[42]

This pietistic or 'spiritualistic'[43] outlook derives from conceiving the Christian life as a life apart, cut off from the world and from the ordinary activities of the human community. Historically speaking, it derives from a reduction of the Christian idea to a religious spirituality. The idea that taking to heart the basic demands of the Gospel message 'means leaving normal life is a conclu-

---

40 *The Way*, 301.
41 *The Forge*, 572.
42 *Friends of God*, 74. Cf. also *Christ Is Passing By*, 98.
43 *Conversations*, 113.

sion that is only valid for people who receive from God a religious vocation, with its *contemptus mundi*, its disdain for the things of the world. But to try to make this abandonment of the world the essence or summit of Christianity would obviously be absurd.'[44]

This sort of outlook may also derive from a kind of clericalism which, without involving leaving the world altogether, makes the Christian life 'a kind of world apart', and which consists in 'going to church, taking part in sacred ceremonies, being taken up with ecclesiastical matters'.[45] Christian life comes to be seen as the preserve of '"pure", extraordinary people, who remain aloof from the contemptible things of this world, or at most tolerate them as something necessarily juxtaposed to the spirit while we live on this earth'.[46] This gives rise to a very common temptation 'to live a kind of double life. On one side, an interior life, a life of relation with God; and on the other, a separate and distinct professional, social and family life, full of small earthly realities. No! We cannot lead a double life. We cannot be like schizophrenics, if we want to be Christians. There is just one life, made of flesh and spirit. And it is this life which has to become, in both soul and body, holy and filled with God. We discover the invisible God in the most visible and material things.'[47]

Therefore, the idea that 'the Catholics are penetrating all sectors of society' makes no sense; lay people, ordinary Christians, 'have no need to "penetrate" the temporal sphere, for the simple reason that they are ordinary citizens, the same as their fellow citizens, and so they are *there* already'.[48] And for the very same reason, that is, by virtue of the 'unity of life', the circle of fam-

---

44 *Conversations.*, 66.
45 Ibid., 113.
46 Ibid.
47 Ibid., 114.
48 Ibid., 66.

ily life and the wider sphere of social life are in no sense two different or opposed worlds.[49]

2. Putting Christ at the summit of all human activities

a. An eager sense of being responsible for the world and all creation

'The Lord wants his children, those of us who have received the gift of faith, to proclaim the original optimistic view of creation, the "love for the world" which is at the heart of the Christian message. So there should always be enthusiasm in your professional work, and in your effort to build up the earthly city.'[50] Now, it is true that 'Many things, whether they be material, technical, economic, social, political or cultural, when left to themselves, or left in the hands of those who lack the light of the Faith, become formidable obstacles to the supernatural life. They form a sort of closed shop which is hostile to the Church. You, as a Christian—a research worker, writer, scientist, politician or laborer, or whatever—have the duty to sanctify those very things. Remember that the whole universe—as the Apostle says—is groaning as in the pangs of labor, awaiting the liberation of the children of God.'[51] Christ on the cross set this freedom in motion once and for all; it is up to Christians to bring about the 'consecration of the world'[52] through co-redemption: 'We must, each of us, be *alter Christus, ipse Christus*: another Christ, Christ himself. Only in this way can we set about this great undertaking, this im-

---

[49] *Conversations*, 87: 'Q. Monsignor, the presence of women in social life is extending far beyond the sphere of the family, in which they have moved almost exclusively up to now. What do you think about this development? What, in your opinion, are the main characteristics that women have to develop if they are to fulfill their mission? A. Firstly, let me say that I do not think there need be any conflict between one's family life and social life.'

[50] *The Forge*, 703.

[51] *Furrow*, 311.

[52] *Conversations*, 70.

mense, unending task of sanctifying all temporal structures from within, bringing to them the leaven of redemption.'[53] In other words, 'by his death on the Cross, Christ has drawn all creation to himself. Now it is the task of Christians, in his name, to reconcile all things with God, by placing Christ, at the peak of all human activities.'[54]

b. Sanctification of the world by the citizen and by the Christian worker

We children of God, who are citizens with the same standing as others, have to take part "fearlessly" in all honest human activities and organizations, to make Christ present in them. Our Lord will ask a strict account of each of us if through neglect or love of comfort we do not freely strive to play a part in the human undertakings and decisions on which the present and the future of society depend.'[55] For Blessed Josemaría Escrivá, due to the unity of life and the secularity that is part of the lay Christian's make-up, there is no room for derogations, exemptions or privileges claimed in the name of another world, or for the false humility of not claiming one's rights. The Christian is not an ex-patriate:[56] 'Carry all your duties as a citizen. Do not try to get out of any of your obligations. Exercise all

---

[53] *Christ Is Passing By*, 183.

[54] *Conversations*, 59. Cf. *The Forge*, 685 as also *The Way of the Cross*, eleventh station, point for meditation 3: 'How beautiful are those crosses on the summits of high mountains, and crowning great monuments, and on the pinnacles of cathedrals...! But the Cross must also be inserted in the very heart of the world. Jesus wants to be raised on high, there: in the noise of the factories and workshops, in the silence of libraries, in the loud clamour of the streets, in the stillness of the fields, in the intimacy of the family, in crowded gatherings, in stadiums...Wherever there is a Christian striving to lead an honorable life, he should, with his love, set up the Cross of Christ, who attracts all things to himself.'

[55] *The Forge*, 715; see also the entire chapter on 'citizenship' in *Furrow*.

[56] *Christ Is Passing By*, 99: 'In this history, which began with the creation of the world and will reach its fulfilllment at the end of time, the Christian is no expatriate. He is a citizen of the city of men, and his soul longs for God. While still on earth he has glimpses of God's love and comes to recognize it as the goal to which all men on earth are called.'

your rights, too, for the good of society, without making any imprudent exceptions. You must give Christian witness in that, too.'[57]

This restoration of the world through the sanctification of men and of the world is brought about mainly through work: 'We must not forget that God created man *ut operaretur* (Gen 2:15), to work, and others (our family and our country, the whole human race) also depend on the effectiveness of our work.'[58]

However, 'we must not offer God something that is less perfect than our poor human limitations permit. The work that we offer must be without blemish and it must be done as carefully as possible, even in its smallest details [. . .]; in short, it must be complete and faultless.'[59] 'Your work must be done well, mindful of others' needs, taking advantage of all advances in technology and culture. Such work fulfills a very important function and is useful to all mankind, if it is motivated by generosity, not selfishness, and directed to the welfare of all, not your own advantage: if it is filled with the Christian sense of life.'[60] The social impact of the work one does is a function of 'a spirit of service, a desire to contribute to the well-being of other people'.[61] The work a woman does in the home (not that she is the only one to work there) 'is a social contribution in itself and can easily be the most effective of all [. . .]. Through this profession—because it is a profession, in a true and noble sense—they (women) are an influence for good, not only in their family, but also among their many friends and acquaintances, among people with whom they come in contact, in one way or another. Sometimes their impact is much greater than that of other professional people.'[62]

---

57 *The Forge*, 697.

58 *Friends of God*, 169.

59 Ibid., 55.

60 *Christ Is Passing By*, 166.

61 Ibid., 51.

62 *Conversations*, 88 and 89. Cf. also *The Forge*, 702.

c. Human advancement through Christian apostolate

If 'Our professional vocation is an essential and inseparable part of our condition as Christians,'[63] the imperative need for apostolate in order to enable mankind to attain its fullness in Christ will be met mainly through 'professional' work: 'I often feel like crying out to all those men and women in offices and shops, in the world of the media and in the law courts, in schools, on the factory floor, in mines and on farms and telling them that, with the backing of an interior life and by means of the Communion of Saints, they should be bringing God into all these different environments, according to that teaching of the Apostle: "Glorify God by making your bodies the shrines of his presence".'[64] For 'Our Lord wants men and women of his own in all walks of life. Some he calls away from society, asking them to give up involvement in the world, so that they remind the rest of us by their example that God exists. To others he entrusts the priestly ministry. But he wants the vast majority to stay right where they are, in all earthly occupations in which they work: the factory, the laboratory, the farm, the trades, the streets of the big cities and the trails of the mountains.'[65]

This lay apostolate, born directly of the commitment acquired through Baptism, is a joint development of nature and grace, of the natural and the supernatural; it is not a kind of adjunct, but, rather, part and parcel of the 'unity of life': 'who ever said that to speak about Christ and to spread his doctrine, you need to do anything unusual or remarkable? Just live your ordinary life; work at your job, trying to fulfill the duties of your state in life, doing your job, your professional work properly, improving, getting better each day. Be loyal; be understanding with others and demanding on yourself. Be mortified and cheerful. This will be your apostolate.'[66]

---

63 *Friends of God*, 60.
64 *The Forge*, 945.
65 *Christ Is Passing By*, 105.
66 *Friends of God*, 273.

'Strive to ensure that those human institutions and structures in which you work and move with the full rights of a citizen, are in accordance with the principles which govern a Christian view of life. In this way you can be sure that you are giving people the means to live according to their real worth; and you will enable many souls, with the grace of God, to respond personally to their Christian vocation.'[67]

It goes without saying, but Josemaría Escrivá often spells it out, that this call to arms of Christians who want to take Christianity and their social obligations seriously, is something that essentially involves the freedom of each individual person, because there is no responsibility without freedom:[68]

'Do not forget, my sons, that I always speak of a responsible freedom.'[69]

IV. Personal freedom is essential in the Christian life

In the course of a homily he gave on November 22, 1970, the feast of Christ the King, we find this extraordinary statement: 'I have spent my whole life preaching personal freedom, with personal responsibility. I have sought freedom throughout the world and I'm still looking for it, just like Diogenes trying to find an honest man. And every day I love it more. Of all the things on earth, I love it most. It is a treasure that we do not appreciate nearly enough.'[70] This vibrant love for freedom,

---

67 *The Forge*, 718.

68 *Christ Is Passing By*, 27. All his exhortations to the service of others (for example, *The Forge*, 144), the duty to provide the common good and avoid absenteeism (*The Forge*, 714), the need to take an active part in state or private associations in one's respective country (*The Forge*, 717), are subordinate to the exercise of one's freedom.

69 *Conversations*, 117

70 *Christ Is Passing By*, 184.

which is evidenced on almost every page of his writings, is grounded, as Blessed Josemaría saw it, on an extremely clear doctrine, and also on his own experience of suffering, and that of the work he founded: the chapter on the 'citizen of the two cities' in Cesare Cavallieri's long interview with Bishop Alvaro del Portillo gives some instances of these experiences.[71]

1. The freedom of persons, and the truth that sets one free

a. The two stages of freedom: 'Veritas liberabit vos'

'Throughout my years as a priest, whenever I have spoken, or rather shouted, about my love for personal freedom, I have noticed some people reacting with distrust, as if they suspected that my defence of freedom could endanger the Faith. Such faint-hearted people can rest assured. The only freedom that can assail the Faith is a misinterpreted freedom, an aimless freedom, one without objective principles, one that is lawless and irresponsible. In a word, licence.'[72] Thus, human freedom has two stages:

— the faculty of choice (that is part of what it means to be a human being, and God respects it);

— man's exercise of that freedom, in line or not with goodness and truth, with the will of God.

The first is a great good, 'which makes man capable of loving and serving God'.[73] It is 'a gift from God',[74] who has chosen to 'run the risk of our freedom'.[75] 'The Lord does not destroy man's freedom; it is precisely he who has made us free. That is why he does not want to

---

71 Cf. A. del Portillo, *Intervista sul fondatore dell'Opus Dei*, conducted by Cesare Cavallieri (Milan, 1992).

72 *Friends of God*, 32.

73 *Conversations*, 104.

74 *Christ Is Passing By*, 24.

75 Ibid., 113.

wring obedience from us. He wants our decisions to come from the depths of our hearts.'[76] 'God does not want slaves, but children. He respects our freedom.'[77] This freedom is something which Blessed Josemaría Escrivá always describes as 'personal' ('personal freedom, which I defend and will always defend with all my strength . . .')[78] in order to show that collective and public freedoms are the extension of personal freedom and, at the same time, to indicate that every human person deserves respect on account of the dignity which this freedom rightly confers on him or her: 'We have a duty to defend the personal freedom of everyone, in the knowledge that "Jesus Christ is the one who obtained that freedom for us" (Gal 4:31). If we do not so behave, what right have we to claim our own freedom? We must also spread the truth, because *veritas liberabit vos*, the truth makes us free, while ignorance enslaves.'[79]

And here the second stage of freedom comes into play; it is a stage which involves the redemptive renewal of mankind, because, as Blessed Josemaría is never afraid to say, 'where there is no love of God, the individual and responsible use of personal freedom becomes impossible'.[80] To do his thought justice we would really need to reproduce here whole pages of his homily 'Freedom, a gift of God', which is a veritable jewel of Christian anthropology and practical moral theology. We will give the thread of his argument by a series of quotations: 'Thus we come to appreciate that freedom is used properly when it is directed towards the good; and that it is misused when men are forgetful and turn away from the Love of loves. [. . .] Christ himself gives us the answer: *veritas liberabit vos*, the truth will set you free. By itself, however, freedom is insufficient: it needs a guide, a north

---

76 *Christ Is Passing By*, 100.
77 Ibid., 129.
78 *Friends of God*, 26.
79 Ibid., 171.
80 Ibid., 29.

star [. . .] Reject the deception of those who settle for mouthing the pathetic cry of "Freedom! Freedom!" Their cry often masks a tragic enslavement, because choices that prefer error do not liberate. Christ alone sets us free, for He alone is the Way, the Truth and the Life.'[81] People who do not choose the freedom that sets them free include those who worship their own freedom, those who are indecisive, and those who reject God; these three kinds of behavior all lead to the same result—slavery, in the guise of freedom. The first-mentioned do not use the freedom that is theirs: 'They look at it, they set it up, a clay idol for their petty minds to worship. [. . .] Their freedom turns out to be barren, or produces fruits which even humanly speaking are ridiculous. A person who does not choose, with complete freedom, an upright code of conduct, sooner or later ends up being manipulated by others. He will lead a lazy, parasitic existence, at the mercy of what others decide. [. . .] "No one is forcing me!", they obstinately repeat. No one? Everyone is coercing their make-believe freedom which refuses to run the risk of accepting responsibility for the consequences of its own free actions.' Secondly, you have 'the indecisive and irresolute person (who is) like putty in the fingers of circumstances. Anyone and anything can mold him according to its whim, particularly his passions and the worst tendencies of his own nature wounded by sin.'[82] Finally, 'He who sins against God keeps the freedom of his will to the extent that he is free from coercion, but he has lost it in that he is no longer free from blame" (St. Thomas Aquinas, *Quaestiones disputatae, De malo*, q. 6, a. 1).[83] 'Slavery or divine filiation, this is the dilemma we face. Either we are children of God or we are slaves to pride, to sensuality, to the fretful selfishness which seems to afflict so many souls.'[84]

---

81 *Friends of God*, 26.
82 Ibid., 29.
83 Ibid., 37.
84 Ibid., 38.

b. *'Freedom of consciences' and respect for persons*

Starting out from this dual dimension of freedom—free will and opting for truth—Blessed Josemaría liked to make a distinction between 'freedom of consciences' and 'freedom of conscience'. Apropos of the latter expression, commonly used to mean the autonomy of the person, it needs to be stressed that it is 'inaccurate to speak of *freedom* of conscience, thereby implying that it may be morally right for someone to reject God. We have already seen that it is in our power to oppose God's plans for salvation. It is in our power, but we should not do it.'[85] This principle not only shows disregard for the objective moral law, the will of God, but it also undermines the integrity of one's own conscience: 'Freedom of conscience: no! How many evils this lamentable error, which permits actions against the dictates that lie deepest within oneself, has brought about in nations and individuals. Freedom "of consciences", yes: for it means the duty to follow that interior command...ah, but after receiving sound formation!'[86]

Freedom of consciences is a natural right guaranteeing religious freedom to all, the Church included, in human society; for there are those who, 'in the name of a false freedom ask Catholics "to do them the favour" of going back to the catacombs';[87] and there are also those who 'fear—and oppose!—Catholics being simply good Catholics',[88] even to the extent of the organized oppression of believers by tyrannical and totalitarian regimes.[89] On the contrary, 'I defend with all my strength the *freedom of consciences*, which means that no one may licitly prevent a man from worshipping God. The legitimate hunger for truth must be respected. Man has a grave obligation to seek God, to know him and worship him,

---

85 *Friends of God*, 32.
86 *Furrow*, 389.
87 Ibid., 301.
88 Ibid., 931.
89 Cf. *The Forge*, 259.

but no one on earth is permitted to impose on his neighbor the practice of a faith he does not have; just as no one can claim the right to harm those who have received the Faith from God.'[90] Here we have a condemnation of any recourse to violence, a rejection of any type of tyranny, because it is 'opposed to human dignity'.[91] 'How sad it is to have the mentality of a Roman emperor, failing to understand the freedom other citizens enjoy in the things God has left to the free choice of men.'[92]

Finally, in 'Christian respect for persons and their freedom',[93] a poignant homily, because one can detect the autobiographical element behind every line, the founder of Opus Dei denounces hypocritical attacks on the elementary rules of morality and the natural law as evidenced in many contemporary lifestyles. In our societies, where views and opinions are given world-wide exposure by the media, bad-mouthing and calumny have become powerful weapons against physical and moral persons. What begins with imagining evil where there is none, and causing groundless suspicion, ends up with giving vent publicly to rash judgment: 'Setting their prejudices up as criteria, they are quick to criticize anybody and slow to listen. Afterwards perhaps, out of "openmindedness" or "fair play", they extend to the accused the possibility of defending himself. Flying in the face of the most elementary justice and morality—for he who accuses should bear the burden of proof—they "grant" the innocent party the "privilege" of proving himself blameless [. . .].' Then he refers to the fact that everyone has a basic natural human right to be treated with respect, and he goes on: 'Those who impugn the reputation and honor of others show that they are ignorant of some truths of our Christian faith and certainly do not have an authentic love of God.'[94]

---

90 *Friends of God*, 32.
91 *Conversations*, 53.
92 *Furrow*, 313.
93 *Christ Is Passing By*, 67–72.
94 Ibid., 68, 69 and 72.

2. Unity of faith, and freedom of opinion

The relationship between respect for persons and recognition of freedom-truth brings us to another relationship—that between unity of faith and Christians' freedom of opinion. Here too Blessed Josemaría has very practical and clear things to say in response to the confusion and disorder which usually arise when people dogmatize on temporal questions and relativize the truths of faith.

a. *There are no dogmas in the area of matters of opinion*

'Only in faith and morals is there an indisputable standard: that of our Mother the Church.'[95] 'As Christians, you enjoy the fullest freedom, with the consequent personal responsibility, to take part as you see fit in political, social or cultural affairs, with no restrictions other than those set by the Church's Magisterium. The only thing that would worry me, for the good of your souls, would be if you were to overstep these limits, for then you would have created a clear opposition between your actions and the faith you claim to profess, and in that case I would tell you so, clearly.'[96] The freedom that belongs to Christians is also endangered by those who 'degrade man, by denying the value of the Faith and putting it at the mercy of the grossest errors'.[97] That is what happens when political criteria are applied, inappropriately, to Catholic belief and morality: 'there are practicing Catholics who even seem devout and perhaps have sincere convictions, yet who are naively serving the enemies of the Church. Into their very homes, under various names, invariably wrongly used (ecumenism, pluralism, democracy) has insinuated itself the worst adversary—ignorance.'[98]

---

95 *Furrow*, 275.
96 *Friends of God*, 11.
97 Ibid.
98 *Furrow*, 359.

Faith and morals are not things decided by majority vote, in the light of circumstance: they are not the outcome of opinion or negotiation: 'holy intransigence' has to apply in doctrinal matters.[99] But, as far as persons and their free opinions are concerned: 'No one has a right to impose non-existent dogmas in temporal matters.'[100] 'The fact that someone thinks differently from me (especially in matters which are open to personal opinion) in no way justifies an attitude of personal hostility, or even coldness or indifference.[. . .] When the value of freedom is fully understood and the divine gift of freedom is passionately lived, the pluralism that freedom brings with it is also loved.'[101]

b. Respect for legitimate pluralism

'How determined some people are to make everyone behave the same way, to turn unity into amorphous uniformity, drowning freedom.'[102] There are some who 'have a one-party mentality, in politics or in the spiritual sphere',[103] and prominent among that sort of people are those who want to confine religion within a single political straightjacket: 'I do not approve of committed Christians in the world forming a politico-religious movement. That would be a crazy thing to do, even if it were motivated by a desire to spread the spirit of Christ in all the activities of man';[104] for 'nothing is further from the Christian faith than fanaticism—that unholy alliance of the sacred and the profane, whatever guise it takes.'[105] In the Church this one-party outlook could be seen in certain contemporary forms of clericalism; so much so that Blessed Josemaría even said, in an 1968 interview in *L'Osservatore romano*, that it consti-

---

99 *The Way*, 397 and 398.
100 *Conversations*, 77.
101 Ibid., 98.
102 *Furrow*, 401.
103 *Conversations*, 50.
104 *Christ Is Passing By*, 183.
105 Ibid., 74.

tuted 'one of the greatest dangers threatening the Church today'. Ignorant of 'one of the divine requirements of Christian freedom and led by false arguments in favor of greater effectiveness,' this sort of thinking imposes on Christians a uniformity which threatens to 'commit the hierarchy in temporal questions (thus falling into a clericalism which though different is no less scandalous than that of past centuries)'.[106] Blessed Josemaría denounces very forthrightly this ecclesiastical propensity to yield to the temptation of having 'one way only'; it shows him to have been a precursor of the promotion of rights and freedoms within the Church: 'We should flee like the plague from that approach to pastoral work and the apostolate in general which seems to be no more than a revised and enlarged edition, in the sphere of religion, of the one-party system.'[107]

It would be equally intolerable if the Christian, in his private affairs, were to make use of the common faith to try to impose his own free choices in temporal matters on other Christians: 'It would never occur to such a Christian to think or to say that he was stepping down from the temple into the world to represent the Church, or that his solutions are "the Catholic solutions" to problems. That would be completely inadmissible! That would be clericalism, "official Catholicism", or whatever you want to call it. In any case, it means doing violence to the very nature of things.'[108]

Taking issue with that sort of one-party spirit (in its various forms) Blessed Josemaría championed the development of a Christian lay outlook, proposing the application of ethical principles as old as the Gospel, and like the Gospel new: 'You must foster everywhere a genuine "lay outlook", which will lead to three conclusions: be sufficiently honest, so as to shoulder one's own personal responsibility; be sufficiently Christian, so as to respect

---

106 *Conversations*, 59.
107 Ibid., 99.
108 Ibid., 117.

those brothers in the Faith who, in matters of free discussion, propose solutions which differ from those which each one of us maintains; and be sufficiently Catholic so as not to use our Mother the Church, involving her in human factions.'[109]

V. Conclusion

For these goals to be achieved 'the prejudice must be rejected that the ordinary faithful can do no more than limit themselves to helping the clergy in ecclesiastical apostolates. It should be remembered that to attain this supernatural end men need to be and to feel personally free with the freedom Christ won for us.'[110]

This means that all the baptized should strive to improve their Christian formation, to free themselves from the most basic of evils, one that is ever-present—ignorance: "You need formation, because you need a profound sense of responsibility, if you are to foster and promote the activity of Catholics in public life and do so with the respect that everyone's freedom deserves, reminding each and every one that they have to be consistent with their faith.'[111]

---

109 *Conversations*, 117.
110 Ibid., 34.
111 *The Forge*, 712.

By way of conclusion

*Bishop Alvaro del Portillo (1914–1994),
Prelate of Opus Dei and Chancellor of
the Roman Atheneum of the Holy Cross*

In response to the request of the organizing committee of the Theological Symposium on the teachings of Blessed Josemaría Escrivá de Balaguer held in October 1993, I am happy to write these short reflections for inclusion in the Proceedings.

I do not intend to address subjects already discussed by those who read papers. Instead, I hope that what I have to say will help to highlight some of the essential features found in all Blessed Josemaría's writings. Like his entire life and work, these writings have special spiritual and therefore theological significance. In these pages I shall follow the order in which subjects occur in the papers of the symposium—the call to holiness, the spiritual life, and sanctification in the world.

The papers and round-table discussions have, from different angles, thrown light on the huge doctrinal horizon opened up by Blessed Josemaría. He has in fact left us an extremely rich spiritual heritage and one involving great intellectual and apostolic perspectives. The vigor and beauty of his spiritual writings will become increasingly more evident, thanks, among other things, to his influence in the area of theological thought.

Thanks to the light cast by the charism and specific spirituality of the founder of Opus Dei, in the seventy-five years that have gone by so far, and thanks to the grace of God, countless fruits of Christian life in all spheres of society have come to maturity. Thanks to the impetus given by his preaching on the universal call to holiness and apostolate, an ever more vital and rich mobilization has taken place of Christians committed to a radical following of Christ in the context of daily life. Those years have seen the birth and consolidation of initiatives in the field of education and social welfare, projects to do with school and university training and professional and social formation and the like. In other words, Blessed Josemaría Escrivá's teaching has become a living thing, an inspiration for countless ordinary Christians who want to give glory to God and serve mankind by means of their everyday work, done in all kinds of settings, but done always striving to attain human perfection.

This is something one must keep in mind so as not to fall into an obtuse, abstract way of thinking; and it has been the backdrop of the entire symposium which has just completed its work—life as the interpretative tool of doctrine. This is also the framework into which I should like to set these present thoughts of mine which, as I have already said, are designed simply to outline a few essential themes. I am particularly conscious of something the Holy Father John Paul II said in his address to those taking part in the symposium: 'Josemaría Escrivá de Balaguer, like other great figures in modern Church history, can also be a source of inspiration for theological thought. In fact, theological research, which has an irreplaceable role of mediation in the relationship between faith and culture, professes and is enriched by drawing on the Gospel, under the impulse of the experience of Christianity's great witness. Blessed Josemaría, without a doubt, should be included among them.'[1]

What more could be said to the theologians taking part in the symposium? These words of the Pope are extremely stimulating. They also inspire what I have to say as I reflect on the fruits which, to the benefit of the Church and of society, have grown and undoubtedly continue to grow,

---

1 John Paul II, Address to those attending (this symposium), October 14, 1993, 4: see p. 17 above.

abundantly, from the work of theological research undertaken by specialists from the world over into the doctrinal principles which inspire the spiritual testimony of Blessed Josemaría.

I. Holiness in the world

In the Holy Father's address, a passage from *The Way* is quoted which other speakers have also referred to. It says, 'A secret, an open secret: these world crises are crises of saints. God wants a handful of men "of his own" in every human activity. And then . . . *pax Christi in regno Christi*—the peace of Christ in the kingdom of Christ.'[2] These words, so concise and so deep, sum up one of the central teachings of Blessed Josemaría. So, it is perfectly understandable, and to a degree foreseeable, that they should have been used as a point of departure for reflection and dialogue at different stages of the symposium. I too want to touch on them, at the very beginning of what I have to say.

If we bear in mind its global content, the quotation reveals first and foremost the supernatural intensity of the way their author looked at the world and at what was happening in it. These are ideas written at a particular time in contemporary history, in a context marked by particular kinds of difficulty; but they have permanent validity. They go back to the beginning of the thirties, an especially critical time for Spanish society, yes, but also for the whole world. And yet, read today and with reference to present circumstances, over seventy years later, these words do not need to be adapted in any way to continue affecting our conscience: they proclaim a truth which the passage of time seems unable to change. The whole world, the space that God has given the human creature, furrowed though it is by a multitude of unforeseen events deriving from man's freedom, is observed by Blessed Josemaría with a depth

---

2 *The Way*, 301.

which manages unfailingly to grasp, in Christ, what really matters.

His way of looking at things is serene, positive, reflecting the brightness of God's love for man and for creation which the saints seem to share in a special way. One thing that shows the rightness of his approach is the sobriety of the words he uses to express the inexpressible; the sobriety which one notices in point 301 of *The Way* refers to an invisible reality, but one obvious to the eyes of faith, something historically unfinished, and yet already perfect, something earthly and also eschatological—the beloved and still awaited reality of the Kingdom of Christ. To the installation and spread of that Kingdom among men and through men, in all creation, Blessed Josemaría had devoted all his energies from the time he was a young man.

That passage in *The Way*, like many passages in his writings, is viewed from the perspective of the development of the Kingdom of Christ on earth, for the glory of the Father and the good of mankind. The ejaculatory phrase, *Regnare Christum volumus*,[3] whose biblical content becomes clear when one links it to Luke 19:12–14 and 1 Corinthians 15:24–25, was selected by Blessed Josemaría as a kind of summary to describe the apostolate of the ordinary Christian in the world.

In the heart and mind of the founder of Opus Dei this 'slogan' often occurs with two others, both of them full of resonances and strongly evocative of the spirit God entrusted to him: *Deo omnis gloria!*, a cry of filial love, which evokes Jesus Christ's absolute self-giving to the will of the Father,[4] and *Omnes cum Petro ad Jesum per*

---

3 Cf. *The Way*, 11; *Furrow*, 292; *The Forge*, 639; see also *Christ Is Passing By*, 179; *The Way*, 301, 906; *Furrow*, 962; *The Forge*, 372, 822 and 857.

4 See *The Way*, 780; *Furrow*, 647; *The Forge*, 611, 639 and 1051. Cf. also *Friends of God*, 12, 114, 164 and 196; *The Way*, 80, 252, 617, 779, 782–4, 804; *Furrow*, 509, 552, 555 and 721; *The Forge*, 87, 122, 247, 255, 327, 334, 353, 704, 737, 852, 920, 921, 1033.

Mariam!, which encapsulates a commitment of life that refers to the central features of Catholicism.[5]

Regnare Christum volumus!, Deo omnis gloria!, Omnes cum Petro ad Jesum per Mariam! From the outset of the ecclesial mission of the founder of Opus Dei these three aspirations intone on Blessed Josemaría's lips a canticle of faith, hope and love, an unceasing prayer to which, in due course, countless voices have re-echoed; in fact they have become ejaculatory prayers which are raised to heaven from all parts of the globe. But it is not a prayer made up of words alone. The example of the founder's life has taught his children, and those who draw inspiration from his spirituality, to prove their words by the testimony of their deeds—deeds of loyalty to Christ and his Church, a conscious decision to help the redemption through on effective commitment to their apostolic mission. All this, then, goes to make up the program of Christian holiness to which point 301 of *The Way* refers.

In the 'open secret' which these words proclaim, and which provides a diagnosis of a perennial need of human society, elements distinct in themselves come together to produce a clear, succinct judgment: 'these world crises are crises of saints'. The meaning of this statement, so steeped in Christian certainty that it might seem a paradox if read with purely rational logic, becomes evident only in the light of faith. From the point of view of natural reason, one might think that it was simply offering spiritual solutions to much more complex temporal problems. In fact, a person with faith readily intuits that that is not the meaning to be given to the term 'crisis', either in this passage in *The Way* or in the Gospel sources from which it derives.

If one looks at human realities from the viewpoint of faith, and therefore sees them in terms of the intimate connection between revealed truth and the salvation of man, 'world crises', in the sense of social disorders of

---

5 See *Christ Is Passing By*, 139; *The Way*, 833; *The Forge*, 647.

whatever type, are primarily man-caused. They are, basically, evidence of a disorder which may not be easy to see but which is as real as that that emerges on the surface of history—a disorder which lies in people's hearts. So, one can see there is a causal connection between world crises and crises of saints, insofar as social disorders are the inevitable consequence of moral disorders, and the solution of the former depends on that of the latter.

A view of the world and its problems such as that revealed by this point of *The Way* is, then, fully a part of the Christian concept of man and his activity. There is nothing negative about it; it is very positive; it is trying to bring about lasting solutions. The ever-present reference of the natural to the supernatural arises from its obvious intimate and gratuitous connection with the order of divine causality: material creation is designed by God for man; and man has been created, in Christ, so that he can have personal communion with God. The spirit of Christianity contains a deep awareness of the transcendental dimension that gives meaning to all creating things. God created the world to have an essential reference to the human person, who, in turn, is called to follow his vocation as a son of God with full freedom. The spiritual heritage left by Blessed Josemaría is a worthy example of that Christian spirit; which is why, in the words of the Holy Father, it has a place among the great Christian testimonies. The text of *The Way* which we are discussing confirms this.

An awareness of the transcendental meaning of the world does not suppress or weaken the natural substance of things, by 'spiritualizing' them in an artificial way; it respects that substance in its entirety and defends it against possible reductionist ideas. The world needs saints not in order to be superficially de-naturalized and turned into something it is not, but to be led in an appropriate way towards its mysterious fullness, which can only be attained in the fullness of the glory of the sons and daughters of God.

The point of *The Way* which we are discussing goes on to make other significant statements: 'God wants a handful of men "of his own" in every human activity. And then . . . *pax Christi in regno Christi*—the peace of Christ in the kingdom of Christ.' These words confirm and even reinforce what came before them, by bringing in the subject of the 'Kingdom of God'. One needs to carefully work out the exact theological content of the words just quoted; they fully respect the nature of things and of human activities and, at the same time, they give them a substantial supernatural reference. This is the very first thing one notices in men of God—who are committed, come what may, to be saints—and in their activity in the world: for they strive as vigorously as they can to bring about the true and gradual development of the world, which thereby takes shape as the Kingdom of Christ.

The holiness we learn to seek through the teachings of Blessed Josemaría has this essential quality: it is a holiness *in the world*. Being 'in the world' is not meant to mean that the world just happens to be the place where holiness grows and matures: in other words, the world is not just the external framework of 'spiritual' activity. On the contrary, the expression 'holiness in the world' means that created things have an active presence, a specific role, in the process of sanctification: for the very simple reason that each created thing is in itself the object of human activity, its reason-of-being. Man develops as a person in the world through his relationship with other human beings and through work, that is, through his action in the various activities which go to make up the connections the human person has with the rest of creation. So, in this same world and in these very activities, without denaturalizing his relationship with created things, man grows in holiness and, with the help of grace, is becoming ever more like Jesus Christ, the Son of God made man.

In this sense, and going back again to point 301 in *The Way*, one can see why 'God wants a handful of men "of his own" in every human activity'. These people 'of his own' refer to man, not to activities. These activities are (ought to be, as society becomes gradually Christianized) the ordinary simple actions of human beings (each person with his or her own specific role and responsibilities), and they don't have to change their nature or significance just because they are actions done by people in whom the Holy Spirit dwells and works.

This shows us very vividly the value which created things have, not only in themselves but above all by virtue of the fact that our world was lived in and sanctified by Christ. In this world, through the gift of the Paraclete sent to men, there is at work 'the radiant, universal force of the Redeemer's grace', as the Pope observes in his address, commenting on a well-known statement of Blessed Josemaría's: 'Speaking with theological rigor [. . .] one cannot say that there are realities [. . .] which are exclusively profane; for the Word of God has made his dwelling among the sons of men, he was hungry and thirsty, worked with his hands, knew friendship and obedience, experienced sorrow and death.'[6]

This reference to the Christological meaning of created reality, which already in and through itself manifests the dominion of Christ, is deeply consistent with the proclamation of the universal call to seek Christian holiness in the midst of the world's activities, cooperating in the mission to spread, until the end of time, that dominion—the Kingdom of Jesus Christ—throughout the earth.

---

6 Cf. John Paul II, Address cited in fn. 1; the phrase from Bl. Josemaría is from *Christ Is Passing By*, 112.

II. Being sons and daughters of God. Being Christ

Holiness in the world is nourished by and rooted in an essential and profound sense of divine filiation which a Christian has in Christ. If the first postulate—*being in the world*—could be defined as an external quality of the vocation to holiness proclaimed by Blessed Josemaría, the second—the fact that it is rooted in a *sense of divine filiation*—must be taken to be the key, internal quality par excellence, the most characteristic, most important, quality.

For the founder of Opus Dei his life and mission got its meaning mainly from his consciousness of being a son of God. 'My life,' he exclaims in one of his homilies, 'has led me to realize in a special way that I am a son of God and I have experienced the joy of getting inside the heart of my Father, to rectify, to purify myself, to serve him, to understand others and find excuses for them, on the strength of his love and my own lowliness.'[7] Everything about him radiated this conviction and rested on this foundation: his life of prayer and penance, the exercise of his ministry as a priest, his vast apostolic activity . . . , all aspects of his life in the world were marked by the seal of divine filiation.

If his life was supernaturally sealed with that divine spirit, one can say that his spirituality also bears that imprint as one of its essential features. This is something to which we should give time and thought. How could a theologian study his teachings without paying special attention to this essential aspect? This is a matter of exceptional importance and one highlighted already during the symposium; I wanted to refer to it too, but only, as I said, to draw attention to one central aspect of it. I shall deal particularly with the mutual relationship there is between filiation and love for the Cross.

In Blessed Josemaría's spirituality, the sense of divine filiation is inseparable from a sense of the Cross, insofar as it is an awareness, on the one hand, of a grace

---

7 *Friends of God*, 143.

which conforms a person to Christ and, on the other, of a gift which one should be using all the time in one's effort to follow Christ truly, making no concessions. The founder of Opus Dei lived a sense of divine filiation as to share filially in the work of salvation by identifying himself with the will of God our Father. Thus, being a son of God in Christ brings with it the grace to take up the redeeming Cross every day, thereby discovering the true meaning of our life and the things we do. Being a son of God also involves being called to imitate Christ, to model all creation (and above all the minds and hearts of men) on the model and through the salvific sign of the Cross, which imprints on us the seal of a total identification with the paternal will of God.

Over the course of the symposium some words of Blessed Josemaría were quoted which I too should like to bring in: 'When the Lord dealt me those blows, around the year thirty-one, I didn't understand why. And then, suddenly, in the midst of that great bitterness, (came) those words: 'you are my son' (Ps 2:7), you are Christ. And all I would do was say over and over again: *Abba, Pater! Abba, Pater! Abba! Abba! Abba!* Now I see it as a new light, as a new discovery: as one sees, with the passing of the years, the hand of the Lord, of divine wisdom, of the Almighty.

'You did this, Lord, to make me see that having the Cross means finding happiness, joy. And the reason—I see it now more clearly than ever—is this: having the Cross means being identified with Christ, it means being Christ, and therefore, being a son of God. [. . .]

'The Cross: that is where Christ is, and you have to lose yourself in Him! There will be no more suffering, no more hardship. You mustn't say: Lord, I can't go on, I'm a wretch . . . No! that is not true! On the Cross you will be Christ, and you will feel like a son of God, and you will cry out: Abba, Pater! How happy to find you, Lord!'[8]

---

8 Meditation, April 28, 1963: *Registro Histórico del Fundador* (RHF), 20.119, p. 13.

By way of conclusion

This text, whose biographical and spiritual significance is obvious, expresses very vividly the connection between divine filiation and the Cross. The words 'having the Cross means being identified with Christ, it means being Christ and, therefore, being a son of God' seem to be the very nucleus of the passage. At the very center of this, one can see the power the Cross has to play in shaping a Christian's life: having the Cross means being Christ, being a son of God. And one cannot remain indifferent to this invitation to take up the Cross, in order to conform the world to Christ, in order to be Christ. Being a son of God and having the Cross entails carrying it, taking its weight on one's shoulders, making it present, working under its blessed weight, flooding the world with its redemptive energy and its light, the light of the loving Son, dead and risen.

Blessed Josemaría followed this way of the unity between filiation and Cross (Christ's highway) throughout his life, ever more intensely as he grew older, as one can sense by just looking at the text I have transcribed. His spiritual teaching, which reflects his own experience of God and of God's plans, reveals at every step his conviction that the Cross is the only way to go for whoever wants to follow Christ in all circumstances.

In a text going back to 1955, he wrote: 'And now I would like you to engrave deeply on your mind and upon your heart—so that you can meditate on it often and draw your own practical conclusions—the summary St. Paul made to the Ephesians when he invited them to follow resolutely in our Lord's footsteps: "Be imitators of God, as very dear children, and walk in love, as Christ has loved us and delivered himself up for us, a sacrifice breathing out fragrance as he offered it to God" (Eph 5:1–2).

Jesus offered himself up in a holocaust of love. What about you, who are a disciple of Christ? You, a favoured son of God; you, who have been ransomed at the price of the Cross; you too should be ready to deny yourself.'[9]

---

9 *Friends of God*, 128–9.

From the passages in his preaching which deal with the identification of the Christian with Christ, let us listen to this one, from 1967: 'I beg our Lord to help us make up our minds to nourish in our souls the one noble ambition that matters, the only one that is really worthwhile: to get close to Jesus, like his Blessed Mother and the Holy Patriarch St. Joseph did, with longing hearts and self-denial, without neglect of any kind. We will share in the joy of being God's friends—in a spirit of interior recollection, which is quite compatible with our professional and social duties—and we will thank him for teaching us so clearly and tenderly how to fulfill the Will of our Father who dwells in heaven.'[10]

Anyone who attends the school of Blessed Josemaría learns from the outset an important lesson for our activity as Christians in the midst of society, and discovers, immediately too, how to put that lesson into practice. It could be summarized as follows: we will offer our brethren witness to Christ if we ourselves are another Christ, if we identify ourselves with him, if we assimilate his filial spirit by taking up the Cross, as he did. 'On the Cross you will be Christ, and you will feel like a son of God.'

The essence of Christian witness is passing on to others one's own lived experience of God as Father, of the love he shows us, and of the Cross of Christ and its salvific value. Here lies the effectiveness of the influence the sons and daughters of God in Christ are called upon to exercise on society. This is the mission which, as Christians, we should carry out in the context of our everyday occupations. 'It is the task of the millions of Christian men and women who fill the earth to bring Christ into all human activities and to announce through their lives the fact that God loves everyone and wants to save everyone. The best and most important way in which they can participate in the life of the Church, and indeed the way which all other ways presuppose, is by

---

10 *Friends of God*, 300–1.

being truly Christian precisely where they are, in the place to which their human vocation has called them.'[11]

III. Putting Christ at the summit

In the spiritual language of Blessed Josemaría, the expression 'putting Christ at the summit of all human activities',[12] and other similar expressions,[13] is used as a summary of the apostolic duty Christians have. In some way, they form a compendium of the entire apostolic substance of his writings, as the following statements, for example, confirm: 'This is the secret of the holiness which I have now been preaching for so many years. God has called on all of us to imitate him. He has called you and me so that, living as we do in the midst of the world—and continuing to be ordinary everyday people!—we may put Christ at the summit of all honest human activities.'[14]

The expression 'put Christ at the summit of all human activities' is to be found even as he was taking his first steps as a man with a mission to found Opus Dei, and it illustrates the apostolic purpose contained in his foundational charism. In the soul of Blessed Josemaría the expression is linked to John 12:32, which provides a key to its interpretation. Many sources can be offered to show this, but I think it suffices to refer to a text Blessed Josemaría wrote in 1931, in which he describes a supernatural experience which occurred when he was celebrating mass on the feast of the Transfiguration of our Lord, in the diocese of Madrid: 'The time of the Consecration came', he writes in an autobiographical account: 'at the point of raising the Sacred Host, without losing

---

[11] *Conversations*, 112.

[12] Cf., for example, *Conversations*, 59; *The Forge*, 685; *Christ Is Passing By*, 156 and 183.

[13] 'At the summit of all noble realities' (Letter, September 4, 1951, no. 3); 'at the center of everything' (*Christ Is Passing By*, 105).

[14] *Friends of God*, 58.

the proper recollection—I had just mentally made the offering to merciful Love—there came to my mind, with exceptional force and clarity, those words of Scripture *et si exaltatus fuero a terra, omnia traham ad meipsum* (Jn 12:32). Normally, in the presence of something supernatural, I feel afraid. Then comes the *ne timeas!*, it is I. And I realized that it will be the men and women of God who will raise up the Cross by means of Christ's teachings on the pinnacle of every human activity. . . . And I saw the Lord victorious, attracting all things to Himself.'[15]

As one can see in this fragment, explicitly, and as one can read into other passages, the raising up of Christ is intimately connected with the raising up of his redemptive Cross—that instrument chosen by God to show men his mystery of salvation and glorification. Raising up the Cross is, then, a Christian task of primordial importance: the task of 'the men and women of God.'[16]

In the teachings of Blessed Josemaría the sanctification of the world is conceived and described as something done in line with this program—'putting Christ at the summit of all human activities', 'at the center of everything'. It consists, then, in inserting all earthly activities into the spiritual dynamism which emanates from the Cross of Christ. Sin having been conquered, and men having been redeemed, the world too, through the holiness and sanctified work of the sons and daughters of God, is set on the road to sanctification, in the sense that the development of the world is oriented towards the end which was its original reason-of-being—the showing forth of divine Goodness and Beauty, the proclamation of God's loving fatherhood, and his glorification.

This teaching raises quite a variety of questions which need to be thought about and developed theologically. To highlight here some particular points, especially linked to the general plan of the symposium and the lines

---

15 'Apuntes íntimos', 217, 7 August 1931.
16 Cf., for example, *Christ Is Passing By*, 156 and 183.

its work took, I should like to touch on one aspect which is obviously important, and which has many significant formational and pastoral effects.

I shall choose one of the many passages that I could pick, to introduce what I want to say:

'Since you want to acquire a Catholic or universal outlook, here are some of its characteristics:
— a breadth of vision and a deepening insight into Catholic orthodoxy, into the things that are permanently valid;
— a proper and healthy desire, which should never be frivolous, to present anew the standard teachings of traditional thought in philosophy and the interpretation of history;
— a careful attention to trends in science and contemporary thought;
— and a positive and open attitude towards the changes current in society and in ways of living.[17]

This passage is a very good example of the truly Catholic, universal, outlook of the founder of Opus Dei, but it also throws light on the content and tone of the formation which, through his life and his teaching, he passed on to those who, seeking Christian formation, approached him or centers of Opus Dei throughout the world.

It is easy enough to see the way this universal outlook, open to the widest horizon, is delineated in this passage, if we draw attention to two extremes: a) the richness of Catholic orthodoxy, on which the teaching is based and which it explores as a 'permanently valid' part of its essence; and b) a careful and creative attention to trends in contemporary culture and to changes in society and ways of living. The relationship between these two poles is not one of dialectical opposition, conflict or mutual rejection, but rather of intrinsic affinity.

---

17 *Furrow*, 428.

In the point from *Furrow* which we are commenting on, the subject is set in the context of formation, as a counsel given someone who wants to assimilate a particular approach to things. This means that the desired synthesis between Christian spirit and the cultural and intellectual world, between the Gospel and the various cultures, needs first to happen in persons themselves. Here again we find a teaching of Blessed Josemaría's on which he always placed a great emphasis in his preaching and writing: to sanctify the world personal sanctity is needed. In the prodigious amount of work he did over the course of his life to give formation to people, this conviction was ever-present.

The works from *Furrow* which I have quoted outline only 'some characteristics' of this formation and therefore do not go into any detail.

From the very beginning the text refers to 'Catholic orthodoxy'. This alludes to the certainty of the doctrine of the Faith, and the total fidelity one should have to the Church. I think it is appropriate to point out that this allusion occurs in a very 'dynamic' context: he sees the doctrine as a source which is ever being renewed—something perennially new. In Blessed Josemaría Escrivá's thought orthodoxy is not something sclerotic and lifeless, able only to produce static intellectual and spiritual attitudes, which impoverish the Christian life. Quite the contrary: he sees orthodoxy as something alive and dynamic, ceaselessly oriented to giving new stimulus to evangelization and new vitality to the Church, opening up new frontiers for the spread of the Kingdom of God.

So, as Blessed Josemaría sees it, one should use 'the standard teachings of traditional thought' as a first step towards a vigorous renewal (in the best sense of the word, of course).

This reference to traditional teaching (one would expect no less of a serious professional) implies that the truths found there have to be treated with due respect but they also need to be thought about and worked on, in order to draw from them their fullest meaning. A

Catholic intellectual who has apostolic spirit should not be content with taking over the 'permanently valid' content of our cultural resources, clinging to the way it is formulated (as if that were the only thing that could save him, as if it were something fixed, immovable, unimprovable). If one adopted that approach, one would run the risk of cutting oneself off from dialogue with the contributions made by contemporary thought, to which, on the contrary 'careful attention' should be given.

On the other hand, this attitude of careful attention does not mean total acceptance, even though it certainly calls for a positive, favourable, and open intellectual attitude. So, we are as far away from an attitude of fear, suspicion or defensiveness towards new ideas simply because they are new, as we are from any slavish kowtowing to the latest great insight. On the contrary: we find here a serene, constructive attitude to the world, one of the most fundamental constituent elements of which is its intellectual content. In this connection it is interesting to see what he says about the positive sciences—the fact that he recognizes the considerable role they have to play in shaping the outlook of an age.

In our text, love for the world also includes a 'positive and open attitude towards changes current in society and in ways of living'. Instead of the kind of wariness towards change which was a feature of certain intellectual climates at times, the position taken here is a favourable one, and it realizes that changes tend to come about not so much by a quiet process of evolution, but quite often through sudden unexpected developments. Undoubtedly, in taking a positive attitude to those changes, Blessed Josemaría was not unaware of the anti-Christian forces which underlay many of them. It simply shows his love for the world, this real world which he happened to live in; and it also shows that he wants to do everything possible to lead it back to God. What he is saying here (so positively) can help us avoid the danger of loving an imaginary world, a world of the past, rather than the world it is up to us to sanctify. The fact of the matter is that it is here, among the things which go to make up an ordinary life, a life knit into the lives of our contemporaries, that Christ wants to reign and should reign. Here is where he is calling us to serve him and to use all our talents when doing so.

To conclude these thoughts, I return to the paragraph I mentioned at the start, taken from our Holy Father John Paul II's address to those attending the symposium. After quoting point 301 of *The Way*, the Pope says: 'How much power this doctrine has in terms of the arduous and at the same time appealing work of the new evangelization, to which the entire Church is called! In your congress you have had the opportunity to reflect on various aspects of this spiritual teaching. I invite you to continue in this work because Josemaría Escrivá de Balaguer, like other great figures in modern Church history, can also be a source of inspiration for theological thought. In fact, theological research, which has an irreplaceable role of mediation in the relationship between faith and culture, professes and is enriched by drawing on the Gospel, under the impulse of the experience of Christianity's great witness. Blessed Josemaría, without a doubt, should be included among them.'[18]

Among the members of the Opus Dei prelature, priests and lay people, men and women, all over the world, there are many whose job is 'intellectual' rather than manual. Through the magnanimity which is part of the spirit we have received through Blessed Josemaría, and trying to imitate the love for the Church and the world which he passed on to us, and with the help of theological reflection, they should continue to serve the Church in its 'new evangelization'. In the hope that God will continue to bless that work, I offer it today, in the name of all, to the Blessed Virgin, Seat of Wisdom, through the intercession of Blessed Josemaría Escrivá.

---

18 John Paul II, Address (cited in fn. 1), 4.